Greasing the Wheels

Using Pork Barrel Projects to Build Majority Coalitions in Congress

Pork barrel projects would surely rank near the top of most observers' lists of Congress's most widely despised products. Yet political leaders in Congress and the president often trade pork for votes to pass legislation that serves broad national purposes, giving members of Congress pork barrel projects in return for their votes on general interest legislation. It is a practice that succeeds at a cost, but it is a cost that many political leaders are willing to pay in order to enact the broader public policies that they favor. There is an irony in this: Pork barrel benefits, the most reviled of Congress's legislative products, are used by policy coalition leaders to produce the type of policy that is most admired: general interest legislation. This book makes the case that buying votes with pork is an important way in which Congress solves its well-known collective action problem.

Diana Evans is Professor of Political Science at Trinity College in Hartford, Connecticut. She has published articles in leading journals in political science on political action committees and congressional decision making, congressional elections, and congressional oversight of the bureaucracy. She is past president of the New England Political Science Association.

Greasing the Wheels

Using Pork Barrel Projects to Build Majority Coalitions in Congress

DIANA EVANS

Trinity College

PUBLISHED BY THE PRESS SYNDICATE OF THE UNIVERSITY OF CAMBRIDGE
The Pitt Building, Trumpington Street, Cambridge, United Kingdom

CAMBRIDGE UNIVERSITY PRESS
The Edinburgh Building, Cambridge CB2 2RU, UK
40 West 20th Street, New York, NY 10011-4211, USA
477 Williamstown Road, Port Melbourne, VIC 3207, Australia
Ruiz de Alarcón 13, 28014 Madrid, Spain
Dock House, The Waterfront, Cape Town 8001, South Africa

http://www.cambridge.org

First published 2004

Printed in the United States of America

Typeface Sabon 10/13 pt. *System* LaTeX 2ε [TB]

A catalog record for this book is available from the British Library.

Library of Congress Cataloging in Publication data available

ISBN 0 521 83681 6 hardback
ISBN 0 521 54532 3 paperback

For Steve

Contents

Tables and Figures

TABLES

FIGURES

Acknowledgments

I am indebted to many colleagues and friends for their comments, criticisms, and wise advice on this book. Some read and commented on the entire manuscript; others read and commented on portions of it; still others provided advice on specific problems. In alphabetical order, they are Janet Box-Steffensmeier, Larry Evans, Richard Fenno, Morris Fiorina, Mark Franklin, Adam Grossberg, Gary Jacobson, Kenneth Koford, Frances Lee, David Mayhew, Bruce Oppenheimer, David Rohde, Douglas Rivers, Richard Smith, and Christopher Zorn.

Of all of those on this list, I owe special thanks to Dick Fenno and Mark Franklin for their careful reading of the whole manuscript. Both have a special talent for simultaneously criticizing and encouraging; they kept me on track right until the end. I am deeply grateful for their help.

In addition, I wish to thank the many congressional staffers, lobbyists, and administration officials – all of whom were promised anonymity – who kindly shared with me their insights and experience concerning the politics of the pork barrel.

I also would like to thank the talented Trinity students who served as my research assistants: Bill Dennen, Marion Guill, Ann Mulcahy, Melissa Prober, Joan Savage, and Leslie Soler. Thanks also to my friend and colleague Trinity sociologist Noreen Channels, who provided an objective eye when I needed help with editing in the early stages of the project.

I also owe thanks to Trinity College for providing me with generous financial support throughout the life of this project in the form of research leaves and expense grants, as well as funds for the occasional unanticipated interview trip to Washington.

I have drawn on several of my earlier publications in this book. Portions of Chapter 3 are drawn from "The Distribution of Pork Barrel Projects and Vote Buying in Congress," in *Congress on Display, Congress at Work*, ed. William T. Bianco (Ann Arbor: University of Michigan Press, 2000). Portions of Chapter 4 are taken from "Policy and Pork: The Use of Pork Barrel Projects to Build Policy Coalitions in the House of Representatives," *American Journal of Political Science* 38 (November 1994): 894–917, Blackwell Publishing; also "Reconciling Pork-Barrel Politics and National Transportation Policy: Highway Demonstration Projects," in *Who Makes Public Policy? The Struggle for Control between Congress and the Executive*, eds. Robert S. Gilmour and Alexis A. Halley (Chatham, N.J.: Chatham House, 1994); and "Congressional Oversight and the Diversity of Members' Goals," by permission from *Political Science Quarterly* 109 (Fall 1994): 669–688. The 1990 interviews relating to the highway bill were conducted as part of a larger project examining congressional-executive relations with respect to program management, sponsored by the National Academy of Public Administration. The results of that study were reported in *Beyond Distrust: Building Bridges between Congress and the Executive* (Washington: National Academy of Public Administration, 1992).

It is customary to thank one's spouse for showing tolerance during a project such as the one that produced this book. I am happy to say that there is no need for me to do so; there was never a moment when my husband, Steve Gephard, made me feel that he was marshaling his considerable patience and tolerance. Instead, he gladly gave me his constant encouragement and enthusiastic support, in addition to preparing many a dinner when I could not bear to tear myself away from "just one more (and one more, and one more) logit analysis" or "just a couple of more paragraphs." To Steve I give my heartfelt thanks.

Of course, none of those on whose help I relied bears the slightest responsibility for any remaining shortcomings of this book.

I

Introduction

In 1985 and 1986, Congress undertook the largest reform of the U.S. tax code since World War II. The goal of the reformers, particularly President Ronald Reagan, was to reduce personal income tax rates by raising corporate tax rates and closing most loopholes for wealthy individuals and businesses (Birnbaum and Murray 1987, p. 22). One of the key players in that process was former Representative Dan Rostenkowski of Chicago, chair of the House Ways and Means Committee. To pass the legislation in the committee required both political skill and resources, and his were considerable. The *New York Times* described how he did it:

> On a Friday morning in November . . . , hours before the Ways and Means Committee was to vote . . . , Mr. Rostenkowski sat with a list in the committee's library and began calling other members to tell them of special tax breaks he had sneaked into the bill just for them. They included favorable tax treatment for stadiums in Cleveland, Miami and the Meadowlands in New Jersey, for waste-treatment plants in New York City and on Long Island, for a convention center in Miami, for parking garages in Memphis and Charleston, S. C., for St. Luke's Hospital and New York University in Manhattan, and, not surprisingly, for a savings and loan association in Chicago. Members who planned to vote against the bill got nothing for their districts. (Rosenbaum 1994)

Rostenkowski's horse trading is part of the tradition commonly known as pork barrel politics. It is a phenomenon with a long and widely despised history in the lore of politics. Yet the *New York Times* article that described the congressman's strategy in a manner that invited the reader's disapproval also noted its richest irony: By giving out a few new tax breaks, euphemistically called "transition rules," to key representatives, Rostenkowski played a central role in passing a broad reform of the tax code that "struck at the nerve of the nation's most powerful lobbyists and special interests and . . . was widely applauded by many of the same advocates of clean government who found Mr. Rostenkowski's methods so objectionable" (Rosenbaum 1994).

The irony is this: pork barreling, despite its much maligned status, gets things done. Simply put, that is the overriding thesis of this book. To be sure, it is a practice that succeeds at a cost, but it is a cost that many political leaders are willing to pay in order to enact the broader public policies that they favor. The pages that follow explore the complexities and subtleties of what pork barreling political leaders accomplish and how they do it, but the arguments are at heart an elaboration of this theme: Pork barrel benefits are used strategically by policy coalition leaders to build the majority coalitions necessary to pass broad-based, general interest legislation. Leaders do so by tacking a set of targeted district benefits onto such bills, using the benefits as a sort of currency to purchase legislators' votes for the leaders' policy preferences, much as political action committees make campaign contributions in the hope of swaying members' votes. In so doing, policy coalition leaders may even overcome the strictures of party loyalty, using pork to lure members of the other party away from their own leadership. The irony of this coalition-building strategy is that pork barrel legislation, the most reviled of Congress's legislative products, is used by coalition leaders to produce the type of policy that is most admired: general interest legislation.

Pork barreling is not the only way in which leaders create majority coalitions for general interest bills, but, especially in certain policy areas, it is an important one. This book explores the strategies by which leaders use pork barrel benefits to form majority coalitions and analyzes the impact of these strategies on the decisions of the legislators who receive the benefits. Additionally, to see how the process operates in the real world, the book examines the use of pork barrel benefits to pass a number of major pieces of legislation, including highway bills, the North American Free Trade Agreement (NAFTA), and an array of appropriations bills. The case studies include bills in both the House of Representative and the Senate during years of both Democratic and Republican control.

The pork barrel is a popular metaphor for projects and favors for legislators' districts. Although the origin of the term is somewhat murky, it probably derives from the pre–Civil War South, when on holidays slave owners set out barrels of salt pork for their slaves, who were frequently undernourished. The resulting frantic rush for the barrel inspired the unflattering popular image of much better-fed politicians grabbing benefits for their constituents with the fervor of starving slaves scrambling for food. The term was used in Congress as early as the 1870s to describe legislation containing projects for members' districts (Ashworth 1981; Safire 1988). Seen in this light, descriptions of pork barrel politics typically are overlaid with moral opprobrium.

The pejorative term "pork barrel politics" is frequently replaced in the scholarly literature by the more neutral term "distributive politics," which refers to the process by which distributive policy is made. Definitions of the latter vary somewhat, but the following is satisfactory for our purposes: Distributive policy targets discrete benefits to specific populations such as states and congressional districts but spreads the costs across the general population through taxation. Such benefits have so little policy connection to each other that changing or even removing one district's benefit from a bill would have no impact on the benefits given to other districts (Shepsle and Weingast 1981, p. 96), although it might diminish the bill's prospects of passage by reducing its supporting coalition. Packages of such benefits, according to Theodore Lowi, "are characterized by the ease with which they can be disaggregated and dispensed unit by small unit more or less in isolation from other units and from any general rule" (Lowi 1964, p. 690).

The scholarly literature on distributive politics focuses on omnibus pork barrel bills, legislation that consists of nothing but distributive projects. By contrast, this book focuses on the use of distributive benefits to win votes for general interest legislation, defined here as broad-based measures that affect the whole nation or a large segment of it. General interest legislation need not, by this definition, fall evenly on all districts or individuals; all that is necessary is that it affect all districts or all of those in a broad category. Nor does this definition imply that general interest legislation is in the "public interest." Losers might well outnumber winners, or the total costs might be greater than the total benefits. All I mean is that such legislation provides a collective benefit, defined as a "good, such that if any person . . . in a group . . . consumes it, it cannot feasibly be withheld from the others in that group" (Olson 1965, p. 14). The "group" in this case extends far beyond individual congressional districts. The argument of this book is that distributive benefits are added to general interest bills as "sweeteners" to buy the votes of enough members to create a majority coalition in favor of such bills.

The two terms, "distributive" and " pork barrel," will be used interchangeably here, despite the fact that some scholars do not treat them as synonymous. Rather, they define pork barrel policy as that subset of distributive policy that is inefficient, where the costs of the policy exceed the benefits (Ferejohn 1974, p. 235; Shepsle and Weingast 1981; Baron 1991). However, I do not employ that distinction here, where the point is to explicate the political uses of distributive politics in policy making, not its economic implications. The efficiency or inefficiency of a policy, while economically important, is rarely central to decisions in Congress about whether to request or provide benefits. More important, although some members of Congress routinely oppose distributive policy because of its presumed inefficiency, most members ignore the distinction in practice, as the case studies in this book show. Their incentive to do so stems in part from the fact that project costs in the form of money spent in a member's district can be reinterpreted politically as benefits to the district. As those costs are shared nationally by all taxpayers (Shepsle and Weingast 1981), a legislator normally has little reason to care about the economic efficiency of his or her own project or of any bill that contains it (Weingast, Shepsle, and Johnsen 1981). Furthermore, the readiness with which federal agencies claim that a project's benefits equal or exceed its costs highlights the practical difficulties of making judgments about project efficiency in any case (Maass 1951).

Pork barrel or distributive policy dates from the earliest years of the Republic. In the eighteenth and nineteenth centuries, Congress's distributive policies consisted mainly of projects of physical improvement such as lighthouses, roads and canals, dams and harbors; the classic source of those benefits was rivers and harbors legislation. The purpose of such projects was described in 1888 by James Bryce, who wrote that "grants from the federal treasury for local purposes" were routinely employed by members of Congress seeking to secure their renominations (Bryce 1959, p. 40). Today distributive benefits are found in nearly all policy areas, especially in appropriations bills, where targeted funding is granted for a broad range of purposes, including highway interchanges, supercomputers for universities, detention centers for illegal immigrants, and studies of agricultural pests, such as fire ants.

However, with the advent of the environmental movement, some of the more traditional types of pork barrel projects, such as dams and river and harbor dredging, have aroused considerable public opposition for their negative environmental impact. More broadly, John Ferejohn (1974, pp. 52–54) shows that district projects can impose local costs in addition to offering benefits. In those cases, the emergence of opposition depends on whether the costs are concentrated, falling on those who may already be organized and thus capable of quick action, or dispersed, falling on those who are less likely to be organized. If river navigation is improved for barges by dredging, other commercial interests, such as trucking, consequently may lose business, producing winners who will support and losers who will oppose a district project. Similarly, dams destroy upstream wildlife habitat, stimulating opposition from environmental groups. Congress has adapted, responding to such opposition with what has been called "post industrial" pork, which includes money for such things as environmental cleanup projects and university research, otherwise known as academic pork (Starobin 1987; Savage 1999).

Clearly, pork barrel politics occurs because members of Congress believe that district benefits enhance their chances for reelection. In studies of distributive politics, the electoral connection is axiomatic. In his study of Congress's allocation of water projects, Ferejohn speculates that there are three reasons why such projects are valuable to members. All of those reasons are related either directly or indirectly to reelection. First, members believe that bringing home projects gives them a record of constituency service on which they can campaign. A second and related benefit is that assiduous attention to constituents can help to create an impression of invulnerability, redirecting to more opportune targets the ambitions of high-quality potential election challengers. Third, like old-time machine politicians, members of Congress can buy with projects the freedom to do as they wish, or as their party leadership wishes, on issues of more importance to them on Capitol Hill (Ferejohn 1974, pp. 49–51). In other words, they can buy leeway for their activities in Congress (Fenno 1978) with the credit that pork barrel service earns for them with constituents.

In mass media accounts of pork barrel politics, the tone is typically critical, with an emphasis on the self-serving aspects of "bringing home the bacon." Journalist Brian Kelly quoted a White House aide's cynical comment: "If you're a congressman and you want to get reelected – and you do because it's a pretty great job despite all the whining you hear from them – then you give things to the people who can vote for you. In return they keep electing you. The hell with what it means for the rest of the country" (Kelly 1992, p. 6). The electoral benefits of pork may be concentrated or dispersed within the constituency. When organized interests or businesses benefit, as they do, for example, when the project entails highway construction contracts, the benefits can be said to be concentrated. When benefits go (perhaps simultaneously) to a large group of unorganized constituents, as would a new highway interchange that relieves downtown congestion, the benefits are dispersed. In either case, members of Congress expect to profit electorally. Where benefits are dispersed, they expect to be rewarded with the votes of grateful constituents. When benefits are concentrated, they may receive a smaller direct electoral reward but gain substantial campaign contributions, which, incumbents hope, eventually can be parlayed into votes.

The following sections present views of pork barrel or distributive politics as seen from quite different perspectives. First, the journalistic view is the most familiar to political observers; it is a largely negative view of pork barrel politics. While the journalistic perspective provides insight into the distribution of pork barrel projects, it generally fails to place the use of such projects in a broader strategic context. In particular, journalists typically overlook the utility of pork barrel benefits for crafting broad-based legislation. Second, in the realm of scholarship, I examine important literature on the theory of distributive politics, as well as literature that deals with how Congress passes general interest bills and how that literature treats pork barrel politics. I argue that this literature also fails to recognize fully the use of pork barrel benefits for passing general interest legislation.

THE JOURNALISTIC VIEW OF PORK BARREL POLITICS

Journalistic reports of the impact of pork barrel politics suggest that bringing large amounts of money home to the district can indeed protect members of Congress. Well known in the 1970s was Pennsylvania's Eleventh Congressional District, an impoverished coal-mining area whose citizens showed their gratitude to the colorful Representative Daniel Flood by reelecting him after his indictment on various bribery and corruption charges. Flood was beloved not only for his theatrical style, but also for the millions of dollars in benefits that he funneled to the district as vice chairman of the Defense Appropriations Subcommittee. After pleading guilty to reduced charges, Flood left Congress in 1980 (Kelly 1992, pp. 72–74).

Next door in Pennsylvania's Tenth District, Joseph McDade's constituents similarly benefited from his position on the Appropriations Committee. The Greater Scranton Chamber of Commerce estimated in 1992 that federally financed projects valued at $420 million were currently under construction in the district, nearly all of them due in large part to McDade's efforts. In 1992, he too was indicted, in this case on five counts of bribery, racketeering, and other corruption charges, including allowing his son to accept $7,500 in tuition money from a defense contractor.

Like the voters of the Eleventh District, McDade's constituents gave him the benefit of the doubt, reelecting him twice by large margins during his unsuccessful legal challenges to the indictment. As the mayor of Scranton said about the tuition payments, "Maybe Joe didn't know his son was getting a scholarship" (Hinds 1992). When he was finally acquitted of all charges during his 1996 reelection campaign, his constituents reelected him again; he retired in 1998.

Brian Kelly's *Adventures in Porkland* (1992) offers a number of examples of what the author considers pork barrel profligacy. He traces, among other things, the battle over an item in an agriculture appropriations bill that earmarked $500,000 to make a memorial of Lawrence Welk's childhood home in Strasburg, North Dakota. The effort to remove that item from the budget was one of the few successful attacks on hundreds of pork barrel projects in appropriations bills in 1991. However, a project that survived the winnowing process was Senator Ted Stevens's (R-Alaska) $25 million supercomputer for the University of Alaska. On paper, this was an unremarkable if expensive example of the increasingly common practice of earmarking money for scientific research for specific universities. Kelly notes that this project, part of Senator Stevens's plan to harness the solar energy that creates the aurora borealis, evidently, if surprisingly, passed the "laugh test" that a source told Kelly was being applied to appropriations project requests that year; that is, projects that "sounded just too downright stupid for words [were] going to get cut out" (Kelly 1992, pp. 206–207). Despite passing that test, Stevens's project evidently was the object of some skepticism: "One.... physicist noted that to collect the energy would require an antenna stretching from Mount McKinley to Mount Fuji, and then it would power nothing more than a microwave oven" (Savage 1999, p. 172).

The obvious appeal of distributive politics notwithstanding, Congress has long had its anti-pork crusaders. A group composed of members of Congress and representatives of nonprofit taxpayer groups attempted to purge the 1991 appropriations bills of what they considered the most egregious examples of pork. Led by Representatives Tim Penny (D-Minn.) and Harris Fawell (R-Ill.), this group called themselves the "Porkbusters." They introduced legislation in 1991 to cut 325 projects worth $1 billion from that year's appropriations bills (Kelly 1992, p. 56). Despite their best efforts, hundreds of the projects that they tried to kill survived, and a number of Porkbusters were embarrassed on the floor by Appropriations Committee members, who pointed out that the sponsors themselves had benefited from the committee's largesse in the past. Nevertheless, the group continued to introduce legislation to remove large numbers of projects from spending bills. Perhaps not surprisingly, it enjoyed only modest success (Pound 1994; "Who Ya Gonna Call?" 1997).

The Porkbusters worked closely with the nonprofit Citizens Against Government Waste (CAGW), a group formed in the wake of the Reagan administration's Grace Commission (named for its chair, industrialist J. Peter Grace) to seek out government waste. Grace himself went on to become co-founder of CAGW in 1984, along with columnist Jack Anderson. That organization's major activity is to track projects earmarked for states and congressional districts in annual appropriations bills and publicize them at a press conference held jointly each year with members of Porkbusters. In an effort to attract maximum coverage, the press briefing is clearly designed as theater:

> Rep. David Minge, D-Minn., co-chairman of the House's self-proclaimed Porkbuster Coalition, joined other budget hawks at a news conference, where they were flanked by a pig eating novelty dollar bills and a person in a pink pig suit. The Citizens Against Government Waste put out the "2000 Congressional Pig Book," which lists members of Congress who secured funding for more than 4,000 home-state "pork" projects worth $17.7 billion. ("Minnesota Ranks Near the Bottom" 2000)

Despite Congress's continued enthusiasm for distributive benefits, press accounts of the 1994 congressional elections suggested that there may be a limit to the degree to which pork barrel projects can inoculate incumbents against electoral defeat. In those elections, thirty-five Democratic House incumbents were defeated by Republican challengers. If that year was remarkable for the number of incumbents unseated, it was also noted in the press for the defeat of a number of members who for years had showered their districts with federal benefits. Once considered invulnerable, representatives such as House Speaker Thomas Foley and Texas Democrat Jack Brooks were defeated. In a pre-election visit to Brooks's district, reporter Michael Wines quoted the representative's description of some of the reasons for his forty-two years of electoral success:

> The big Pontiac glided past a local television station ("Helped them with the FCC."); a brief stop at the intracoastal canal in nearby Port Arthur ("I widened it; deepened it."); a pause at the seawall ("Forty, fifty-million dollars").
>
> Later he fired up a cigar and cruised past the site of the new Federal prison ("2,000 jobs, $150 million") and Lamar University at Beaumont, where a cigar-clutching statue honors the 71-year-old Congressman whose labors elevated the school from backwater junior college to four-year university. (Wines 1994)

But such successes may have played differently with voters in 1994 than in the past; they certainly did not save Jack Brooks. As an analysis in the *New York Times* noted, "Once there was a time when clout and seniority were good.... [But] worthwhile local projects are no longer easily distinguishable from simple pork in the minds of many voters...." (Toner 1994).[1]

Notwithstanding the Republicans' loud condemnation of pork barrel politics during the 1994 election campaigns, Republican freshmen in the 104th Congress quickly began to serve their constituencies in the traditional manner. For example, George Nethercutt (R-Wash.), who unseated Speaker Thomas S. Foley by depicting him as a pork barrel politician, quickly became a strong advocate of farm subsidies in his agricultural district once in office (Wines 1995). Additionally, a *New York Times* tally of 1995 awards of highway and urban mass transit projects by the House Appropriations Committee's transportation subcommittee shows that Republicans and Democrats alike received projects, but members of the congressional majority, the Republicans, received considerably more than the Democrats (Wines 1995), despite the party's denunciation of pork barrel politics in the 1994 election campaign.

By the fall of election year 2000, the *Los Angeles Times* reported that things were back to normal:

> ...the more aggressive Republican approach has been to provide vulnerable incumbents opportunities to address their districts' local concerns. And that, in turn, has meant that year-end appropriation bills are laden with local projects. "You can't point to a single vulnerable incumbent who hasn't been taken care of in the appropriations process," boasts Tony Rudy, deputy chief of staff to House Majority Whip Tom DeLay (R-Texas). "Since Day One, we've asked our vulnerable members what they need and how we can help them get it. These guys don't have to run a one-size-fits-all race." (Hook 2000)

The kind of pork barrel politics that is the focus of this book – trading projects for members' votes for broad public policy – is characterized in the media as negatively as any other pork barrel deal. For example,

[1] For members of Congress devoted to this vote-winning strategy, a cautionary note is sounded by a national poll of the voting age population in which respondents indicated that the most important aspects of the job of a member of Congress was to pass laws on important national problems and to help people with the bureaucracy. Bringing money or projects to the district was last on the list. Moreover, a majority of that survey's respondents said that they would prefer for their representatives to help to reduce the deficit by not bringing benefits back to the district, even if other members continue to do so (Hibbing and Theiss-Morse 1995). The academic literature that addresses the priority that voters give to pork barrel benefits is addressed more fully in the next chapter.

President Clinton received a considerable amount of bad press for buying the votes of members of the House of Representatives for the North American Free Trade Agreement (NAFTA). As one account described that effort, ". . . the vote on NAFTA last month came down to old-fashioned bribery" (Anderson and Silverstein 1993, p. 752).

Nevertheless, a description of former Public Works and Transportation Committee Chair Robert Roe's generosity to his colleagues reveals the benefits in terms of personal power: "The bills that went before his subcommittee were his personal handiwork, and drew votes from legions of members owing him a personal debt" (Davis 1987, p. 2594). This and similar accounts typically leave the impression that although it may be legal, such vote buying is corrupt and immoral, as legislators sell out the national interest for something as trivial as a highway or, in the case of NAFTA, favorable treatment for their district's farmers, such as broomcorn growers and tomato farmers.

However, there is some recognition that, as this book argues, such spending can help speed the passage of legislation of national importance: "Pork has . . . come to play a role in passing major bills with sweeping national impact. . . . As part of such deal making, those trying to pass a given bill will sweeten it by adding dozens and sometimes hundreds of items of interest to individual members" (Kelly 1992, p. 11). And "when applied with skill, pork can act as a lubricant to smooth passage of complex legislation"; "perhaps the most time-honored rule of pork-barreling is that any member getting a project is duty bound to support the rest of the bill" (Starobin 1987, p. 2583 and 2587).

The New Republic, almost alone among journalistic publications, recognized the strategic use of pork and went so far as to praise it as a tool for creating majority coalitions:

> Even if every single pork barrel project really were a complete waste of federal money, pork still represents a very cheap way to keep our sputtering legislative process from grinding to a halt. In effect, pork is like putting oil in your car engine: it lubricates the parts and keeps friction to a minimum. This is particularly true when you are talking about controversial measures. (Cohn 1998, p. 23)

Similarly, Ellwood and Patashnik (1993), themselves academics, writing in *Public Interest*, praised the practice, arguing that it allows legislators to take risky actions for the public good and protect themselves from electoral retaliation. Yet none of these authors systematically examines how pork is used to gain votes or the effectiveness of this strategy for passing general interest bills. Nor does the scholarly literature on distributive politics, discussed in the following section, do so.

THEORIES OF DISTRIBUTIVE POLITICS

A careful reading of any serious newspaper shows that congressional leaders exert great effort to enact public policy of national scope; moreover, political parties struggle over competing visions of the public good. The following section of this chapter and Chapter 2 analyze the serious difficulties that Congress faces in its efforts to pass general interest legislation and how the distribution of pork barrel projects helps them to do so. Yet despite those problems, journalistic accounts show that Congress traditionally has had little trouble taking collective action to provide legislative packages made up exclusively of distributive or pork barrel benefits, defined earlier as benefits that are targeted to discrete populations, such as a geographic area, and paid for through general taxation.

A large and distinguished body of scholarship focuses explicitly on the passage of purely distributive legislation. Formal theories of distributive politics examine legislative bargaining to pass omnibus bills that provide distributive benefits for a majority of legislators' districts. Such bills are composed of nothing but pork barrel benefits and therefore do not include general interest provisions. Formal distributive theories assume, first, that members seek distributive benefits for their constituents in order to get reelected (e.g., Rundquist and Ferejohn 1975; Weingast 1979; Shepsle and Weingast 1984).[2] Second, they assume that legislatures operate under majority rule arrangements; thus, in order for any member to secure a pork barrel project, a majority must receive them. After all, no one has a direct personal interest in other members' projects, but each has a strong interest in his or her own; therefore, each member has an incentive to vote for other legislators' projects in exchange for those members' votes for his or her own. In a majoritarian institution, each project must obtain the support of at least 50 percent plus one of the members present and voting in order to pass. The way to achieve that is to give at least a minimal majority of the voting members a personal interest in voting for other members' projects by including in the bill projects for all members of the prospective majority. The resulting legislation consists of an omnibus bill of pork barrel projects.

[2] However, it should be noted that the more general theories of distributive politics are not inconsistent with a variety of motivations. See Shepsle and Weingast 1994.

Formal theories concentrate in part on the important question of the size of the majority – minimal versus universal – whose members will receive projects and thus vote for the bill. Theorists have debated the equilibrium size of such pure distributive policy coalitions. On one hand, it is argued that the victorious coalition for distributive legislation will be minimal winning, in which only a bare majority of members gets projects (Buchanan and Tullock 1962; Riker 1962; Riker and Ordeshook 1973; Snyder 1991). The incentive to join such a coalition is that the total benefit pie, which is paid for by all taxpayers, is divided up fewer ways.

Others argue that omnibus pork barrel bills will be passed by universalistic coalitions (Barry 1965; Ferejohn 1974; Mayhew 1974; Weingast 1979; Shepsle and Weingast 1981; Niou and Ordeshook 1985), which form when legislators "seek unanimous passage of distributive programs through the inclusion of a project for all legislators who want one" (Weingast 1979, p. 249). A norm of universalism develops out of members' uncertainty as to whether they will be included in any given minimal winning coalition, because the number of such potential coalitions is very large and, without a structurally induced equilibrium, equally likely to form. Each legislator worries about the risk of not being in the benefit-winning coalition that finally does emerge and losing his or her seat as punishment for not bringing home the bacon. A universalistic approach obviously minimizes this uncertainty and maximizes the legislator's chances of getting an electorally beneficial project; an institutional norm of universalism therefore produces a greater expected net benefit for each member than a minimal winning coalition. Thus, it is argued that members prefer universalistic distribution of government benefits.

However, the role of distributive benefits in passing general interest legislation is typically not recognized in the formal literature on distributive politics, largely because it ignores general interest legislation altogether. An exception is found in the work of Groseclose and Snyder (1996), who employ the language and analytic approach of distributive theories but develop implications for a more general theory of distributive politics. They derive a model in which leaders attempt to buy as cheaply as possible votes for their preferred policies, of whatever type. Although the point is not explicit, in their model the legislative package need not consist only of a set of pork barrel projects; rather, it could contain as its base a general interest policy, such as NAFTA, an example to which they refer but do not examine empirically.[3] Like other theorists, they are primarily concerned with the size of winning coalitions and the price that must be paid for members' votes.

Despite the general lack of attention to the use of special projects by leaders to win votes for their broad public policy goals, scholars have recognized that legislative coalition leaders use logrolling for broader purposes than benefits targeted to individual districts. For example, it has long been known that supporters of agricultural commodity programs and backers of the food stamp program created legislative majorities by supporting each other's broad-based programs (Ferejohn 1986). Likewise, supporters of different agricultural commodities, each one of which affects numerous districts but by itself would be unlikely to win majority support, have created majority coalitions by voting for subsidies for each others' commodities (Stratmann 1992). Logrolling also occurs among supporting coalitions for bills of even more general interest, including consumer protection and minimum wage legislation (Kau and Rubin 1979). These and other studies established empirically that logrolling occurs on several types of policies, not just for packages of individual projects aimed at single congressional districts. More to the point of the argument made here, the scholarly literature refers to – but, except for the start made by Groseclose and Snyder (1996), does not systematically examine – the role of distributive benefits in the passage of general interest legislation.[4] Thus, although there is some recognition that trading individual pork barrel benefits for votes occurs, scholars have not fully considered the strategies by which it is done nor examined such exchanges using data from cases in which it was attempted.

[3] Groseclose (1996), making a similar theoretical argument, does test the vote-buying hypothesis empirically, if indirectly (lacking data on specific favors used to buy votes), but uses as his case the Byrd Amendment to the 1990 Clean Air Act, which would have provided benefits to coal miners who lost their jobs due to the Clean Air Act. Although it would have benefited people in more than one state had it passed, this amendment meets the definition of distributive benefits, in that it was targeted to a discrete group of geographically concentrated people. Thus, that paper does not provide an example of the use of distributive benefits to pass general interest legislation, although the argument itself could be applied to such cases.

[4] However, a systematic support-buying strategy for broad-based legislation has been studied in the executive branch, where officials build legislative coalitions by distributing some of the benefits under their control to members of Congress who can help their programs. Arnold (1979) found that executive agencies allocate district benefits so as to maintain supportive congressional coalitions for the agencies' programs, attempting to buy at least tacit acquiescence from program opponents and active assistance from supporters.

In fact, the major dilemma faced by Congress is how to achieve collective action to pass general benefit legislation, given the individualistic impulses generated by the desire to be reelected. The argument of this book, an argument generally neglected by the literature on distributive politics, is that pork barrel benefits help policy coalition leaders to resolve that dilemma, one which is faced by any legislative body organized, like the U.S. Congress, on the basis of geographic representation with, during most of the twentieth century, relatively weak formal mechanisms for enforcing party discipline, compared with parliamentary democracies and some state legislatures. The solution that is examined systematically here is that legislative leaders form coalitions to support major general benefit legislation by buying enough votes to create a majority.

However, some scholars have proposed other theories of how Congress achieves majority coalitions; in several of these approaches, distributive benefits play a role, albeit a less central one than the role described in this book. The following section examines, first, the nature of the collective action dilemma and, second, several prominent theories of how that dilemma is resolved and the role that distributive benefits play in the process. In the following chapter, I develop my own model, one in which distributive politics plays a more central role than in these theories, and show how that model advances our understanding of the process of creating majority coalitions in an individualistic legislature.

PORK BARREL POLITICS AND THE COLLECTIVE ACTION DILEMMA

Collective action simply consists of the coordinated activities of two or more individuals (Sandler 1992, xvii). Of course, it is well known that the larger the size of the group needed to take collective action, the more difficult it is to do so on the merits; that is, the more people there are who share a collective goal, the harder it is to organize them for action, because in large groups, each potential member has an incentive to free-ride on the efforts of others (Olson 1965). In a legislature, collective action by a majority is normally required for the body to make authoritative decisions; in some cases, an extraordinary majority is required, as it is to override a presidential veto or, in the Senate, to cut off debate. However, collective action does not necessarily produce collective benefits or general interest legislation. In fact, most of the literature on distributive politics concerns how Congress takes collective action to provide distributive benefits, as discussed earlier.

Finding incentives to get Congress to take collective action to provide general benefits is more problematic. The difficulties involved in doing so comprise Congress's collective action dilemma, the major symptom of which is that members of Congress have more incentive to pass pork barrel bills than general benefit legislation. The source of the problem, it is argued, is the reelection goal, whose primacy has for several decades been a fundamental premise of the literature on Congress. As David Mayhew contends, "[reelection] has to be the *proximate* goal of everyone, the goal that must be achieved over and over if other ends are to be entertained" (Mayhew 1974, p. 16). To be sure, important work has considered additional goals, specifically making good public policy and gaining influence in the House or Senate (Fenno 1973); but the electoral goal in particular drives the distribution of benefits to constituents (Fenno 1973; Ferejohn 1974; Murphy 1974; Shepsle and Weingast 1981; Fiorina 1989), even if it does not motivate everything that members of Congress do.

Given the importance of reelection, the supreme challenge for Congress arguably is to provide itself with incentives to engage in collective action to achieve broad national goals. The problem is most vividly illuminated by David Mayhew (1974) in his elegant extended essay on the impact of the reelection goal on Congress members' behavior and the resulting implications for public policy. Mayhew argues that, on its own, the reelection incentive gives rise to a bias toward particularized (i.e., distributive or pork barrel) legislation, as it is for such benefits that members believably can claim credit and are held individually accountable by the constituents and interest groups who determine their reelection chances. Such credit claiming is believable because pork barrel benefits are of a relatively small scale and are precisely targeted; constituents therefore reasonably believe, with the member's encouragement, that no one else cares enough about the district to bother to provide them (Mayhew 1974, p. 54).

Members of such a radically individualistic body need never take action to form coalitions to pass nonparticularized or general interest legislation, because their constituents do not hold them personally responsible for broad-based policies. Electoral benefits arise from merely taking positions on general interest legislation, not from mobilizing to pass it. On the other hand, in the arena of distributive benefits, members must actually work to get concrete results for their supporters in order to obtain electoral rewards.

These incentives create a collective action problem: In large legislative bodies, the impact of most members' individual contributions to passing broad-based legislation is so dilute that there is no incentive for them to devote time to it, especially as that time could otherwise be spent servicing constituents and special interests with targeted benefits. Rather, in the arena of general interest legislation, there is a strong incentive for members to free-ride on the contributions of others. For the legislature as a whole, the problem then becomes how to ensure that someone has an incentive to provide collective benefits in the form of general interest legislation.

Several prominent theories of congressional organization and legislative strategy deal with this collective action dilemma, particularly as it pertains to general benefit legislation. These analyses each delineate different means by which Congress channels members' reelection concerns into incentives to take collective action for the collective benefit, thus resolving the reelection/collective goods dilemma. They all link the resolution of the collective action problem to its source, the reelection goal, as I do. However, those analyses differ in their identification of the solution that Congress has devised to deal with the dilemma.

The first approach to a resolution is found in Mayhew's own analysis of the electoral incentive, where he takes account of Congress's exploitation of a further incentive, individual power, as a means to resolve its collective action dilemma. A second approach highlights the role of congressional leaders, showing how they manipulate members' behavior, using the reelection goal to induce them to support policies that provide collective benefits. Additionally, informational and partisan theories take as their primary object of study how Congress organizes itself more broadly to pass legislation, particularly general benefit legislation. The remainder of this chapter briefly summarizes the major arguments and conclusions of each of these approaches to the collective action dilemma and examines how they incorporate distributive benefits. All of them include a role for such benefits to some extent, but in none of them are distributive benefits as central to the resolution of the dilemma as they are in my argument, which I develop further in Chapter 2.

The Electoral Incentive

Mayhew argues that to solve the collective action problem created by the reelection incentive, it was necessary for Congress to create positions of extraordinary internal power that give some members a reason to provide for what he calls institutional maintenance. Those positions reward members who take time away from reelection-enhancing distributive politics to appropriate money for broad national programs, to attend to the tax code, and (in the House of Representatives) to regulate floor procedures.

Specifically, the House gave unusual power and influence to the members of the "control" committees, which at the time of his study consisted of the Appropriations, Ways and Means, and Rules Committees (Mayhew 1974).

Why would reelection-seeking legislators find it wise to grant selective incentives to some of their own to attend to broader legislative matters, especially when those power committees are intended in part to restrain members' pork barrel tendencies? Mayhew argued that they did so because "if members hope to spend careers in Congress, they have a stake in maintaining its prestige as an institution" (1974, p. 145), and the reelection logic, if left alone, would threaten the prestige and ultimately the power of Congress itself. That is, an institution that operates unfettered by concern for collective goods would tax barely at all and spend the country into oblivion because electoral rewards attend both kinds of policy making. Moreover, individual members usually can evade blame for the collective impact of such policies. Therefore, through membership on committees that confer disproportionate individual power, the House provides selective incentives for some of its members to supply the collective benefit of congressional prestige by protecting the federal treasury and bringing order to House floor proceedings. Paradoxically, in this view, the first collective good that an individualistic, reelection-oriented legislature must provide is its own institutional power and prestige. The distributive impulse thus generates the need for Congress to exploit other goals in order to provide collective goods.

However, Mayhew's solution to the dilemma is limited to two key areas of policy making, those most fundamental to the functioning of government: taxation and spending. My own view is that policy coalition leaders resolve the problem in many policy areas by turning the very distributive impulse that Mayhew implicitly criticizes to the task of making general interest legislation, using the particularized benefits that damage the institutional reputation of Congress to save it.

The Policy Modification Strategy: Arnold's Theory

In contrast to Mayhew, Douglas Arnold, in his ground-breaking analysis of legislative strategy, argues that the drive for reelection can lead members of Congress to seek either distributive *or* general benefits, depending on how the leaders of policy coalitions manipulate the decision-making process. Distributive benefits play a role in his theory but are not used in the targeted way in which they are in the model presented in this book, in which policy coalition leaders give projects to individuals to gain their votes. Arnold sees three main strategies by which leaders form majority coalitions: persuasion, procedural methods, and modification of legislative proposals (1990, pp. 92–115). All of these strategies have the potential to help leaders resolve the collective action dilemma. Persuasion consists of acting to change the policy preferences of relevant actors and persuading legislators that it would be to their electoral advantage to support the policy. Procedural strategies involve the use of legislative procedures in ways that make support for the leaders' preferred policies appear electorally advantageous or at least not disadvantageous for members.

The third strategy, modification of policies, comes the closest of the three to the vote-buying model presented in this book. The policy modification strategy involves changing the policy to attract a larger supporting coalition without altering it so much that the leaders themselves can no longer support it. For example, leaders may transform a comprehensive proposal to one that is incremental in its approach, a strategy that was followed by supporters of national health insurance when they settled for partial solutions to health care needs with Medicare and Medicaid (Arnold 1990, pp. 108–115).

Another modification technique, one that is more to the point of this book, is to change the allocation of distributive benefits to attract additional key coalition leaders or inactivate potential opposition leaders. Such members are awarded disproportionate distributive benefits, typically by broadening the categories of eligible benefit recipients so that the districts of key members qualify. However, Arnold argues that coalition leaders do not target individual members with exclusive benefits:

> When promoting proposed programs, coalition leaders have only a few geographic strategies available, since they do not yet have any specific benefits to promise individual legislators. All they can do is try to affect legislators' general expectations by modifying a program's character. (1990, p. 114)

Because such benefits are normally given out to congressional districts by bureaucrats (also see Arnold 1979), he argues that coalition leaders use strategies of modification to increase the *probability* that any one member's district will receive distributive benefits in the bureaucratic allocation process, rather than by directly providing such benefits. That can be done in one of two ways: by liberalizing the eligibility criteria to enlarge the geographic scope of the program or by increasing the number of shares to be given out by the agency. He notes, for example, that the Johnson administration found it necessary to broaden the categories of cities that would qualify for the model cities program in order to ensure that some small cities would be included; it did so to attract Edmund Muskie as a coalition leader in the Senate (1990, pp. 108–114).

However, Arnold's version of policy modification is necessarily an indirect approach to buying votes, one that makes it more difficult for coalition leaders strategically to target key members of Congress. Instead, leaders must cast a wide benefit net that will capture a supporting coalition of somewhat indefinite size and composition in order to snare the needed committee chairs and other key members. Another implication of this strategy, one that limits its efficacy, is the following: Because benefits are not individually targeted to the districts of specific members, leaders cannot easily enforce the terms of the trade by threatening to remove traitors' benefits in conference committee. Eliminating a category of benefits to punish a traitor might also punish a loyal friend whose district falls into the same category, which leaders are likely to be reluctant to do. Additionally, broadening the number of categories of beneficiaries, as Arnold notes, dilutes the benefits in all categories, reducing the vote-buying power of any one benefit (1990, pp. 114–115).

Due to the resulting insufficiency of incentives to comply with leaders' wishes, this strategy entails a potential free rider problem: In a large legislature, members who might receive a benefit if the program passes can afford to vote against the program, knowing that failure to support it is unlikely to affect materially their district's chances of getting a significant benefit. And even if members support the program as a whole due to a high probability that their districts will benefit, those benefits, along with a low risk that betrayals will be punished, give members less incentive to be loyal to *all* of the leaders' positions, including those that do not relate directly to the benefit in question. That is because it is difficult to use broad categories of benefits (whose advantages are often diluted, as described above) to gain members' support not only for the bill itself, but also for the leaders' positions on any amendments. Benefits more sharply targeted to individuals solve that problem. That is because, using Arnold's approach, leaders are unlikely to eliminate benefits for a whole category of members just to punish one legislator for not supporting them on an amendment, especially if that member voted for the underlying bill. By contrast, it is quite feasible to eliminate a pork barrel benefit that was targeted to a specific member in punishment for betrayal on an amendment. In his brief discussion of the addition of transition rules for individual legislators in the 1986 tax reform bill, Arnold does recognize that leaders influenced individual members' votes by inserting benefits for their constituents; he quotes Senate Finance Committee Chairman Robert Packwood (R-Ore.) as saying committee members would not receive transition rules unless they voted for his bill (1990, p. 218). Yet such individual vote buying is not fully incorporated into his theoretical discussion. The sort of policy modification that Arnold describes there, a strategy of targeting benefits to classes of districts rather than to individual ones, is a blunt instrument compared with the insertion of projects for individual members. Additionally, in Arnold's analysis, this strategy is available only when the policy proposal confers distributive benefits in the first place. On the other hand, giving benefits to individual members (as opposed to categories of districts) in return for their support is something that can be done regardless of the nature of the policy in question, as Chapter 2 explains.

Thus, although Arnold's analysis of how coalition leaders resolve the collective action dilemma does not exclude individual vote buying, it also does not fully develop and explore that strategy.

The Informational Approach

Although informational theory is not explicitly aimed at showing how Congress resolves its collective action dilemma, it provides important insights into both that question and the role of pork barrel benefits. Like other theories of congressional behavior and policy making, the informational theory of legislative organization is based, at least implicitly, on the reelection incentive. According to this approach, lawmakers organize their legislatures to reduce uncertainty about the effects of the policies that they pass. As Thomas Gilligan and Keith Krehbiel (1990) assume, legislators know what policy outcomes their constituents want, but are uncertain about which legislation will produce those results. Thus, they organize themselves into specialized committees that have an incentive to provide accurate information about likely policy outcomes so that all members can vote for the policies that will produce effects that their constituents desire. Implicit in this formulation is the recognition that members want reelection and that constituents cast their votes on the basis of policy effects. There is no specification as to what type of public policy is involved; it could be distributive or general interest policy.

Nevertheless, the issue of the disproportionate distribution of benefits looms large in informational theory. Krehbiel (1992) derives "informationally efficient" committees, which are legislative committees that share their information about policy effects with the rest of the legislature. The trick of legislative organization is to design committees so that they have no incentive to be uninformative or, failing that, to provide incentives for committees to be informationally efficient. Krehbiel argues that one way in which legislatures achieve this goal is to select committee members who do not exhibit a high demand for the committee's policies, as such members would try to gain most of the benefits of the committee's output for their own districts or conceal information about the policies for their own benefit. Heterogeneous committees, which have members on both sides of the issue spectrum, are more likely to be informationally efficient, thus transmitting information that is inherently more credible to the rest of the legislature. Where committees do allow extreme or high-demanding members to join, it is because they can specialize at a lower cost than other members due to their greater incentive to gain information about the policy area.

Informationally efficient committees are rewarded. Because their information about policy effects can be trusted by other members, they are more likely to get restrictive rules on the floor, thus limiting the extent to which their legislation can be amended; that, in turn, increases the chances that their bills will pass in the committee's preferred form. A restrictive rule also allows committee members to add distributive benefits for their districts to the bill without risking a pork barrel free-for-all on the floor (Krehbiel 1992, pp. 95–101). These benefits serve, in effect, as a reward to committee members for specializing and disseminating accurate information. When committees are not composed entirely or even largely of high-demanders, the legislature can tolerate some degree of distributive advantage to committee members because they are not likely to be unduly greedy.

In contrast to distributive theory, where pork barrel benefits are the point of the legislative process, Krehbiel argues that in informational theories,

> Pork is not the do-all and end-all of legislative behavior, legislative organization, or legislative policy outcomes.... distributional issues merely form the basis of conflict. To be sure, conflict is a major part of what makes legislative politics fascinating, and distributive policies are sometimes useful currencies with which to pay off hardworking committee members who contribute to informational efficiency in the legislative process. However, information theories place distributive politics in a different perspective. Pork may be a lubricant for the legislative machine, but it is not the machine's main product. (Krehbiel 1992, p. 95)

Thus, distributive benefits *are* used in exchange for something in informational theories. That something is not votes, however; it is committee members' time, effort, and truthful communication. In informational theory, in order to gain floor passage, especially under a restrictive rule, the policies proposed by committees must pass the test of being superior to the status quo in themselves (without pork barrel sweeteners) in the eyes of the majority of the legislature. By contrast, when members' votes are bought with pork barrel benefits, the policy to which they are attached need not be superior to the status quo in the majority's eyes if the distributive benefits that the members receive are more salient (and more appealing) than the underlying policy.

Thus, the informational theory of congressional organization does not encompass the use of pork barrel benefits to purchase votes for general benefit legislation that cannot get a majority on the basis of its own provisions. Yet if leaders keep such legislation free of pork, they deprive themselves of an important tool of legislative strategy. As the data in this book show, when coalition leaders buy votes for general interest legislation with pork, they can grease the legislative wheels, distributing it wherever it is needed, not just to committee members for doing the institutionally beneficial thing. Moreover, leaders can pass legislation with provisions that they favor, but which alone may not be able to garner a legislative majority.

Partisan Approaches

Gary Cox and Matthew McCubbins (1993) and David Rohde (1991) address the problem of unrestrained legislative individualism in partisan rather than institutional terms, seeing the party caucuses and their leaders in the House of Representatives as the source of collective action. Like Mayhew, Cox and McCubbins acknowledge that without selective incentives there is little individual inducement for legislators to make sacrifices to achieve collective goals. However, quite unlike Mayhew, who argues that members can evade individual responsibility for collective outcomes, their argument suggests that the potential effect of members' radical individualism is damage to each one's chances of reelection. That is because legislators' electoral fates depend not only on their own individual records and qualities, but also on their parties' records of achievement. They argue that legislators are held individually accountable by the voters for the record of the party of which they are members (Cox and McCubbins 1993, pp. 109–110).

Knowing this, legislators give their party leaders powers that help the leaders to enforce some degree of party loyalty and therefore individual accountability for the party's record. Those leaders make and enforce deals to pass collective benefit legislation that is designed to gain or maintain majority status for their party. Cox and McCubbins join Mayhew in locating leaders' power primarily in their ability to structure the control committees: They exercise a relatively high degree of control over who serves on those committees, rewarding loyal members with prestigious appointments; majority party leaders also exercise some degree of control over the choice of committee chairs. The chairs, in turn, have two kinds of individual incentives to shepherd the party's collective benefit legislation to passage: First, success helps to secure their leadership status; second, they get a share of any distributive benefits that they give out to other party members to close rifts in the party over the broader legislation (Cox and McCubbins 1993, pp. 123–125).

In this way, partisan theory explicitly takes account of particularized benefits as rewards. However, while distributive benefits serve as useful selective incentives, Cox and McCubbins do not develop fully the implications of trading benefits for votes. Party leaders presumably could buy the votes of only a few members of their caucus. Those members might be, in Krehbiel's terms, pivotal voters, or those who are essentially indifferent between the proposed policy and the status quo (Krehbiel 1998, p. 99). But if they are nearly indifferent, why would they not go along with a public policy that would help their party stay in power? Why would they need, in addition to that incentive, a pork barrel benefit? Of course, there might well be additional caucus members initially slightly opposed to the bill who could be brought around by a pork barrel benefit. For that to happen, those members must calculate the risks of supporting a policy that their constituents presumably also oppose somewhat in return for a local benefit. If the value of the local benefit outweighs the cost of the larger policy, they can afford to sell their votes, even in Cox and McCubbins's world where constituents vote in part on the basis of the party's national performance. In any event, while Cox and McCubbins recognize that pork helps leaders to form majority coalitions, they do not develop the circumstances under which members would find it worthwhile to sell their votes. Indeed, the authors acknowledge the restricted role of distributive benefits in their theory: "We think that the debate over the strength of party as an influence on voting behavior has focused too narrowly on the meting out of tangible rewards and punishments by leaders" (1993, p. 156). However, in their focus on party agendas, they neglect the function of distributive benefits in bringing along members of the opposing party, a role that is explored in Chapter 2.

In developing the theory of conditional party government, Rohde (1991) argues that House leaders obtain strong powers over their party when there is broad agreement within the caucus and conflict between the parties over many policy issues. Majority party leaders are enabled to exercise their powers fully when there is intraparty consensus and interparty conflict *on a particular issue*, a circumstance that he calls "conditional party government." Under those conditions, the majority party can press its policy agenda, as internal consensus exists only on an issue that will not cost members reelection or their own majority status. Yet even when the majority party enjoys broad agreement but not unanimity on a policy issue, its leaders still may lack sufficient votes to pass it; under those circumstances, the leadership is authorized to use its powers to bring into line recalcitrant members. Those powers exist primarily in the form of incentives made available to the House Democratic leadership during the 1970s reform era, such as heightened control of committee assignments and the rules governing floor debate (Rohde 1991, pp. 28–36), along with similar powers later assumed by the Republican leadership (Aldrich and Rohde 2001). Although the theory of conditional party government does not stress the use of distributive benefits to draw support from recalcitrant members, that technique could function here as it would in Cox and McCubbins's theory.

Overall, partisan theorists allow that pork can be used to rein in majority party members who can afford to sell their votes this way (and some cannot, due to strong district opposition). Thus, pork can be used to expand the number of issues on which conditional party government is possible. However, those theorists do not acknowledge that it can also bring in minority party members. In addition, in the hands of committee leaders or the president, pork can even separate majority party members from their own floor leaders. That is, leaders who have access to pork barrel benefits can work in opposition to party leaders, enticing members to defect in return for a district benefit. A notable example of presidential influence against the majority party occurred on the 1993 NAFTA vote in the House, when President Clinton worked against his own party's majority leader and whip to gain acceptance of NAFTA. The president's use of distributive benefits to win votes for NAFTA is examined in detail in Chapter 5.

Summary

Although each of these theoretical approaches to how Congress legislates general benefits incorporates distributive benefits to a greater or lesser degree, none of them treats fully the use of pork barrel projects as a solution to the problem of making collective benefit legislation in an individualistic, single-member-district-based legislature.

Additionally, pure distributive theories conceive of pork as something that is legislated for its own sake, so that for any member to receive a project, a majority must receive them. In this narrow world, no one has any incentive to worry about passing general interest legislation, as everyone focuses on benefits for his or her own constituents. Moreover, distributive theories typically ignore the role of legislative leaders in assembling the oversized coalitions that many scholars have found in the real world of distributive politics. Rather, the coalition-building process implicit in these theories is one in which rank-and-file members, responding to their own electoral needs, forge agreements with each other to form majorities to acquire distributive benefits. By contrast, I argue that legislative leaders are the key actors in assembling coalitions to support all kinds of legislation.

Two of the approaches summarized in this chapter bear similarities to the argument of this book: partisan theories and Arnold's policy modification strategy. Both take account of the role of leaders in assembling majority coalitions. However, my argument is that the use of pork to gain votes is not necessarily tied to partisanship; indeed, it is a coalition-building technique that transcends the bounds of partisanship, giving those in a position to use it considerable ability to reach across party lines in search of allies. Moreover, I conceive of vote buying as a more precisely targeted and therefore a more effective strategy than does Arnold, a strategy that can be used to pass many types of legislation.

However, I should stress that the coalition-building approach presented here is not intended as a substitute for any of these other theories, but rather as a complement. As Shepsle and Weingast (1994, p. 153) and Rohde (1994) argue, the major approaches to understanding congressional policy making are not mutually exclusive, but rather share a number of complementarities. The one offered here should be seen as one of a number of ways in which Congress deals with its major dilemma.

THE STRUCTURE OF THE BOOK

The chapters that follow develop more fully my own argument that the judicious distribution of pork barrel benefits is an important technique for forming majority coalitions for general interest legislation; I also test the empirical implications of that argument. Chapter 2 presents a systematic explication of the ways in which leaders pursue the vote-buying strategy and how legislators respond to it. I describe two alternate strategies by which policy coalition leaders might distribute pork in order to secure members' votes. First, they could make a careful calculation of just how many additional votes they need for a bill and give benefits only to that number of members (the minimal winning coalition approach). Alternatively, they could give pork universally, or at least to supermajorities, in order to increase the certainty of majority support for all of their positions, even on unforeseen developments during the bill's legislative progress. This chapter also considers the possibility that members themselves, seeing that special benefits are available to those who play their cards right, conceal their true intentions on a bill that they already support in order to more effectively bargain for benefits, resulting in the distribution of pork to supermajorities of members. Finally, Chapter 2 explores the likelihood that members who receive such benefits honor their bargains and support the legislative preferences of the leaders who bestowed them.

Chapters 3 through 6 consist of case studies of the use of distributive benefits in general interest bills. These cases provide an opportunity to test many of the propositions developed in Chapter 2, allowing an assessment of the utility of this analysis of one important means of resolving Congress's collective action dilemma. The empirical data permit examination of the applicability of the arguments in Chapter 2 to both the House and Senate; in Democratic- and Republican-controlled congresses and across a time period in which parties were both increasingly polarized and internally unified (i.e., the requirements of conditional party government were increasingly met). To the extent that the arguments hold across houses and changes in partisan control, we can be confident of their generality. To the extent that that is not the case, we must consider competing explanations for the passage of general interest legislation.

Chapter 3 examines how committee leaders allocated highway demonstration projects in two major highway reauthorization bills by the House Public Works and Transportation Committee; specifically, that chapter analyzes systematically what factors determined the distribution of project awards, that is, who received projects in bills that otherwise distributed funds by formula. The chapter analyzes the 1987 highway bill, the first reauthorization in which committee leaders included large numbers of projects for individual members (as opposed to the traditional formula allocation of highway funds), and the 1991 bill, the next program authorization. This data allows an exploration of increases over time in the numbers of such projects and the forces that drove the change. More specifically, this chapter analyzes the evidence for the argument that members strategically concealed their true preferences on the second (1991) bill in order to get a project, once they became aware, as a result of the projects in the 1987 bill, that leaders were willing to use projects to win their votes.

Chapter 4 goes further with the highway bills, examining the impact of highway projects on the roll call votes of the members who received them. It provides the first test of whether or not pork barrel projects do in fact buy votes for broad-based measures and, if so, whether they are as effective the second time that leaders use them, when members may be concealing their true support for the bill, as the first time, when members are more likely to state their sincere voting intentions.

Chapter 5 examines the vote-buying strategy in the hands of the president; specifically, it analyzes the use and effectiveness of special benefits promised by President Clinton to members of the House in the difficult but ultimately successful battle to gain its approval of NAFTA. Chapter 6 considers the use of this strategy in the Senate, which traditionally is reputed to find individual pork barrel projects less advantageous than other methods of distributing benefits to constituents. This chapter analyzes the insertion of special projects into Senate appropriations bills in three different congresses and the impact of those projects on senators' floor votes. One set of cases is taken from a Democratic congress; the other two are from Republican-controlled congresses. The comparison of congresses dominated by different parties allows consideration of the question of whether Republicans and Democrats use pork barrel projects for the same purpose and to the same effect.

The final chapter summarizes the results across cases, houses of Congress, and parties, and reaches conclusions about the merits of the arguments presented in Chapter 2. It also considers the impact of the vote-buying strategy on the public policies that it is intended to help to pass. I do not reach judgments as to whether legislation passed with this technique is good public policy. My argument is that distributive benefits help leaders pass general interest legislation that they themselves favor. Additionally, to assess the generality of the findings in this book, this chapter explores the question of when and how often this coalition-formation technique can be used. Finally, the chapter examines the implications of this coalition-building strategy for majoritarian democracy. Briefly, the argument is that when some legislators' votes are bought with pork barrel benefits, the general interest policy to which the benefits are attached need not be to the liking of the majority of Congress. Thus, although vote buying is one solution to the problem of passing general interest legislation, it paradoxically may undermine majoritarian government on broader policy issues.

A word about terminology is in order here. The use of the term "vote buying," along with the corollary of "vote selling," may seem to imply corruption. I do not intend that implication. The expression is, rather, a convenient metaphor for the exchange of a distributive benefit that is, like money, disaggregable, for support for a broad, general interest policy. However, such exchanges, when they occur, are qualitatively different from buying and selling votes for money (i.e., taking bribes) or campaign contributions. The latter activities are both corrupt and illegal: It is a violation of federal criminal statutes for members of Congress to take something of value for *themselves* in exchange for performing an official act (18 USC 201). By contrast, it is neither illegal nor, in my view, corrupt for members of Congress to decide to trade their votes on national policy for constituency benefits. That is because, unlike the hard cash that might change hands in a bribery scheme, the distributive benefit is intended for members' constituents. Naturally, members hope to receive their constituents' support in return for what they do for them, whether the benefit is local or national, but that is the nature of representation. In the sort of vote buying that I describe in this book, when policy coalition leaders offer such exchanges, legislators have an obligation then to consider the trade-off between the local interests of their constituents and more broad-based interests (many of which, to be sure, their constituents also care about). Tension between local and national interests is inherent in geographically based legislative bodies, and representatives would be remiss if they did not balance their constituents' immediate local interests with their interest in the national policy for which members are asked to provide their votes. Whether such trade-offs produce good public policy is a matter for debate; the final chapter takes up that question.

Thus, this book explicates an important technique by which legislative leaders attempt to overcome the electorally induced individualism of members of Congress and to persuade them to pass general interest legislation. Ironically, they do so by playing to precisely the feature of legislative politics that causes the collective action dilemma in the first place: members' desire for reelection and the resulting incentive to gain pork barrel benefits for their constituents.

2

Pork Barrel Politics and General Interest Legislation

The argument of this book is that one important strategy by which policy coalition leaders create legislative majorities for controversial general interest legislation is to buy legislators' votes, one by one, favor by favor. Doing so not only helps leaders to unite their party; it also can draw members of the other party away from their own caucus. Where attainment of a secure majority on the merits seems doubtful, distributive benefits provide the extra margin of support to compensate for pressures that otherwise might persuade members not to vote for such a bill. This strategy is particularly interesting for its use of the sort of policy that is most reviled by observers of Congress – pork barrel policy – to pass the type that is most admired – general interest policy.

Before proceeding to a discussion of the process of acquiring votes with distributive benefits, it is worthwhile to elaborate on the definition of general interest legislation. In Chapter 1, I defined such legislation as broad-based measures that affect the whole nation or a large segment thereof. This definition of general interest legislation is somewhat similar to Douglas Arnold's definition of general benefits. Arnold requires that in order to be general in their impact, policies must "fall uniformly on members of society" (Arnold 1990, p. 26). Subsumed by this definition is breadth of impact: Such policies obviously affect everyone. But aside from pure public goods, most policies do not have a truly uniform impact; even Arnold's examples, which include economic growth and stable prices, are unlikely to be truly uniform in their effects on all socioeconomic levels. Therefore, I prefer to stress the breadth, rather than the uniformity, of a policy's effects.[1] As this implies, there is a great deal of territory between the extremes of pork barrel and general interest legislation, and policy coalition leaders can use pork to gain votes just as easily for policies in that middle range as for general interest policy. However, the legislative challenge with which this book is concerned is the collective action dilemma faced by Congress in passing general interest legislation, not policies in the middle range of impacts.

Winning support for general interest legislation with pork barrel benefits is a strategy that can be used by any leader of a policy coalition: committee and subcommittee chairs, party leaders in each house of Congress, and the president. Clearly, the need to buy votes depends on the size and unity of a party's caucus. If the caucus has a large majority and is tightly unified on most matters, vote buying with pork is likely to be unnecessary. If, on the other hand, the party is heterogeneous and fragmented or in the minority, vote buying becomes more necessary in order for party leaders' preferences on general interest legislation to prevail. Even as congressional party leaders' powers have grown (especially in the House) over the past twenty years (Aldrich and Rohde 2001), there are still advantages to using the carrot of pork barrel benefits rather than the stick of party discipline to gain compliance with leaders' policy goals. In that manner, leaders can pass general interest policies that they believe will redound to the party's overall benefit in subsequent elections. It should be noted, however, that this is a strategy most available to the majority, as it is more likely to control distributive benefits.

Committee leaders can use pork for the same purpose, but their goals may differ from those of their party leaders. Committee leaders may not be in tune with their own party leadership on a given issue within their jurisdiction; if they can distribute pork, they are more able to pursue an independent course, defying their leadership in order to attain their own policy preferences. Of course, the more sanctions the leadership possesses to use against rebellious committee chairs, the less likely such a strategy is. But to the extent that chairs hold their positions independent of caucus leaders, they can use this strategy more freely, without fear of the ultimate sanction, loss of the chairmanship. When chairs are elected by caucus, they can actually gain independence from their leaders by distributing pork. No wonder the Republican leadership, having just attained the majority

[1] My definition of distributive benefits is analogous to Arnold's definition of benefits to groups or geographic areas; that is, such benefits are concentrated on one segment of the society (Arnold 1990, p. 26). For reasons explained below, I concentrate on geographic benefits.

in the House in 1995, sought to weaken committee chairs by imposing six-year term limits and initially banning the distribution of pork by appropriations subcommittee chairs (Green 1995).

THE CONDITIONS FOR USING PORK TO BUILD MAJORITY COALITIONS

Regardless of who the policy coalition leaders are, I assume that four conditions must exist in order for them to pursue this coalition-building strategy. First, they must have access to sufficient distributive benefits to trade for members' support for their favored legislation. For committee leaders, some jurisdictions are more useful than others in this regard. For example, the House committees on International Relations and the Judiciary have less opportunity to distribute pork than the Transportation and Infrastructure (formerly Public Works and Transportation) Committee and the Appropriations Committee, due to the nature of the matters under their jurisdictions.

A second necessary condition for implementing the vote-buying strategy is that leaders must be willing to use it. This circumstance should not be taken for granted, despite the obvious appeal of pork barrel benefits. An example of one who was not so willing was Representative Norman Mineta (D-Calif.), when he took over the chairmanship of the Aviation Subcommittee of the Public Works and Transportation Committee in 1989. That subcommittee previously had been known for its generous distribution of pork barrel projects; however, Mineta, who was known to oppose such projects, held fast against their inclusion in the bills reported under his leadership (Duncan 1989, p. 132).

Third, I assume that rank-and-file members who sell their votes on general interest legislation for a pork barrel project are motivated by the reelection goal. If they otherwise would oppose the bill but agree to trade their vote for a project, they must care more about the project and its impact on their reelection than about the general interest provisions of the bill to which the project is attached.

Fourth, policy coalition leaders who use this strategy are not driven by their own electoral goals to pass the underlying general interest legislation. Instead, they are motivated by the other two commonly recognized goals, making good public policy or achieving internal influence (Fenno 1973).

The third and fourth conditions deserve some elaboration. Restating them together, when leaders buy votes with pork barrel benefits, they take advantage of rank-and-file members' electoral goals to pass bills that the leaders favor; however, the leaders themselves are motivated by other goals. The idea that leaders use members' desire for reelection is not new. Scholars have long recognized that they do so in a variety of ways to gain members' support for legislation, as noted in Chapter 1 (Arnold 1990; Cox and McCubbins 1993). The assumption that underlies this hypothesis, that legislators desire reelection, has been central to much of the theory concerning congressional behavior for several decades, not only among distributive theorists (e.g., Fiorina 1989; Mayhew 1974; Rundquist and Ferejohn 1975; Weingast 1979; Shepsle and Weingast 1984), but also among those who acknowledge other goals in addition to reelection (e.g., Fenno 1973; Dodd 1977). Much of the plausibility of the reelection assumption rests on the fact that in legislative institutions where power and influence increase with seniority, successive electoral victories are necessary in order for legislators to achieve any of their other goals.

Whether pork barrel benefits confer an electoral advantage is a matter of scholarly controversy. For example, there is evidence that federal spending in a member's district has no significant impact on reelection outcomes (Feldman and Jondrow 1984; Frisch 1998; Stein and Bickers 1995, pp. 130–134). But in individual-level analysis, there is evidence that distributive projects have both direct and indirect effects on voters' choices. The indirect effect operates through an increase in voter awareness of new grants, which results in an increase in an incumbent's popularity, which in turn positively affects the incumbent's share of the vote (Stein and Bickers 1995, pp. 133–134). Additionally, there is evidence that members who narrowly won open seat elections enjoyed more new distributive benefits in the first four months of their terms than other members; those high levels of new awards early in their terms in turn reduced their chances of facing high-quality challengers in the next election (Bickers and Stein 1996). However, there is some indication that the electoral advantage conferred by pork barrel benefits accrues more to Democrats than to Republicans (Alvarez and Saving 1997; Bickers and Stein 2000), perhaps because it is expected more of Democrats (Alvarez and Schousen 1993).[2] Similarly, there is disagreement about the impact of district service, including distributive benefits (Evans Yiannakis 1981; Fiorina 1981a, 1989; Johannes and McAdams 1981), but members of Congress themselves clearly believe

[2] There is also evidence that electoral advantage depends on the "fiscal consistency" displayed by the incumbent. Sellers (1997) finds that fiscal liberals in districts that receive high levels of federal spending win reelection by higher margins than fiscal conservatives in high-pork districts. That is, the voters appear to punish members who preach fiscal austerity but bring home the bacon anyway.

that district service is helpful in building their reputations. For this belief, there is persuasive evidence (Cain, Ferejohn, and Fiorina 1987). Thus, consistent with both theoretical scholarship and much of the empirical literature on pork barrel politics, I assume that members of Congress seek distributive benefits as a way to aid their constituents and thereby boost their own reelection chances.

However, a persistent puzzle is posed by reelection-based theories of congressional behavior: What motivates potential policy coalition leaders to devote resources to pass general interest legislation that will not disproportionately benefit their districts? Presumably, their constituents will not particularly thank them for such efforts, compared with their gratitude for distributive benefits. As noted in Chapter 1, both informational and partisan theories deal with this problem in part by allowing party leaders or committee members to receive distributive benefits for devoting time to the legislative enterprise, as such benefits reduce the opportunity costs of building coalitions to pass broad-based legislation. In those theories, the solution to the dilemma, like its source, is reelection-based.

However, even that solution begs the question of the source of the original motivation to make good public policy. I agree with Mayhew (1974) that there is little direct electoral payoff to individual members for time devoted to passing collective benefit bills. That is not to say that their constituents necessarily are indifferent to national problems. However, members can make points with their constituents as easily by simply taking positions on national issues as by working on solving them behind the scenes, as typical constituents (unlike attentive elites) lack the Washington-insider information that they would need to discover whether or not there was action behind the talk. It can therefore be argued that it is irrational for reelection-driven members to engage in legislative work on issues that do not offer concentrated benefits to constituents or to interest groups (Mayhew 1974, pp. 114–115).

Nevertheless, it makes sense to assume that members have other goals in addition to reelection; by serving in Congress, they wish to accomplish something. Their other goals may consist of a number of things, but as Richard Fenno persuasively demonstrates, internal influence or power and the desire to make good public policy certainly are among them. Likewise, Lawrence Dodd (1977) argues that members want to "make a mark" in a policy area, which can be seen as a combination of Fenno's good public policy and influence goals. Arnold (1990, p. 8) identifies a similar motivation, altruism, meaning among other things that policy coalition leaders care about a particular public policy area.

Thus, we arrive at the fourth condition: that leaders' efforts to pass general interest legislation must be motivated by their goals of good public policy or power and influence rather than reelection; reelection itself is taken care of by other, perhaps related, activities. Although leaders may compensate themselves for the opportunity costs of their efforts to pass general interest legislation by inserting into the bill special benefits, perhaps disproportionate ones, targeted to their own districts, this possibility does not negate the role of nonelectoral motives in their efforts to pass broad-based legislation. After all, there are simpler ways to gain constituency benefits than by doing the spade work needed to pass major legislation, ways that leave more time for other reelection-enhancing activities. Thus, it is reasonable, even necessary, to assume that goals other than reelection, such as making good public policy and gaining influence in the House or Senate, motivate the extensive behind-the-scenes work needed to make national policy. It is not necessary to specify whether the good public policy and influence goals operate together or alone on any one legislative effort; all that matters here is that policy leaders' goals in working to pass general interest legislation are primarily nonelectoral.

Nevertheless, here again, the motivation for party leaders may differ in degree, at least, from those for other policy coalition leaders, such as committee chairs. Party leaders seek to pass general interest legislation to improve the party's public record in a way that will result in the reelection of its incumbents and help to capture some seats currently held by the other party. By doing so, they increase their own chances of retaining their leadership positions and, if they are not in the majority, gaining control of the chamber itself (Cox and McCubbins 1993, pp. 109–112, 125–135). Thus, for leaders themselves, the motive for mobilizing to pass general interest legislation is not their own reelection; rather, it is some combination of power and good public policy (the latter, in this case, in the eyes of the electorate).

How do these motives work for other policy coalition leaders, especially committee chairs? To the extent that committee and subcommittee chairs are chosen for their adherence to their caucus's policy preferences, as they are to some extent in both parties in the House, the motivation to promote the preferences of the majority of the caucus is the same as that of the party leaders themselves. That is, if they deviate too far from caucus preferences, they risk losing their leadership positions. On the other hand, they are not as responsible individually for the public record of their party as the top leaders, so they are likely to face greater temptation to seek public policy that conforms to their own policy preferences, as long as it falls within the boundaries of what the caucus is willing to tolerate. The exceptions are likely to be the chairs of the committees whose jurisdictions encompass those issues that define the differences between the parties and thus its public record, such as Appropriations, Budget, and the tax-writing committees (Ways and Means in the House and Finance in the Senate) and, of course, the Rules Committee in the House. The chairs of those committees and their subcommittees probably have less freedom to deviate from caucus preferences than others because they are responsible for the matters that largely comprise the party's identity. For other committee chairs, the balance between party goals and their own policy preferences may be tilted to a greater degree in favor of their own preferences. In any case, they, like party leaders, also are motivated by nonelectoral goals.

The president is the exception to the condition that policy coalition leaders are motivated by nonelectoral goals. He is the one figure who is held responsible by the public for collective benefits, especially the condition of the economy and (when events bring it to the forefront) national security; in other words, the president is held responsible for results. As Gary Jacobson says, "uniquely among elected officials, presidents can profit politically by producing diffuse collective benefits at the expense of concentrated particular interests" (Jacobson 1990, p. 112). Therefore, for presidents the motive for using pork barrel benefits to pass such legislation is, at least in part, electoral.

To summarize the discussion of the third and fourth conditions for using pork barrel benefits to buy votes for general interest legislation: When leaders use the vote-buying strategy, they take advantage of the electoral goals of the members to whom they give benefits. However, except for the president, leaders themselves are motivated by not by their own reelection, which they can provide for much more efficiently by other means, but by some combination of the power and good public policy goals.[3] Returning to my broader argument, pork barrel benefits help leaders to unify fractious caucuses around their position and to undermine the unity

[3] One might argue that ambition for higher office, a goal that Fenno (1973) recognizes but does not deal with, is an electoral goal that would provide leaders with an incentive to mobilize to pass general interest legislation. It could be argued that pork barrel benefits to one's constituents are ill-suited to the need to expand one's constituency in order to run for higher office, while a combination of advertising and position taking on general interest legislation can provide for much of the expansion needed. Yet pork can help by serving the particularized desires of interests that can provide political action committee (PAC) contributions for a run for the Senate or the presidency.

of the opposing party. This is especially true for majority party leaders and chairs, who are more likely to have benefits to give.

Types of Benefits

For leaders committed to certain public policy positions, vote buying has a major advantage over another type of legislative mobilization: It allows a bill's sponsors to pass the measure without altering its central provisions, whereas they otherwise might be forced to compromise on the bill's content to gain support for it. Therefore, because vote buying with pork allows policy coalition leaders to protect the bill's provisions, it gives them more freedom to craft it as they see fit. Of course, in reality, both vote buying and substantive modification of the bill are likely to be used. That is, in the interest of gaining important allies, some alterations usually are made in the central provisions of the bill; but to avoid changes beyond a certain point, projects for individual members may be added to buy those members' votes. Such outright vote buying is especially useful when further changes in the substance of the bill would make it unacceptable to the very coalition leaders who are working for its passage. Moreover, as noted earlier, the strategy is particularly important when other ways of inducing loyalty to leadership desires, such as party rewards and sanctions, are weak or absent altogether. Indeed, vote buying with distributive benefits can enable leaders to cross party boundaries to win votes on both sides of the aisle.

Of course, other sorts of individual favors, often in the form of IOUs, might be used by a coalition leader who does not have ready access to distributive benefits: a promise to appear at a district fundraiser, a committee chair's pledge to hold a hearing in a member's district, the president's commitment to support a member's favorite legislative proposal in the future, or even a tacit understanding that the leader owes the member a favor. However, such trades are difficult to document and therefore are usually not amenable to systematic empirical analysis. The most observable currency consists of distributive benefits attached to the bill under consideration. Because such distributive benefits lend themselves to clear quid pro quo deals on a specific piece of legislation and because they are of a type believed to directly aid members' reelection bids to a degree that, for example, a hearing in the district might not, distributive benefits may be the most effective resource. Thus, benefits explicitly attached to the bill or the accompanying committee report are the main focus of this book.

In addition, the focus here is on pork barrel benefits given to identifiable geographic areas, specifically, members' own districts (or states, in the case of senators), even though such benefits also may be targeted to individuals and interest groups outside the districts of the members who requested them. Beneficiaries of the latter sort may aid members' reelection, typically by making campaign contributions. Definitions of distributive benefits sometimes implicitly extend to these beneficiaries (e.g., Collie 1988, p. 427), sometimes explicitly (Mayhew 1974, pp. 56–57); however, the theoretical literature concentrates on geographic benefits (e.g., Shepsle and Weingast 1981, p. 96). The discussion of beneficiaries in this book is restricted to geographic districts because it is impractical reliably to document benefits given to entities that are not geographically defined.

The remainder of this chapter lays out the vote-buying strategy from the coalition leaders' point of view; it also considers the reactions of the leaders' targets, the legislators whose support they seek.

LEADERS' STRATEGY: FORMING THE COALITION

The key figure in forming supporting coalitions for legislative initiatives is typically a member of Congress in a formal leadership position, who by virtue of that position has access to more of the political resources needed to pass legislation than rank-and-file members. Although policy entrepreneurs are not necessarily restricted to members holding formal leadership positions (Loomis 1988), in order to use distributive side payments to gain votes on general benefit legislation, a legislator must have the capacity to link such benefits with the bill in question. As the preceding discussion suggests, the people with the greatest ability to do this are committee and subcommittee chairs as well as the parties' top House and Senate leaders and the president himself. Therefore, for discussion purposes, the person who is in a position to use distributive benefits to form a majority coalition is referred to as the policy coalition leader or simply the leader. Although that person is likely to hold a formal leadership position, the term is sufficiently generic to include anyone who spearheads the effort to pass a particular bill.

In any public policy area, proposed legislation may originate in one or more of several places. The following brief discussion is not intended to be comprehensive on that score but is meant to illustrate the reasons that coalition leaders might wish to protect a bill's general interest provisions by buying votes with pork barrel add-ons.

Potential policy coalition leaders may begin with their own most-preferred policy. However, it is very unlikely that major legislation modeled strictly on the policy views of one leader could gain a majority on the merits. Instead, the leader most likely must incorporate provisions into the initial version of the bill in response to the demands of desired coalition members. If the leader is a committee chair, he or she may need to respond to party leaders, the ranking minority member of the committee, rank-and-file committee members, or chairs of other key committees. At some point in the process of modifying the bill, the leader may deem further changes unacceptable; from then on, if the bill lacks a majority, the leader must seek a way to gain the votes of more members without doing violence to the bill's provisions. By adding pork barrel benefits targeted to individual legislators, the leader can preserve the bill's central policy provisions, thus simultaneously serving his or her good public policy and influence goals. Because of their divisibility, such benefits can be targeted to the districts of members whose support is needed but might otherwise not be forthcoming.

Additionally, party leaders as well as committee chairs may be expected to pass legislation on behalf of a president of their party; in those cases, their ability to craft the policy to their own liking is probably severely constrained; but they may be under strong pressure to protect key substantive provisions of the bill as ardently as they would if the bill were their own. Similarly, when different parties control the presidency and one or both chambers of Congress, policy coalition leaders may be responsible for passing alternatives to the president's legislative initiatives. In either case, the incentives to add distributive benefits to gain votes for the bill are equally strong.

However, leaders are unlikely to give projects to just anyone who opposes the bill. Rather, they must answer two questions in order to determine to whom to give distributive benefits in return for votes. The first question relates to the overall coalition strategy: how large a supporting coalition do they need, and thus to how many members must they give projects? The second question concerns the allocation strategy: Exactly which members should they target? Should they give benefits to members on the fence or to opponents, to members of their own committees or to key leaders? I argue here that the coalition and allocation strategies are related; that is, the size of the coalition depends at least in part on who controls the allocation process – the leaders or the members who seek benefits, which depends in turn on the availability of full information to the leaders.

Coalition Size

The issue of how many members leaders must help in order to construct a majority coalition becomes rather complicated, as this discussion shows below. There are two options for coalition size: First, leaders can grant projects to a minority of members sufficient to form a bare majority coalition for the bill when combined with those who support it on its merits. This is likely to be the result when leaders exert tight control on the distribution of projects, minimizing the number that they give. Alternatively, leaders can try to maximize support for the bill, giving to anyone who asks, in which case the tendency would be toward a universalistic or at least a supermajority coalition of project recipients, far more than needed to pass the bill. This is likely to occur when control of project allocation is more diffuse, residing to a greater degree with rank-and-file members, who demand a project in return for votes that most of them would have cast for the bill without a project. These two options are analogous, but not identical, to the well-known alternatives for coalition size in the literature on distributive politics – minimal winning and universalistic coalitions – described in Chapter 1.

The empirical literature on distributive politics, like the formal literature, has produced conflicting findings concerning the extent of distribution of pork barrel benefits, although on balance, when Congress distributes benefits to itself, the evidence for oversized (rather than bare majority or minimal winning) coalitions is strong. On one hand, there is evidence that, in the distribution of funds by the federal government (most of it not specifically earmarked by Congress), spending within specific programs does not cover even a near-majority of districts (Stein and Bickers 1995).[4] However, an examination of the *discretionary* distributional decisions made by bureaucrats shows that, to secure their budgets, bureaucrats distribute grants widely to legislators' districts. Because they know they must ask for congressional support repeatedly, they make project grants so as to maximize that support, although even here, a blanket statement that distribution is universalistic is unwarranted (Arnold 1979, pp. 209–210). Finally, research on the decisions that are most analogous to those examined here – how congressional committees distribute benefits across

[4] In the most comprehensive examination of the distribution of federal benefits to date, encompassing virtually all federal distributive and redistributive programs, Stein and Bickers find that across program areas the median number of districts served never exceeds a majority, and very few individual programs benefit more than a majority of districts (Stein and Bickers, 1995, pp. 37–43).

congressional districts – has found allocation to oversized majorities in such areas as public works (Maass 1951; Ferejohn 1974; Owens and Wade 1984; Wilson 1986), appropriations (Fenno 1966), public lands (Fenno 1973), and tax policy (Manley 1970).

By contrast, in the situation analyzed in this book, where leaders need to increase support for a general interest bill, they may find it unnecessary to distribute benefits universally in order to accomplish their goals. In fact, they may not even need to give benefits to a simple majority. This is true when members reveal their true preferences for the bill and demonstrate that there is a base of support on the merits. In that case, leaders may choose to target projects only to the minority of members needed to round up the bill's support to a majority. Here, the decision as to who receives a project is not entirely with rank-and-file members as it is under the simplest assumptions of the formal literature; instead, the leaders determine the size of the coalition.

However, a leader is likely to get only one chance to engage in the sort of efficient and highly targeted vote buying that produces small distributive coalitions. The dynamic of a game changes if players know that it is to be repeated indefinitely; and a minimal winning strategy is not likely to be stable over a series of bills. Thus, even if a committee's leaders followed a minimal winning strategy for one bill, they probably could not sustain it over a subsequent stream of similar bills, because minimal winning coalitions tend, in repeated play, to give way to universalistic coalitions (Weingast 1979; Axelrod 1981). Because legislation is not decided in isolation, the condition of repeated play typically is met. That is, legislative leaders (as well as presidents) produce a continuous stream of legislative proposals. In so doing, they reveal their own strategies for passing bills; thus, leaders have the advantage of surprise only the first time they try to buy votes with pork barrel benefits. The first time they use this approach, they may well succeed in buying votes for a bill using a minimal number of pork barrel benefits. But on subsequent bills, members who did not get a project in return for their votes the first time feel like fools for having "given away" their votes on the earlier bill. Those members now have an incentive to try to take control of project distribution away from the leaders; they do so by concealing their true policy preferences and bargaining for a project regardless of their support for the merits of the second bill, in effect holding up the leaders for a project in return for their votes.

It then becomes increasingly difficult for leaders to obtain accurate information about members' true preferences; and members' concealment of their voting intentions is therefore an effective strategy for getting a pork barrel project. On the second and subsequent bills, a majority of members is likely to bargain for projects, and they will most likely be granted them, as leaders now cannot be certain who would support the bill without one. In fact, an incentive now exists for all who conceivably could support the bill to bargain for a project in return for their votes. From the leaders' point of view, giving projects to these members secures their votes and avoids the risk of alienating them, as members now know that projects are rather freely given in return for votes. Thus, the first time leaders use the vote-buying strategy is their last, best opportunity to give projects to less than a majority of the membership. After that, the number is bound to balloon as the number of *apparent* fence-sitters increases as a result of members' concealing their true opinions about the bill itself and demanding projects. In that situation, leaders have an incentive to play it safe and give projects even to members who they think are bluffing about the possibility of voting against the overall bill without a project.

Moreover, leaders want more than a simple affirmative vote on the bill. In addition, they want it to pass with as few hostile amendments as possible; they want any presidential veto to be overridden; and they want to be able to break a filibuster in the Senate. If amendments do not threaten the provisions that rank-and-file members care about, those members may either support the amendments on the merits or attempt to use their votes on them as bargaining chips with committee leaders. In such cases, the members could promise to vote with the leaders on the bill overall but threaten to vote with the opposition on amendments that do not endanger benefits for their districts or policies that they prefer. In fact, while it may be difficult for most members to conceal their general preferences on recurring legislation on which they already have a voting history, they can much more easily conceal their preferences on individual amendments and credibly threaten to deprive leaders of important victories unless they are given a distributive benefit. Thus, by giving benefits to a supermajority of members, leaders guarantee themselves an extra margin of protection. That is not to say that they grant every single request from every member; to do so would quickly break the bank. However, in the interest of good will, leaders have an incentive to give something to every member who asks. As accurate nose counting becomes impossible, bet hedging seems increasingly wise.

Nevertheless, when distributive benefits are attached to a general interest bill, a truly universalistic coalition, as opposed to an oversized, supermajority coalition, is unlikely. That is because the nondistributive provisions of the bill are likely to require some members to oppose it on ideological or constituency grounds, regardless of whether the member receives a project. And a pork barrel benefit that goes only to part of the district may not be sufficient compensation for a member's taking an ideologically dissonant position or one that is opposed by the majority of the district. For such actions, the net electoral impact, even with a project, could be negative. Indeed, such members may not even seek a project, as they cannot promise to support the bill in return. In turn, failure to support the bill could doom the project, as leaders might well retaliate against them by eliminating it in conference.

In summary, the number of members to whom leaders give pork barrel benefits depends on the degree to which rank-and-file members conceal their true preferences for the bill or hostile amendments to it. The first time leaders use the vote-buying strategy, the sequence of events is likely to help them to minimize the number of projects. That time, leaders have an opportunity to ascertain members' opinions on the bill without complicating matters with the promise of projects. Once an accurate head count is achieved, leaders can then reveal a vote-buying strategy to remedy any deficit of support. But however small the number of project recipients on the first bill, there will be strong pressures toward universalism on the second and subsequent bills, as control of the allocation process slips from the hands of the leaders and shifts to rank-and-file members.

Why do similar universalistic pressures not develop on the first bill on which leaders attempt to buy votes? It does seem possible that once word gets out that leaders are distributing pork, a large majority of members would seek to bargain for a project from the beginning. From the perspective of committee leaders, the fact that they must come before the chamber repeatedly to pass legislation suggests some risk in ever following a minimal allocation strategy. That is, members who did not receive a project might conceivably retaliate on this bill or on subsequent legislation. Thus, even on the first bill in a sequence of distributive projects, one might expect that leaders have an incentive to give projects to far more members than needed to form a majority for the bill.

However, time is a factor limiting the pressure toward universalism during the passage of only one bill. That is, before the word gets out that votes are being bought, there is likely to be a core of members willing to commit early to the leaders' most cherished policy proposals. Those members are poorly positioned to bargain later, when they realize that they might have done so. Additionally, it takes time for members to get a feel for how freely leaders are willing to give out projects, especially when there is a leadership change, such as a new committee chair, or when the majority changes to the other party, as it did in the 104th Congress. Often, legislators see who got projects only after the committee reports the bill. Only then will many realize that projects were given not just to the usual leaders but also to rank-and-file members, perhaps extending even to freshmen. But by then it is too late to deal, especially if the bill comes to the floor under a restrictive rule (in the House) that the committee now has a majority to pass. Additionally, distributive benefits often are not listed in legislative language anyway, presumably because they are too easy for pork barrel opponents to trace. Rather, they may appear only in committee reports as directives to the agency that will administer the law. Thus, even without a restrictive rule there may be little opportunity to add individual projects by floor amendment. Even if it were practical, such amendments appear even more blatantly self-serving than having such projects tucked into report language earlier in the process. For these reasons, opportunities for anyone other than the leaders themselves to add projects at the postcommittee stage are limited. The upshot of all of this is that the first time leaders give out distributive benefits to buy votes, they are likely to need to give them only to a minority of members; on subsequent bills, however, the pressures toward supermajority pork barrel coalitions are likely to be irresistible.

Allocation Strategy

In addition to deciding how many members to whom they should give pork barrel benefits to win votes for their policy preferences, leaders must decide how to allocate projects to individual members of Congress. That is, to which members do leaders give projects? As with the closely related question of the number of projects, the choice of allocation strategy is dependent at least in part on the availability of accurate information on member preferences on the bill; the more information leaders have about members' likely support for the bill, the more precisely they can target the benefits. If leaders have such information and initially find that they lack majority support for the bill, they must begin giving benefits to some nonsupporters. Rather than giving projects to firm opponents, vote buyers are likely to look first to members who are most persuadable: those on the fence. For those who are truly indifferent or conflicted about the bill, a project can serve to convert the calculated benefit of supporting the bill from zero to a net positive.

However, a strategy of giving only to fence-sitters is not likely to be feasible; leaders may also have to give projects to some supporters. As noted earlier, support, particularly on a large, complex bill, is many-faceted. Some members who strongly favor the bill's basic policy provisions on the merits may need inducements to support the coalition leaders' positions on some particulars; otherwise, they may believe that amendments that leaders themselves see as hostile are innocuous or even marginally positive. Indeed, some amendments might actually be attractive to less avid supporters of the bill, especially amendments that weaken controversial provisions and thereby provide political cover from potential criticism at home. Thus, leaders are likely to give projects to weaker supporters whose backing they calculate to be at risk on certain issues, in addition to fence-sitters. The purpose is to extract their loyalty on all votes related to the bill.

Such an approach is not unique: Giving to likely supporters is a strategy typically followed by political action committees (PACs) in their allocation decisions, despite the seeming inefficiency of contributing to those who already generally favor their positions (Handler and Mulkern 1982; Brown 1983; Gopoian 1984; Latus 1984; Wright 1985; Evans 1988).[5] As Hall and Wayman (1990) have shown, such a strategy is more rational than it seems at first blush, for such contributions buy friendly legislators' active efforts to obtain favorable legislative treatment for the PAC, when they might otherwise use their limited time to pursue other priorities. Moreover, giving to members who regularly support them is a strategy for helping to ensure that their friends stay in office where they can continue to help their contributors. A similar rationale may apply when leaders use pork barrel projects to buy support on legislation.

An additional, seemingly obvious means to build a majority coalition would be to attempt to convert opponents of the policy proposal by giving them projects. However, that strategy is both naive and fraught with risk. First, such an approach can work only with members who are not initially so opposed to the bill that they will in any case vote against it or try to undermine it with amendments. Therefore, the number of opponents

[5] In addition, Denzau and Munger (1986) developed a theoretical model of interest group vote buying. In contrast to the findings of empirical studies, they argued that groups are likely to pursue an apparently efficient strategy in which they make contributions only to those members who are on the fence for one reason or another, declining to contribute to those who would vote their way for constituency reasons, as the interest groups do not need to sway the votes of these members. However, their analysis ignores other reasons for giving to one's friends, reasons that the empirical studies make clear.

whom this strategy can convert is limited. Second, giving a project to members who are likely to vote against the bill anyway could tempt other, less opposed members to betray their benefactor as well. For this reason, it does not make sense to give projects to opponents simply to mute their vocal opposition, as some scholars have suggested (Arnold 1979; Hall and Wayman 1990). If district benefits are to be effective as an incentive for loyalty, they cannot be given to those who are sure to vote against the leader's position, even if they do it quietly. After all, there must be some threat of punishment of shirkers, but giving projects to members who are likely to oppose the bill suggests to everyone that the ultimate punishment – withdrawal of projects – is unlikely to be imposed. Such a message fundamentally undermines the purpose for which the projects are given in the first place.[6]

Therefore, the most fruitful allocation strategy for leaders is to give projects to fence-sitters and supporters of the general interest legislation. Clearly, full information about member preferences is necessary for leaders to exercise this degree of targeting of project awards. Thus, when leaders are most likely to have full information about members' stands (i.e., on the first bill on which vote buying is used), we can expect to see one of two possible relationships between members' expected overall support for the bill ex ante and leaders' decision to award them a project. To the degree that leaders attempt to be as efficient as possible in their project awards, the relationship will be curvilinear. That is, as members become more committed to the bill, their support is more secure without a project; as their support becomes less firm, leaders are more likely to see them as responsive to a project; as they become more opposed, giving them a project is futile and even counterproductive. Alternatively, to the extent that leaders seek to buy firm support on all possible votes related to the bill, especially on hostile amendments that even the bill's supporters might be tempted to endorse, the relationship between members' expected support for the bill and the receipt of a project will be positive. As is true with the previous alternative, as members become more opposed, there is less reason for leaders to try to buy their support with a project.

However, on the second and subsequent go-rounds of legislation from the same leader, the relationship between members' probable support for the bill without a project and the award of a project is likely to be weak or nonexistent. That is because, as noted earlier, once leaders have revealed a

[6] With regard to campaign contributions, there is little evidence that such attempts to demobilize one's enemies is effective in any case (Hall and Wayman 1990).

willingness to bargain for votes by giving out benefits, increasing numbers of members, now including strong supporters as well as weak ones and fence-sitters, realize that there is a payoff for strategically concealing their true preferences on the bill. Thus, on the second and later bills, the leaders' safest strategy is to take a more reactive, less systematic approach to allocating projects, waiting for the inevitable flood of requests for projects and granting something to everyone with the clear mutual understanding that there is a quid pro quo: Recipients are expected to support their benefactors on all important votes on the bill. By the time this happens, the rank-and-file members have the whip hand; giving them distributive benefits is the only feasible way to protect the bill.

In devising their allocation strategy, leaders face other considerations in addition to members' likely support for the legislation; a number of other variables influence project distribution. They are partisanship, membership on the committee with jurisdiction over the bill, leadership positions on other important committees and in the chamber as a whole, and electoral vulnerability.

First among these variables is partisanship, specifically, the possibility of partisan bias in the allocation of benefits. If partisan theories are correct, particularly Cox and McCubbins's (1993) theory, which incorporates to some degree the use of pork to win the support of recalcitrant party members, projects should go to members of the majority party. Yet among scholars who have examined this question empirically, some have found a high level of bipartisan benefit allocation (Murphy 1974; Wilson 1986; Stein and Bickers 1995); however, others have found that disproportionate benefits flow to members of the majority party (Anagnoson 1982), especially in congressionally devised formula-based spending as opposed to awards given by bureaucrats (Levitt and Snyder 1997; Lee 2000). There is also evidence of linkage between committee membership and partisan advantage, with majority party members on the committee of jurisdiction receiving a disproportionate share (Carsey and Rundquist 1999). However, it is well established that the degree of partisanship varies among committees (Fenno 1973; Smith and Deering 1990); thus we might expect concurrent variation in the degree to which partisanship affects the distribution of pork barrel benefits.

The Senate Appropriations Committee, one which once was renowned for its bipartisanship along with its House counterpart (Fenno 1966), is today increasingly partisan (Marshall, Prins, and Rohde 1997). Accordingly, Balla, Lawrence, Maltzman, and Sigelman (2002) have found evidence for a much more subtle form of partisan bias in earmarking funds to higher education by that committee than previously had been recognized. In a process that they call "partisan blame avoidance," Balla et al. found that the Appropriations Committee majority gives earmarks to senators of both parties. However, when it comes to the actual dollar amounts of those earmarks, majority party members were significantly more generous to their own. The rationale was not exactly one of universalism. Rather, it was the inoculation of members of the majority party against charges of wasteful spending by making the minority complicit in the earmarking process. At the same time, giving higher dollar amounts to their own members allowed the majority to have its cake and eat it too, the cake being an extra measure of any electoral benefits that flow from such spending.

However, the extent to which there is likely to be a partisan bias depends on the reason for which projects are given out. When leaders distribute projects to buy members' votes for general interest legislation, there is no reason to expect a partisan bias. On the contrary, such awards provide leaders with a means to overcome partisan differences on public policy, giving members of the opposite party a reason to vote for the bill. They will also, of course, give to their own party members, as failure to do so while giving to the other party's members would be likely to provoke resentment in their own caucus, tempting some of the latter to vote against the committee on some matters. Thus, leaders are likely not only to give to members of their own party to overcome disagreement, as Cox and McCubbins argue; they are likely to give to members of the other party for the same reason. Thus, vote buying can shore up the unity of the party of the vote buyers, but it offers the additional advantage of undermining the cohesiveness of the other party.

In addition to using project awards to overcome the strictures of partisanship, leaders need to seek the support of members who can be especially helpful to the bill's chances of passage. If the coalition leaders are committee or subcommittee chairs, it is important for them to have their committee members behind them on the floor. A united front, particularly a bipartisan one, is extremely helpful on the floor of the House or Senate, in part because noncommittee members take voting cues from their own party's members on the committee (Matthews and Stimson 1975; Kingdon 1989). If both parties on the committee can be united, potential opponents outside the committee have less credibility in their efforts to build an opposition coalition. Thus, we can expect committee and subcommittee leaders especially to favor members of their own subcommittee and committee with project awards.

This rationale for a procommittee bias in project awards differs from, but is reinforced by, that found in much of the literature, where it has been argued widely that committees give a disproportionate share of benefits to their own members because the committees themselves tend to be composed of those with a high demand for the policies within their jurisdictions (Shepsle 1978, pp. 246–248; Weingast and Moran 1983; Weingast and Marshall 1988; Adler and Lipinski 1997; Adler 2000; Hurwitz, Moiles, and Rohde 2001). Others have disputed this claim and found evidence to the contrary (Cox and McCubbins 1993, pp. 60–82; Krehbiel 1992). At the very least, there certainly is evidence that committees vary in the degree to which they are composed of high-demanders (Adler and Lapinski 1997; Adler 2000), depending in part on the committee's jurisdiction (Hall and Grofman 1990; Cox and McCubbins 1993). Moreover, the fact that committees vary in importance to their members' reelection goal reinforces the finding that committees vary in the extent to which they are composed of high-demanders (Fenno 1973; Bullock 1976; Smith and Deering 1990); high-demanding behavior is most likely to manifest itself on committees that attract members for electorally relevant, constituency service reasons. With respect to whether or not committee members are actually favored in the allocation of funds, as opposed to their level of demand for funding, previous results are mixed. While some have found a procommittee bias (e.g., Plott 1968; Ferejohn 1974, pp. 190–191, 234; Arnold 1979, pp. 207–208; Weingast and Marshall 1988; Frisch 1998, pp. 85–87), others have found mixed or negative results (Goss 1972; Rundquist and Griffith 1976; Ray 1980a, 1980b; Wilson 1986; Hird 1991). As noted earlier, there is also evidence that majority party committee members benefit disproportionately (Carsey and Rundquist 1999).

Whether or not committees are composed of high-demanders, committee chairs are likely to award projects to their members in order to provide the members with greater incentive to give solid, bipartisan support for passing the leaders' favored legislation, thus smoothing the path on the floor of the House or Senate. To the extent that committees are composed of high-demanders, that tendency is reinforced by the members themselves, as they are likely to request larger numbers of projects.

If the purpose of including such benefits is to buy the support needed to pass the committee's version of the bill, the help of other key leaders is needed, especially that of chamber leaders who not only control floor consideration of a committee's bill but increasingly preside over postcommittee adjustments to its provisions (Sinclair 1997). Additionally, leaders of other committees and subcommittees important to the bill's success are likely to be favored. In particular, overlapping jurisdictional claims on the legislation, even if they do not result in its referral to committees other than the coalition leader's own, can pose risks on the floor. While it may be necessary to mollify other committee chairs by changing the content of the bill, giving them distributive benefits could help to reduce their objections and the need to change key provisions. Previous research suggests that chamber and committee leaders are indeed advantaged in the allocation of benefits in distributive policy (Ferejohn 1974, p. 234; Anagnoson 1982; Hird 1991).

Finally, leaders may find a particular opportunity to buy the votes of members who are electorally vulnerable. As noted earlier in this chapter, the evidence concerning the electoral impact of federal spending in a member's district is mixed, but members themselves evidently believe that it is helpful; otherwise, they would not seek distributive benefits so assiduously. Consistent with members' own apparent assumption that pork barrel projects help to protect their seats, it is likely that the smaller a member's winning margin in the previous election, the more likely leaders are to target them with a project in return for their vote.

Thus, the coalition and allocation strategies taken together result in two closely linked models of vote buying. The first time policy coalition leaders use the vote-buying strategy, they have the most control that they will ever have over project awards, and they are likely to give projects to less than a majority of members as they seek to round up support over and above that which they have already ascertained exists. To the extent that they have enough information about member preferences to follow an active strategy of selecting project recipients, they can be expected to give projects to the following legislators: those whose support is strategically essential, that is, members of the committee of jurisdiction and top leaders of other key committees, as well as floor leaders, members who are on the fence, supporters, especially weak supporters, and if needed, weak opponents, as well as electorally marginal members.

On the other hand, when leaders choose to follow the less risky strategy of responding to all of those who come to them for a project, as they must do on bills subsequent to the first one on which they use the vote-buying strategy, members' views on the bill will have little bearing on their chances of getting a project. That is because members now have an incentive strategically to conceal their true preferences in order to bargain for a project. However, the other variables, especially committee membership and leadership position, are all still likely to play a role in some form, as coalition leaders target those who may be especially helpful to their efforts to pass their favored version of the bill. While key members may be no more likely to get a pork barrel benefit, they may nevertheless get a larger number or more valuable benefits than members whose support is less likely to have a multiplier effect. When leaders follow this more passive strategy, the coalition of project recipients is likely to grow quickly to a supermajority from the first to second bill. Chapter 3 tests the hypotheses developed in this section with data from two federal highway bills.

MEMBERS' RESPONSE: VOTE SELLING

Chapters 4 through 7 focus on how the receipt of a distributive benefit influences members' roll call votes. Although their responses to a leader's vote-buying strategy were discussed earlier, it is useful to summarize those points separately here. One of the conditions for vote buying to succeed is that rank-and-file members must care more about pork barrel projects than the bill to which they are attached. Nevertheless, in the initial stages of the process of attempting to pass a bill on its merits, before the pork-for-policy trades begin, there is a group of legislators who support the bill as it is. They might support it because it benefits their districts as members of some class of districts covered by the legislation (as opposed to getting some particularized benefit for which they can claim exclusive credit). In addition, they could support a bill on the basis of their own views of what makes for good public policy, especially in areas that do not touch their constituents in any significant way. Although legislators must remain within the boundaries established by constituent opinion, those boundaries tend to be wide on nondistrict-related issues (Kingdon 1989, p. 68), and members of Congress have considerable leeway to cast votes according to their own policy views. Moreover, when their party's views are not inconsistent with their own, members have reason to follow the party leadership on issues that are of major importance to the party's program and therefore its reputation and electoral fortunes (Rohde 1991; Cox and McCubbins 1993). Thus, the merits of a bill consist of factors such as its district relevance (without individual distributive benefits), the member's own policy views, and the position of the party. The merits may strongly dictate the member's support or opposition to the legislation; by such considerations the initial count for and against a particular bill is created, as long as members do not conceal their true views.

However, some members may not be able to support the bill under any circumstances. This group would include those whose districts are directly damaged by the legislation or whose constituents have strong negative views about the policy itself. Additionally, definite opponents would include members with a strong ideological opposition to the bill or a long history of voting against such legislation. For members in any of those situations, to vote for the bill after receiving a project would be to expose themselves to criticism later for betraying their constituents or their ideology (a potent charge when the member's ideology is consistent with their constituents' views). For such members, not only will pork barrel benefits not make up for their defiance of constituency will but accepting benefits may backfire if it looks like a cynical attempt to buy off the voters. Not only will distributive benefits not buy their support, but such legislators are likely to try to defeat the bill or, failing that, to undermine it with amendments.

But when a proposed general interest bill is not relevant to any of their goals and members are indifferent among policy alternatives (Kingdon 1989), or when there is some conflict among goals, members' votes are likely to be up for grabs. In such cases, the ability to take a pork barrel benefit back to the district in return for a vote might be sufficient to resolve the impasse for those members and convert a bill that is a matter of indifference or worse, conflict, into a net electoral benefit. Of course, the same rationale applies to members who support the legislation's basic aims but whose support for the leaders' positions on secondary issues, which might come up in amendments, might not be so firm. Those members also might be willing to offer support on such matters in return for a project.

What about situations in which members demand projects despite the fact that they support the bill overall anyway, as they are likely to do on second and subsequent bills on which leaders use the vote-buying strategy? In these cases as well, members who get a project are more likely to support the coalition leaders' positions on all aspects of the bill, including hostile amendments (recall that those amendments may not threaten the aspects of the bill that those members support). But if such amendments threaten the leaders' preferences, leaders will expect project recipients to vote against them, and those members have every incentive to do so.

Considering all of these effects of members' possible prior positions on a particular piece of general interest legislation, the expected impact of attempted vote buying on the behavior of individual members of Congress is as follows: All other things being equal, benefit recipients are more likely than nonrecipients to support the leader's position on the bill, the rule under which it is considered (in the House), amendments, and veto overrides.

Incentives to Honor the Agreement

Once the bill has reached the floor and members' projects are already either in the bill or in the committee report, what is to prevent them from violating their promises and voting against the leaders? There is a strong expectation that legislators honor their promises to each other, but such expectations are more likely to be met when there is a mechanism to enforce them. In this case, the enforcement mechanism is the threat that leaders will remove the offender's project in conference committee as a punishment for violating the obligation, be it implicit or explicit, to support the leadership position (Shepsle and Weingast 1987a, 1987b; Longley and Oleszek 1989). Legislators who violate their agreements, particularly with powerful leaders or committee chairs, are likely to be made to suffer for their betrayal sooner or later. They will have no further opportunity to atone after the floor vote, so the only way to ensure the inclusion of their projects in the conference committee report is to accede to the leaders' demands in committee and on the floor, remaining loyal on all votes that the leaders care about. Conversely, members who truly cannot support the leaders' positions, whether for constituency reasons or due to their own policy commitments, are unlikely even to request a pork barrel benefit.

CONCLUSIONS

The vote-buying approach to passing general benefit legislation is not inconsistent with recent theories that address the collective action dilemma. However, it is in some respects a more flexible technique, as the pork barrel offers currency with a bipartisan appeal. Although Republicans have more ideological reason than Democrats to oppose such benefits and may receive less electoral advantage from providing them (Alvarez and Schousen 1993), there is journalistic evidence (Goldstein 1995; Ivins 1995; MacDonald 1996), along with my own findings (Chapter 6) that they energetically pursue such benefits. Cox and McCubbins (1993) argue that distributive benefits provide a method for papering over intraparty divisions and hence increase the party leaders' control and make party government more possible. It is my argument that distributive benefits allow leaders to do more; they can in fact transcend party splits by buying the votes of members of the other party for the leaders' favored legislation, especially when those votes are more easily acquired than those of members of their own party. An example of such a party-splitting issue is the North American Free Trade Agreement (NAFTA), where President Clinton, leading the policy coalition, joined Republicans and conservative Democrats in pushing the treaty in opposition to members of the House Democratic leadership. On the other hand, if liberal Democrats had allowed their votes to be bought for a special benefit for their districts, many of them would have risked electoral support at home, especially from unions.

Thus, the vote-buying approach can just as easily undermine as shore up party unity. Moreover, it gives considerable freedom to leaders who have access to particularized benefits. Indeed, the only limitation on this freedom is the increased tendency of party caucuses (in the case of Democrats) and their leadership (especially the Republicans in the 104th and later congresses) to pass over members who stray too far or too often from the party's center of gravity when choosing committee chairs. Nevertheless, the infrequency with which that is done suggests that although committee chairs must be mindful of the party, they generally have a good deal of leeway to use a pork barrel strategy to craft deals that lure members of the other party from their own fold, possibly compensating for losses of support from their own caucuses.

One qualification about the uses of pork is necessary here. The early literature on distributive politics discussed in Chapter 1 depicts the passage of omnibus bills of pork barrel projects for a majority of members. Here, I have described pork as a means to gain support for policy at the opposite end of the spectrum of divisibility of benefits: general interest legislation, which affects all or most of the nation. However, as noted at the beginning of this chapter, there is a vast range of policies between the extremes of pork barrel and general interest legislation, and policy coalition leaders can also use pork to build majority coalitions for legislation in that range. Although there is necessarily much gray area in any definition of the general interest, many issues clearly do not meet even a liberal interpretation of it. For example, during the House debate on the 1987 highway bill, there was a vote on an amendment supported by transportation committee leaders to benefit billboard owners. One would be hard-pressed to say that legislation that pits the profits of an organized group against the federal treasury qualifies as a general interest measure. Yet distributive benefits allowed transportation committee leaders to gain votes for this type of measure just as readily as for other, broader issues related to that bill. Thus, although the focus of this book is on the use of distributive benefits as a way to resolve Congress's collective action dilemma, described in Chapter 1, it should be kept in mind that leaders can use such benefits to create a majority coalition to support any kind of legislation.[7]

Even if the legislation affects the nation as a whole, when leaders buy members' votes for their policy preferences, there is an obvious potential cost: The resulting public policy may be less representative of the views of the majority of members of Congress and the public than it would be if its provisions were determined by members' true policy preferences. Although there are surely policy boundaries beyond which leaders cannot go and still be guaranteed the votes of project recipients, within limits, they can be expected to have the freedom to shape legislation as they wish, once project recipients have obligated their votes.

I do not assert that all legislation is passed this way. Rather, I argue that in a legislature where parties are less than perfectly disciplined on many issues, where members are elected in candidate-centered, geographically based contests, distributive benefits provide an additional way to resolve the inherent difficulties of passing legislation that confers collective benefits. The key to this process of coalition formation is the ironic fact that the same individualistic tendency that ordinarily makes it difficult for Congress to pass general interest legislation is harnessed by coalition leaders to accomplish precisely that purpose.

The following chapters examine the use of this technique by several kinds of actors in a number of different policy areas. By their nature, case studies cannot answer the important questions of how often and in what

7 A related point is that more narrowly drawn legislation, that is, that which is not general interest, may require more than pork barrel benefits to form majority coalitions, even when the four conditions stipulated at the beginning of the chapter for using pork to form majority coalitions are met. In particular, if a program is narrowly distributive in scope (such as price supports for peanut farmers), not offering even the potential for project distribution to many members given its subject matter, and if its overall provisions do not affect a near-majority of districts, supporters of the legislation must go beyond distributive politics to pass it. In such cases, majority coalitions may be built using not only distributive benefits, but also PAC contributions targeted to members who otherwise would have no ideological or material stake in the program. That is, for such programs, another type of individualized benefit is required to create legislative majorities. Stein and Bickers make precisely this argument; and in their empirical analysis they find that PAC contributions are important in winning support for narrow-gauge policies but are much less important in the sort of broad-based programs that I examine here (Stein and Bickers 1995, pp. 90–107). For general interest legislation, winning members' loyalty with distributive benefits is an easier strategy, as a substantial number of members already have reason to support the policy on its merits, particularly the first time around. And on subsequent rounds, leaders simply expand the number of benefits given out in order to ensure their majorities. Thus, there is less need to coordinate with PACs.

policy areas vote buying with pork is used. For reasons explained more fully in the concluding chapter, precise answers to those questions would be virtually impossible to ascertain. I briefly preview that argument here. The case studies in this book involve data that were relatively if not always readily accessible; they were available in part because they involved geographic benefits, which are easier to connect with particular constituencies than benefits to interest groups. But because many instances of the use of pork are not amenable to this sort of analysis, it is necessary to infer the circumstances under which policy coalition leaders use pork barrel benefits to buy votes for broader policy measures. The major repositories for such benefits are the congressional committees that have jurisdiction over the policy areas that offer the potential for particularized benefits. The seven constituency-oriented committees (out of nineteen standing committees as of the 107th Congress) in the House "are the classic pork-barrel committees of the House," as are the nine (out of sixteen) reelection-oriented committees in the Senate (Deering and Smith 1997, p. 75). Most of these committees also deal with at least some general interest policy matters. Thus, a large percentage of committees in both houses are well situated to use pork to influence members' votes on major policy matters. Whether or not they do so is a matter for the painstaking empirical research undertaken in this book. However, the massive data-gathering effort that would be necessary to determine the frequency with which this technique is used runs into additional difficulties – in particular, the fact that some policy-for-pork trades occur across pieces of legislation; in such cases the connection is particularly difficult to establish. The full range of difficulties of establishing the frequency with which this technique is used is discussed in Chapter 7. Nevertheless, the existence and effects of the strategies described in this chapter can be established; we now turn to that.

The next two chapters describe the first of the case studies of this process; those chapters analyze the passage of two federal highway program reauthorization bills. The first bill is a five-year authorization that became law in 1987; the second is the next reauthorization, which passed in 1991. There is a special focus in this book on these two bills, as they provide unique data on the distribution of pork barrel benefits. Data on who gets such benefits are often difficult for scholars to come by, as Congress typically obscures project locations, probably to protect individual members from charges of pork barreling by watchdog groups. Moreover, the data are made even more valuable by the fact that these two highway bills constitute the Public Works and Transportation Committee's first and second uses of this technique to buy support. The 1987 legislation was the first highway bill to contain a large number of such benefits, and the 1991 was the second one to do so. Thus, it is possible to examine the plausibility of the arguments developed in this chapter about the dynamics of the process of coalition formation the first time leaders use pork barrel projects to buy votes, and how (and whether) that process changes on the next similar bill. Chapters 3 and 4 contain that analysis.

3

Who Calls the Shots? The Allocation of Pork Barrel Projects

> All congressmen would score pork if they had the power. But the big guys eat first, then toss leftover scraps to those they favor. And because everyone wants it, a sort of balance of terror emerges where no one will challenge the porkers because they want theirs someday.
>
> (Kelly 1992, p. 6)

Underlying that remark from a member of the White House staff is the assumption that the leaders who dispense pork barrel benefits exercise tight control over the process. This chapter investigates the extent to which that was actually the case in one committee in the House: the Public Works and Transportation Committee, which distributed projects to create majority coalitions for general interest legislation.

It is also clear from the quotation above that some members of Congress are thought to occupy especially advantageous positions from which to do distributive favors for their fellow legislators. Chief among them are committee and subcommittee leaders whose jurisdictions are conducive to the authoritative distribution of pork. By "authoritative distribution" I mean that the committees can actually commit funds rather than merely authorize them; authorization by itself normally does not assure that the money will ever be appropriated and spent. In addition, the tax-writing committees in both houses of Congress have the ability to confer benefits in the form of special tax treatment, which they have been more than willing to do in order to pass their favored broad-based tax legislation, most famously the 1986 overhaul of the federal tax code (Birnbaum and Murray 1987).

The committees that most obviously have the ability authoritatively to distribute pork barrel benefits are the appropriations committees and their subcommittees. However, other committees also have that ability, most notably, those that deal with public works legislation. Scholars have paid particular attention to rivers and harbors legislation under the jurisdiction of the House Public Works and Transportation (later renamed the Transportation and Infrastructure) Committee, the time-honored repository of pork. As its current name suggests, that committee presently has jurisdiction over highway programs, the subject of this chapter, as well as urban mass transit, airport and airway programs, and a variety of rivers, harbors, and other water resource legislation, among other things. Because the committee confers geographically concentrated benefits, members are attracted to it for its constituency service opportunities (Smith and Deering 1990).

With respect to the federal-aid highway program, the committee enjoys an important advantage in the distribution of pork: It has "contract authority," the ability to commit funds from the Highway Trust Fund without appropriations from general revenues. By contrast, the spending approved by most authorizing committees for the programs within their jurisdictions must await action by the Appropriations Committee, which may well opt to fund the programs at lower than authorized levels or not at all. Thus, the Transportation and Infrastructure committee and its Senate counterpart for highways, the Environment and Public Works Committee, have a degree of autonomy unusual for authorizing committees. One advantage of that autonomy is the committee's ability to distribute pork on its own authority.

This chapter focuses on how the leaders of the House Public Works and Transportation Committee gave out their own form of distributive benefits, known as highway demonstration projects, to the districts of individual members. It shows that they did so as part of a strategy to win members' votes for the federal-aid highway program reauthorizations to which the projects were added. Chapter 4 examines the question of whether those projects actually did help to win the votes of project recipients for the highway legislation.

The federal highway program gives money to states to build and maintain their major highways. Because such programs are often characterized as distributive, it is necessary first to specify the sense in which the overall highway program is a general interest program as opposed to a massive package of pork. Recall that general interest legislation was defined in Chapter 1 as broad-based measures that affect the whole nation or a large segment of it. The impact of general interest legislation does not necessarily fall evenly on all districts or individuals; all that is necessary is that it affect all districts or all of those in a broad category. By contrast, distributive legislation consists of disaggregable benefits; unlike benefits given by general interest legislation, these benefits have so little policy connection to each other that changing or even removing one district's benefit from a bill would have no impact on the benefits given to other districts (Shepsle and Weingast 1981, p. 96). Most of the money in the federal highway program is distributed by formula; the only way to change benefits for one state under this arrangement is to change the formula, but doing so for one state's benefit would affect benefits to other states. This characteristic violates a condition of the definition of distributive benefits employed here, a definition common to the theoretical literature on distributive politics (Collie 1988).

The major component of highway reauthorizations concerns the interstate highway system, which was established by the Interstate Highway Act of 1956. The system was initially called the Interstate Defense Highway System, a name that reveals a major general interest justification for the enactment of the greatest public works project in the history of the country. In the wake of World War II and the early years of the Cold War, many argued that in the event of national emergencies, the country needed a national highway network capable of handling large, heavy military vehicles; the model was Hitler's autobahn system. This argument carried considerable weight with President Eisenhower, who had himself been impressed by the autobahns. The president also believed that such a system would promote nationwide economic development and full employment. The huge coalition that pressed for the legislation was, however, commercial, not defense-oriented. Yet it spanned the nation and encompassed the interests of up to one-sixth of all American workers, whose livelihoods were directly connected to the motor vehicle industry, through their manufacture, sales, service, or commercial use (Goddard 1994, pp. 181–190).

Moreover, the impact of the system is pervasive. As Stephen Goddard has argued, the interstate system has had massive effects on how Americans live and work (1994, p. 197). In so doing, it has created a broad, vested interest among the public in constructing, maintaining, and enhancing the highways on which everyone depends so heavily.

The two reauthorizations of the program considered in this chapter and the next included not only these general interest considerations, particularly the impact of an efficient nationwide highway system on the national economy, but also particular provisions that were valued by the leaders of the Public Works and Transportation Committee. Those concerns are discussed in detail in Chapter 4, which considers the specific provisions that committee leaders sought to protect. But for now, it is sufficient to note that the reauthorizations considered here allocated federal dollars to states on the basis of formulas that took into account population and miles of road, that is, extent of territory. Those formulas created obvious net winners and losers, as some states contributed more to the Highway Trust Fund than they received in highway expenditures. The bills were not packages of individual projects, which would, according to the definition of pork barrel benefits, allocate discrete benefits to individual states and districts without any programmatic connection to other allocations. Thus, because the highway program consists of a nationwide, formula-funded system of highways designed to link all major urban areas, the federal highway program must be considered to be a general interest program.

However, also included in those bills in 1987 and 1991 were distributive benefits, known as highway demonstration projects, mentioned earlier. These projects were designed to meet the needs of particular districts, needs that had not been addressed by state departments of transportation, which administer the federal highway program. While these projects ostensibly demonstrated various technological advances in highway design and construction, most actually did nothing of the kind. Rather, they were thinly veiled pork barrel benefits for members' districts. Two examples taken from 1987 highway legislation illustrate the point: A bridge construction project for Patton Island, Alabama, would demonstrate "methods for improving highway transportation and enhancing economic development." Another, for Kansas City, Missouri, would "demonstrate methods by which construction of the first and southern-most phase of a 5-phase highway project will facilitate construction of the full 5-phase project" (PL 100–17, pp. 185–186). These descriptions hardly promise bold innovations in highway design and construction, and one would be hard-pressed to argue that, as described, they demonstrate anything new or interesting, except to those economic interests that stood directly to benefit.

The questions addressed in this chapter concern how demonstration projects were allocated in two highway reauthorization bills passed in 1987 and 1991. The 1987 Surface Transportation and Uniform Relocation Assistance Act was the first highway bill to contain more than a very few demonstration projects. Traditionally, such projects were included in small numbers for a few key leaders. The previous program reauthorization, in 1982, awarded only ten demonstration projects, a number consistent with earlier reauthorizations. By contrast, the 1987 bill contained 152 demonstration projects for both House members and senators (Hornbeck 1994, p. 4). As such, it is a useful starting point for examining the use of distributive projects to pass general interest legislation. An examination of the subsequent reauthorization, passed in 1991, offers the chance to determine whether the process spiraled out of control as a result of the precedent set in 1987, as predicted in Chapter 2.

The fifteen-fold increase in the number of demonstration projects in the space of the five years between 1982 and 1987 indicates that something changed dramatically during the 1980s in the dynamics of passing highway legislation. There was general acknowledgment, both in the media and in interviews conducted for this study, that projects were added to the 1987 bill to smooth its path to passage (Mills 1990, p. 4138). The question is why such projects were not used in significant numbers prior to 1987. After all, logrolling is hardly a new concept, and highway legislation would appear to be an ideal vehicle for that sort of deal making.

The short answer is that the projects were needed to help forge a majority coalition for the highway bill in 1987, a necessity that the bill's sponsors had not faced in previous reauthorizations. Interviews with committee staff members indicated that by 1987, the construction of the Interstate Highway System, which brought massive formula-based benefits to every state, was nearly complete, and committee leaders faced the challenge of reassessing federal highway policy and deciding its direction in the post–interstate construction era. As a result, the consensus behind highway legislation, a consensus that had been forged by decades of widespread interstate construction, was beginning to dissipate as controversy developed around who would win and who would lose in the new era. For that reason, committee leaders found it necessary to adopt a new technique for creating a coalition that would support their policy preferences for the next phase of the federal highway program.

Thus, the 1987 bill provides a useful starting point for analyzing leaders' strategies for passing legislation using distributive projects and the effects of their strategies on members' support for the legislation. The latter question is taken up in the following chapter. This chapter addresses the matter of how demonstration projects were given out in the 1987 bill and how that process changed the next time the committee had to reauthorize federal highway programs, in 1991. Chapter 2 developed the expectation that committee leaders in 1987 would follow a disciplined strategy of project distribution, giving to a minority of members on the basis of a set of variables that would maximize their chances of passing their bill on the floor of the House. Those variables include the chances that members would not support the bill without a project, as well as their ability to cue other members to support the committee position or otherwise facilitate the bill's passage. By 1991, we expect that leaders would have lost control of project distribution as members, seeing that they could extract a price for their support, strategically concealed their support for the bill and demanded a project. Here, we expect that the number of projects would grow explosively and that project distribution would be much less carefully targeted, with members receiving projects regardless of their likely support for the bill.

In this chapter, following a brief description of the history of the committee, I present the results of interviews with people who worked on the two highway bills. Those interviews provide considerable insight into the intentions of and procedures followed by committee leaders as they distributed projects. Second, I analyze project allocation statistically to determine the strategy by which committee leaders distributed them. The focus in that analysis is on the number of members to whom they gave projects and which members they favored.

THE PUBLIC WORKS AND TRANSPORTATION COMMITTEE AND DISTRIBUTIVE POLITICS

The panel long known as the Public Works Committee historically has been considered a prime source of pork barrel benefits; it has distributed its largesse far and wide for many years. Between 1889 and 1913, its predecessor, the Rivers and Harbors Committee, gave projects to more than 60 percent of the House in most congresses. While short of universal distribution, this percentage is also well above that needed to form minimal winning coalitions to pass the committee's bills. Further, over a ten-year period during that era, nearly 85 percent of all districts benefited (Wilson 1986).

Despite its obvious potential for constituency service (or perhaps because of it), the committee long ago developed a set of arguably objective decision rules for distributing benefits. In the case of water projects, during the 1940s Public Works exercised some self-restraint, as it did not authorize projects without a favorable report from the Army Corps of Engineers, which was responsible for project construction. At the same time, however, members of Congress strenuously lobbied the corps, which weighted local interests heavily in its evaluations (Maass 1951, pp. 576–577), a process biased toward approval of local requests.[1]

In the 1970s, the Public Works Committee required, as it had for decades, that proposed water projects receive a 1:1 benefit-cost ratio from the Corps of Engineers before authorizing them. Although the committee was overwhelmingly constituency-oriented, it was also concerned about its programs more broadly. These two concerns produced conflicting impulses: While members' desire to take benefits back home to their districts tended to suppress partisan conflict, their programmatic commitments held the potential to exacerbate such conflict. Thus, the committee developed a set of formulas for distributing funds rather than doing so on an ad hoc, project-by-project basis. The result was that every district received federal benefits; at the same time Public Works could be characterized as a programmatic rather than a pork barrel committee (Murphy 1974). As I argued above, this pattern continued into the 1980s in the federal highway program.

In 1975, surface transportation and aviation policy were transferred to the committee's jurisdiction from the Commerce Committee, and its name was changed to the Committee on Public Works and Transportation. Twenty years later, with the Republican takeover of the House of Representatives, the committee's name was changed again to the Committee on Transportation and Infrastructure, thus removing "public works" and its connotation of pork barrel politics from the committee's title.

Despite the committee's history of awarding distributive benefits to large majorities of members in some program areas, the large-scale distribution of highway demonstration projects to individual districts in 1987 marked a departure from the committee's efforts to maintain ostensibly objective decision rules for spending highway revenues. However, even in 1987, consistent with the committee's program-oriented tradition, very little of the funding provided by the bills examined here was spent on

[1] A contrasting example, one lacking any sort of merit-based decision rule for distributing benefits, is provided by Richard Fenno's (1973) examination of the House Interior and Insular Affairs Committee, part of his seminal study of six committees in the House of Representatives. That committee dealt mainly with the disposition and use of public lands, including issues such as mining and grazing. It processed hundreds of bills each year, operating under a decision rule of passing "all constituency-supported, Member-sponsored bills" (Fenno 1973, p. 58). Committee members realized that cooperation with other members, many of whom also wanted projects, was the best way to ensure passage of their own constituency bills. Presumably, noncommittee members realized the same thing; as a result, during the time that Fenno examined it, the Interior Committee passed most of the legislation that it brought before the House.

demonstration projects; rather, most of it was expended according to formulas that retained generally applied rules for the bulk of the funding committed by the legislation.

To gain insight into why and how committee leaders awarded demonstration projects, as well as their policy commitments during the transition to the post–interstate construction era, I interviewed staff members for the House Public Works and Transportation Committee, as it was known then, and its Surface Transportation Subcommittee concerning the passage of both the 1987 and 1991 reauthorization bills. The interviews were conducted in 1987, 1990, and 1994. In addition, to obtain a more disinterested perspective, I also interviewed staff members on the Senate Environment and Public Works Committee, which did not distribute demonstration projects, and officials at the Federal Highway Administration.

With respect to the demonstration projects themselves, it is not obvious from the public record who received which ones. Although in many instances special projects are not listed in the legislation itself but rather appear in the committee reports, highway demonstration projects are explicitly listed in the legislation as well as the House committee report. Nevertheless, the geographic location of each project was left vague in both sources, as the following examples from the House committee report on the 1987 bill show:

> Paragraph (13) authorizes a project in the vicinity of San Jose and Santa Clara, California, to demonstrate a unified method of reducing traffic congestion where a highway intersects with two other highways in a railroad crossing in a one-quarter-mile segment.
>
> Paragraph (25) authorizes a highway project to replace a ramp which provides access to an industrial area in Cleveland, Ohio, to demonstrate the relationship between infrastructure improvement and economic vitality.
>
> Paragraph (30) authorizes seven highway projects in Cook County, Illinois: (A) to carry out a highway project which demonstrates methods of utilizing a low cost alternative to reconstruction of a one-mile segment of an east-west road between Nagle and Oak Park Avenues, Chicago, Illinois, which is deficient due to soil conditions. . . . (H. Rpt. 99–665, pp. 31–33)

Some projects clearly can be traced to a particular congressional district, which is the case when a city or county is contained entirely in one congressional district. That is true of the first example above, which is easily traceable to California's Thirteenth District. However, in many cases, locating the recipient district takes considerable effort and is in some cases impossible to do definitively, based only on the legislation's wording. The problem is illustrated by the second example above, in which the project is ambiguously described and located in a city that contains more than one congressional district.

Nevertheless, for the purposes of this study, it was necessary to locate each project precisely by congressional district. I did so using data from internal documents provided to me by congressional staff members. The documents designated the districts that received highway demonstration projects in the House Public Works and Transportation Committee's version of each of the two highway bills examined here. Those data provide the basis for the statistical analyses in this chapter and the next.

THE HIGHWAY BILLS

The 1987 highway reauthorization bill had to clear three major obstacles: a number of challenges on the floor of the House, conflict between the House and Senate public works committees over a number of policy issues, and President Reagan's veto. The 1991 reauthorization also faced difficulties, and the account of that bill's passage will show that committee leaders continued to use demonstration projects to win support for the bill, an approach that had served them well in 1987. It will also become clear that the vote-buying pattern established on the earlier legislation had acquired a life of its own by 1991, resulting in an explosion in the number of projects in the 1991 bill, as predicted in Chapter 2. The following account of the committee's project distribution process will describe some of the public policy goals that the committee's leaders hoped to achieve by awarding demonstration projects and the strategy they followed as they did so.

The 1987 Bill

The 1987 federal-aid highway program reauthorization, the Surface Transportation and Uniform Relocation Assistance Act (which also reauthorized urban mass transit programs), became law in the 100th Congress. It initially passed in the 99th Congress as H.R. 3129, but failed in a late 1986 conference with the Senate and was carried over into the early months of 1987; thus I sometimes refer to it as the 1986–1987 bill. Most of the funding in that $88 billion, five-year authorization went to complete the interstate highway system and maintain the federal-aid highway and urban mass transit systems. Two percent of the total cost was designated for highway demonstration projects, yet that spending received the lion's share of the publicity surrounding the legislation.

The bill was moved through the House by the Public Works and Transportation Committee's "Big Four"; that group consisted of the full committee chairman James Howard (D-N.J.) and ranking minority member Gene Snyder (R-Ky.), along with Surface Transportation Subcommittee chairman Glenn Anderson (D-Calif.) and ranking minority member Bud Shuster (R-Pa.). It was a group known for its bipartisan consensus over highway policy. Its members' ability to put partisan rancor aside is exemplified by the relationship between Republican Bud Shuster and Democrat James Howard. During the mid-1980s, Shuster was known for his fiery partisanship on the House floor and in the Budget Committee, but his relationship with Howard was so congenial that *Politics in America* said that "it used to make one wonder if [Shuster] realized Howard was a Democrat" (Ehrenhalt 1987, p. 1303). True to their tradition, the Big Four, along with their staff, crafted a bipartisan bill behind closed doors in the 99th Congress. By all accounts, dominating the process was committee chairman Howard, who, as the former chairman of the Surface Transportation Subcommittee, possessed considerable expertise along with the power of the chairmanship. Nevertheless, according to committee staffers, there was a good deal of internal horse-trading in the interest of presenting a unified leadership front to the committee as well as to the full House.

The broad policy stakes were outlined earlier; but more detail is in order here concerning some of the issues that made consensus formation difficult in the post–interstate construction era. First, there was a fundamental division among states concerning the distribution of funds. Second, there were growing funding difficulties dating from the late 1970s. Third, there were disagreements over new priorities; prominent among them was the amount of funding to be allocated to the rehabilitation of existing highways versus the construction of new ones.

As the consensus around the highway program dissipated, the division among states over the unequal distribution of funds rose in sharper relief than ever before. The source of the schism was the set of formulas, somewhat redistributive in their effect, used to distribute program funds. By 1986 seventeen states, known as donor states, paid more in fuel taxes into the Highway Trust Fund than they received in program funding, while other states received more than they paid. This imbalance in funding was a serious political problem for the committee. Members from donor states had even less reason to continue to support the program than others; not only were their interstate highways mostly complete, but their states continued to suffer a net loss in the tax-to-revenue ratio of the program. In such conflicts, as Frances Lee (2002) persuasively argues, senators have reason to care about such issues more intensely than House members; nevertheless, the floor debate and my interviews suggest that House members from donor states also cared about this inequity. Although the 1987 bill guaranteed those states a minimum allocation of federal highway funds roughly equal to 85 percent of the gas tax revenues collected from them, their funding remained unfavorable compared with other states. Moreover, demonstration projects did not benefit donor states overall as much as other states: For donor states, unlike donee states (whose revenues exceeded taxes paid), the cost of demonstration projects would come out of their guaranteed minimum allocation of highway funds and therefore would not constitute extra funding for construction. However, the projects were still attractive to individual members in donor states, as they could ensure that demonstration projects would be built in their districts as opposed to someone else's, regardless of whether they were paid for with additional money.

There were also growing difficulties in financing the highway program, according to congressional and Federal Highway Administration staff members. Specifically, in the late 1970s, states began spending up to their annual obligation ceilings (the maximum amount of federal money that they were allowed to spend), and as a result there was too little money to build the states' own high priority projects. Additionally, in the 1980s construction costs escalated, creating even more funding constraints. Linked to the overall funding problem was the fact that as long-completed highways aged and deteriorated, their rehabilitation became more important to state departments of transportation than building new ones. Members of Congress, especially those on the House Public Works and Transportation Committee, continued to press for new construction; yet states now had no money to spare for members' priorities. Thus, demonstration projects were highly attractive to representatives as a way to continue building highways. As a respondent at the Department of Transportation (DOT) said,

> During the heyday of interstate construction under normal formula programs, members of Congress had more opportunity to appear at ribbon-cuttings of new roads. Since most of the construction is completed, demonstration projects provide the only opportunities to take credit for highway construction projects.

Thus, to create a majority coalition in support of the reauthorization, Chairman Howard included in the committee bill 100 highway demonstration projects for seventy-six members of the House. Public Works committee staffers were explicit about the policy-oriented, quid pro quo purpose of such projects:

> The committee has found that to get the national policy they think is fair, it's necessary to sweeten the pot a bit, to do things that need to be done nationally.
>
> If [Chairman Howard] could help a member, he did; at the same time, he expected support.

Two former staff members tied demonstration projects closely to the chairman's quest for influence in the House: As one asserted, the ability to hand out demonstration projects was the source of Howard's power. One indication of this is the personal role played by the Big Four in project allocation. Most of the other provisions of the reauthorization bill were drafted by staff; and people seeking to influence the content of the bill normally lobbied staff members first. However, demonstration projects were different. As a committee staffer said, "Some made the mistake of going to the staff first, but the staff liked their jobs, so they sent them to the members." The power to grant such requests was one jealously guarded by members themselves, with Howard retaining the final say.

The inclusion of so many demonstration projects in this bill was a dramatic change, as indicated by the numbers of demonstration projects in earlier program reauthorizations. According to data supplied by the Federal Highway Administration, the previous three program reauthorizations contained very few such projects. The 1973 legislation contained fourteen; the 1978 law contained eight; and the 1982 legislation awarded ten demonstration projects. Those few projects reportedly were inserted for leaders, chairs of key committees, such as Ways and Means (which had jurisdiction over the gas tax), and the leaders of the authorizing committee. By contrast, the final 1986–1987 legislation contained 152 projects, a number that includes projects added for senators in the House-Senate conference committee. It is the 100 projects in the House committee bill that concern us here, however, as they were intended to help pass the bill in the House. As the data analysis shows below, for the first time those projects were given to many categories of members: nonleaders and leaders alike, as well as legislators who were not on the committee.

During the process of distributing projects, at least some members of the House realized that the committee had begun to entertain requests from all kinds of representatives, and many members therefore began to request them. Whether it was stated or not, the quid pro quo was clear; as one former staff member said, the Public Works Committee leadership expected that members who received demonstration projects would support the leaders' version of the bill:

> It's like the godfather: "you came to me, but once I do you a favor, you have to be loyal." The committee doesn't go out and say it's having a sale of demos; *you* go to the committee; it says jump through these hoops, and you get it.

That remark suggests that even on this bill, the Big Four did not carefully target undecided members to receive a project; rather, they responded to member requests. Nevertheless, they were selective about which project requesters received an award: Committee leaders denied projects to members who previously had opposed the committee on key votes. One staffer said flatly, "They kept a list of those who voted against the committee with black dots next to their names. Those people did not get demonstration projects."

Refusal to give projects to those who had opposed the committee in the past could indicate two things: punishment designed to bring those members into line in the future or a judgment about the member's probability of supporting the committee on this bill. Prior votes are, after all, predictors of future votes. The committee would not want to give projects to those who were likely to vote against the bill: At best, it would be a waste of a project; at worst, it would signal other members that loyalty was not really required in order to get and keep a project, thus undermining any discipline that the projects might have produced.

Despite the quid pro quo expectations, House committee staffers argued that the projects were not given without regard to merit. Requesters were expected to justify the projects: "You needed to be able to say how many people died on that curve." The committee kept a notebook containing this supporting information in order to defend its projects against attack on the House floor. A few staffers argued that the projects demonstrated technological innovations, a point vigorously disputed by Federal Highway Administration officials, one of whom said, "Congress tries to couch their projects in legitimate demo terms, but in reality they're almost all old, proven technology." In past years, a higher percentage of the projects had some claim to the "demonstration" project title, according to another DOT respondent: "There were more real demonstration projects, like pavement studies. They were supported by the states, Congress, and the Department. In the '87 bill, there isn't a single real demo."

Whatever their substantive merits, demonstration projects clearly were intended for political purposes. In the end, committee leaders gave projects to a minority of legislators: Seventy-six members, only 17 percent of the House membership, received the 100 projects in that bill. Yet, as Chapter 4 shows, that number was sufficient to ensure passage of the bill and an override of the president's veto. Moreover, with one major policy exception, the bill passed in the form preferred by the committee leaders.

The Senate initially opposed including demonstration projects because they entailed extra spending above most states' allocations and would build projects that were of low priority to state departments of transportation. Just as important, perhaps, the size of senators' own constituencies made such relatively small-scale projects less profitable in an electoral sense than they were for House members. Senators did designate ninety-nine "high priority" projects in their own version of the legislation, but they were very different from demonstration projects. Their construction was not mandated, and their funding would have come out of the state's regular allocation. In fact, the Senate was far more concerned with the formulas by which the money was to be allocated than with individual projects, as formulas affect the entire state. Nevertheless, soon after the beginning of the 100th Congress, the second conference committee worked out a compromise in which the Senate agreed to allow demonstration projects with certain provisions to make them less costly to the Highway Trust Fund. Once it was a forgone conclusion that demonstration projects would be in the bill, Senate conferees added fifty or so projects of their own to those already in the House bill. In 1991, the Senate, aware from the beginning that projects would be part of that bill, held out until conference, inserting their projects at that time.

The 1991 Bill

The 1991 highway reauthorization was called the Intermodal Surface Transportation Equity Act (ISTEA). The problems faced by the leaders of the House Public Works and Transportation Committee in 1991 were similar to but more severe than those they faced in 1986–1987. The last remaining segments of the interstate highway system were essentially complete, and members saw even less benefit in the program for themselves and had less reason to support the reauthorization with its huge amounts of spending. Once again, donor states posed a particular problem. As one staffer said, "[donor] states had bought into the interstate program and were willing to sacrifice, but once it was built, they wanted their fair share." As with the 1987 bill, the Big Four, especially the new committee chairman, Robert Roe (D-N.J.), had specific policy commitments for which he wished to use the projects to purchase support. Those policy priorities are discussed in detail in Chapter 4, but chief among them was a five-cent increase in the federal gas tax, the source of federal highway funds.

By 1991, pressure to reorient federal highway and mass transit policy had grown impossible for the committee to resist. Yet fundamental changes in those policies were bound to exacerbate divisions not only among donor and donee states, but also between urban and rural areas over funding for mass transit versus highways. This time, however, there would be fewer massive construction projects to console the losers. Although there was limited interest in fundamental policy change on the House Public Works Committee, Transportation Secretary Samuel Skinner and Senate transportation subcommittee chairman Daniel Patrick Moynihan (D-N.Y.) each sought to take advantage of the opportunity to engrave their own signature priorities on the program. Skinner wanted to develop new linkages among existing interstates and the roads that feed into them, creating a new National Highway System that would receive priority in the allocation of funds for highway maintenance, rehabilitation, and expansion. Through that program, Skinner sought to give states more flexibility in the use of their funds in exchange for a reduction in the federal share of transportation spending. He also wanted to develop links among different modes of transportation (Mills 1990; *CQ Almanac 1991*, p. 138). However, his plan was unappealing to many in Congress largely because it pertained to existing roads and failed to provide a justification for the construction of new ones.

Moynihan's proposal was similar to Skinner's in that it provided states with a much higher degree of flexibility to shift funds among all modes of surface transportation, including mass transit and railroads. In particular, Moynihan hoped that giving states the ability to transfer funds out of highway programs into other modes of transportation would be a powerful means to reduce congestion and air pollution in cities. However, his plan would have retained a much higher level of federal funding than Skinner favored (Mills 1991b). Moynihan moved the Senate reauthorization bill so quickly that the Environment and Public Works Committee reported it before the House committee had even introduced its own version, thus reversing the House's usual dominance of the process. His speed also caught interest groups by surprise, making it hard for them to develop an effective response to his proposals.

Robert Roe, the newly chosen chair of the House Public Works and Transportation Committee, got a late start on the bill, according to a staff member, due to his somewhat unexpected ascension to the chairmanship following the Democrats' ouster from that position of the ailing Glenn Anderson (D-Calif.), who himself replaced the late James Howard. Although Roe was the second-ranking Democrat on the committee, he was challenged for the chairmanship by third-ranking Norman Mineta (D-Calif.). Mineta had recently been chosen chairman of the Surface Transportation Subcommittee, a position from which full committee chairs often rose. Some staffers thought that Mineta, who had refused to grant pork barrel projects in his previous position as chairman of the Aviation Subcommittee, would block highway demonstration projects. However, Roe's selection as full committee chairman ensured that the committee would continue to grant the projects. As one staffer said, Roe "believed in members' right to make decisions about projects"; and "no bureaucrat knew more about projects in Bob Roe's district than Bob Roe." In other words, as members of that committee have often asserted publicly, legislators are just as well qualified to decide where roads should go as state departments of transportation. As *CQ Weekly Report* noted soon after his selection as committee chair, "Roe . . . is an old-style pol whose stock in trade is handing out the kinds of highway projects [Secretary] Skinner hopes to limit" (Mills 1990, p. 4134).

Nevertheless, Roe was not blind to the need to revamp the program, despite his belief that more interstate highways should be built. He backed the administration's advocacy of a National Highway System, although unlike Skinner, Roe saw such a system as a vehicle for funding further highway construction. Although most of the media accounts of the House committee's bill focused on the fight over the nickel increase in the gas tax, one former staffer noted that Roe favored the stress on intermodal transportation in the Senate bill; however, the Senate bill also contained much that the House disagreed with, especially the emphasis on highway repair rather than construction.

Given Roe's orientation in favor of both highway construction in general and demonstration projects in particular, it should come as no surprise that he was more than willing to use such projects to advance his own public policy goals. He was explicit about the quid pro quo – project recipients were expected to support the increase in the gas tax. But he also clearly knew that the bill as a whole, given its redesign of highway policy and the smoldering resentment of the donor states, would face considerable difficulty on the floor of the House (Mills 1991a, p. 1488). Thus, he expected that demonstration projects would be useful in shoring up support for the bill itself, in addition to the gas tax.

Moreover, the demand for projects had been building since the passage of the 1987 bill. The large number of projects in that bill "gave members the green light," as one staffer said, to press harder for projects for themselves the next time around. The distribution of projects in the 1987 bill made it clear that a member did not have to be a leader to get one; even freshmen received them, "so on what basis do you deny them in [the 1991] bill?" The combination of greatly increased demand for demonstration projects, their obvious utility for coalition building, and the new chairman's positive attitude toward them led the committee to look favorably on members' requests. Indeed, in the words of another staff member, unlike in 1987, the committee "sent out the word" that it was handing out demonstration projects, thus making a virtue of necessity.

Because the projects in the 1987 bill had prompted not only a great deal of criticism outside the House but also a presidential veto, the Public Works Committee this time adopted procedures to try to address the concerns about them. First, Roe attempted to change the projects' name, calling them "congressional projects of national significance" (*CQ Almanac 1991*, p. 142). Not surprisingly, the new name failed to catch on, but his attempt to make the change reflected the negative connotations of the term "demonstration project." Moreover, in 1987, many observers thought that the process by which the projects had been awarded lacked any apparent criteria beyond the fact that members wanted them. Thus, Roe required members requesting projects to fill out a three-page questionnaire describing and justifying their requests. According to a staff member, Roe and top committee staffers applied three criteria to the project requests:

1. Had the member provided enough information so that "the project was understandable"?
2. Was there a state or local application for the project?
3. Were there any obvious environmental problems?

Clearly, the first criterion is an extremely loose one; a bad project can be "understandable." With respect to the second criterion, a Senate staffer said that Roe first required a state application, but some important members who wanted a project lacked that, so the criterion was loosened to the point of meaninglessness with the addition of local application; as the staffer said, "all of them have local application." Although there is no evidence that the environmental criterion had been applied in the past, there is also no indication as to how strictly it was applied in 1991.

This more systematic application process was an attempt, however minimal, at an appearance of some control over the process; as such, it may have provided a bit of political cover for both the committee and project recipients against charges of pork barreling. Nevertheless, once it became clear how many more projects this bill contained than the last one, all attempts at inoculation against criticism proved futile.

Like Chairman Howard before him, Roe controlled the distribution of demonstration projects, making the first cut of the applications himself along with a top staff member, only then bringing in the other three leaders for the remainder of the decisions. Staffers noted that most members who asked received something; however, nearly everyone got much less than he or she asked for, perhaps an indication that members had no idea how generous the committee might be and were loath this time to ask for less than it was willing to give.

One of the major questions addressed in this research concerns changes in the size of benefit-winning coalitions over time. Specifically, the expectation here is that once leaders have distributed pork barrel benefits to buy loyalty on one bill, members who did not receive a project that time will feel that they gave their votes away and therefore have an incentive to behave strategically in order to receive a project on the next bill sponsored by those leaders. The result is that leaders must resign themselves to the new strategic environment and give projects to all of the (now greatly increased number of) members who request them. That is not to say that they must give members everything they want. To do so would be unwise in a policy sense, as such demands would absorb more and more of the total funding for the program in question, thus negating the policy-based motivation for awarding the projects in the first place. Additionally, it would be unnecessary to give members everything they requested. Although members want something for their vote, many submit more requests than they really expect or need to receive in return for their support (support that, in this game, many of them would give anyway). But even though members will not get all they request, the changed dynamics of the policy-making process on this second round means that leaders must give projects to many more members and maybe even a larger number of projects to particularly influential members.

Therefore, our expectation is that the growth in the number of projects between the first and second bills will be dramatic, as vote buying on the first bill becomes universally known. That certainly was the case for these two highway bills. The 1987 House bill awarded 100 projects to seventy-six members, or 17 percent of the House, accounting for approximately

2 percent of the total funding. The number of projects in the 1991 bill exploded to 489 projects for 262 members, or 60 percent of the House; the projects accounted for 3.5 percent of the funding in the bill.

While the project awards were designed to cast a broad net, media accounts indicated that they were not evenly distributed across the membership of the House. The Big Four took special steps to ensure that their states fared well. Some 38 percent of the project dollars were to go to New Jersey (the chairman's state), California (the subcommittee chairman's state), Pennsylvania (the subcommittee ranking member's state), Arkansas (the full committee's ranking member's state), and Illinois (*1991 CQ Almanac*, p. 142). Although Illinois was not represented among the Public Works Committee leaders, it was the home of the powerful chairman of the House Ways and Means Committee, Dan Rostenkowski, on whom the Public Works Committee depended (in vain, as it turned out) for the five-cent increase in the gas tax. Thus, it appears that leaders were privileged above others, but it should not be inferred that the bill was merely a means to funnel pork to their districts; as the next chapter shows, the leaders had genuine policy commitments at stake as well.

Although on both bills the leaders used demonstration projects to try to ensure members' support for the broader provisions of the highway bill, they gave projects more sparingly in 1987, although they appear "sparing" only in retrospect. In 1991, unlike 1986–1987, the leaders were very public about both their willingness to give projects to the large number of members now requesting them and their expectation that accepting a project obligated a member to support not only the bill, but also the gas tax increase, and, as Chapter 4 shows, anything else the leaders wanted.

PROJECT DISTRIBUTION STRATEGIES

The first question posed in Chapter 2 concerns the growth in the number of projects from one bill to the next. The expectation was that the number of projects would increase dramatically between the first and second bills on which they were used as a coalition-building device. The second time around, leaders are expected to give projects to a supermajority of members, unlike the first time they distribute projects to gain votes. That occurs because, from the first to the second time that leaders use the vote-buying strategy, the control of project distribution is likely to shift to rank-and-file members, as the latter see that they can extract benefits in exchange for their votes. The result is a massive increase in the number of projects that coalition leaders must give.

TABLE 3.1 *Numbers and Cost of Highway Demonstration Projects in Reauthorization Legislation, 1973–1991*

Year	1973	1978	1982	1987	1991
Number of projects	14	8	10	152	538
Cost in millions	N.A.	N.A.	$426	$1,400	$5,171

Note: N.A.: not ascertained. Data for 1973–1987 are from the Federal Highway Administration; data for 1991 are from the Congressional Research Service (Hornbeck 1994). Project costs (including those for 1982) are presented in 1987 dollars.

The second question concerns the strategies that committee leaders used in distributing demonstration projects. The interviews with those who participated in passing the two highway bills have provided a good deal of insight into that question, but the quantitative analysis in this section makes it possible to determine more precisely whether the pattern of project allocation was consistent with the specific distributive strategies delineated in Chapter 2.

With respect to the number of projects, the data reported earlier documented the numbers in the 1987 and 1991 bills as they emerged from the Public Works Committee. Many more projects were added by the Senate in the conference committees that resolved the differences between the House and Senate versions of the bills. Table 3.1 documents the final numbers of demonstration projects in every highway reauthorization bill between 1973 and 1991. It shows the explosive growth between 1982 and 1987, as 1987 was the first year in which projects were included in significant numbers. More important, it shows that the 1991 bill contained 3.5 times as many projects as the 1987 bill, supporting the argument that the use of such projects, once begun, has an inexorable tendency to grow, as more and more members demand one as the price of their support for the bill.

The second major question is the rationale by which these projects were awarded. Chapter 2 made the case that the first time leaders use this strategy, they give projects to gain the loyalty of members whose full support is potentially available – those who do not need to oppose the legislation for electoral or ideological reasons. Thus, the expectation is that the first time leaders use projects in this way they have the best chance they will ever enjoy to target them according to members' likely support for the bill. In the most efficient application of this strategy, there would be a curvilinear relationship between likely support for the leaders' position and the member's chances of receiving a project. However, as noted in the preceding chapter, potential benefits flow from giving projects to some of those who already have a propensity to support the bill. The advantages of doing so include, most prominently, winning their support on amendments that the leaders, but not the members themselves, care about. Thus, if leaders follow a risk-averse strategy, even this first time, of giving projects both to fence-sitters and likely supporters to solidify their loyalty on all issues, the relationship between likely support for the leaders' positions and receipt of a project is expected to be positive.

The second time leaders use the vote-buying strategy, after they have revealed a willingness to give projects in this way, members have an incentive to conceal strategically their true preferences, either on the bill as a whole, if they can credibly do so, or on amendments that threaten the leaders' policy goals. If they do conceal their preferences, there will be little or no relationship between members' likely support for the bill and their receipt of a project. Additionally, at all times, other variables are expected to affect whether members will receive a project, including the member's position in the House, especially if that position is relevant to the bill's chances for passage.

To determine the impact of members' expected support for the legislation on the probability that leaders will award them a project, it is necessary first to estimate the probability that a member would support the committee's positions on the bill without receiving a project. That is what committee leaders themselves must do if they wish to award projects as efficiently as possible. Following that step, we estimate the impact of a member's expected level of support for the committee position on the leaders' decision to give him or her a demonstration project. The dependent variable here is a member's receipt of one or more projects. The unit of analysis is the individual member of Congress.

Two measures of project distribution were used. One was dichotomous – receipt of a demonstration project – which simply indicates whether the member received any project, regardless of how many. That variable takes a value of 1 if the member received one or more projects and 0 if not. The second measure consists of the actual number of projects that the member received. Each was used as the dependent variable in a separate model of how committee leaders distributed projects. To estimate those models it was necessary to use two-stage estimation techniques in which the member's likely support for the committee's position is treated as an endogenous explanatory variable. A full description of the two-stage estimation techniques used for both models is in the Appendix at the end of this chapter. Here, the results are presented as if they were obtained by simple one-stage procedures.

Both measures of project awards are used here because there is reason to believe that the number of projects a member received was determined slightly differently than whether or not a member received a project at all. Moreover, both measures offer different advantages and disadvantages, which will become clear to those readers who peruse the Appendix. Policy coalition leaders' big decision is to determine to which members they must give something to guarantee their loyalty. That is a dichotomous, yes-or-no decision, and the model using that measure estimates the impact of a number of variables on that decision. It is also possible that some members' votes may have been more valuable than others'; that is, some members may have been able to extract more projects than others because of the extra value of their support. That possibility is also examined here, using the number of projects that members received (if any) as the dependent variable.

The model for project distribution, which is essentially identical for both measures of project awards in both 1986 and 1991, is as follows:[2]

Project *or* N projects = fn(Expected Committee Support, Public Works, Leader, Donor, Previous Election Percentage, Democrat)

"Expected Committee Support" is a variable that measures the degree to which a representative would support the policy preferences of the committee leaders without receiving a demonstration project. For a full explanation of how that variable is measured, see the Appendix. With respect to the other explanatory variables, "Public Works" is a dummy variable that takes the value 1 if the member held a seat on that committee in 1986 or 1991, when the projects were awarded. "Leader" takes a value of 1 if the member was one of the top party leadership or chaired or was ranking minority member of the Public Works and Transportation Committee, its Surface Transportation Committee, or any committee whose support was important to the Big Four: the Appropriations Committee, its transportation subcommittee, the Ways and Means Committee, or the Budget Committee; otherwise, leader = 0. Public Works Committee members and other leaders are expected to be more likely to receive a project than other members and to receive more than other members, given the

[2] The model for Project, the dichotomous dependent variable, contains a right-hand variable, CS Residual, which is necessary in the estimation of a two-stage model in which the dependent variable in the second-stage equation is dichotomous. For a full explanation, see the Appendix.

value of their support as cue givers to other members of the House. If these members support the leaders' preferences on the highway bills, the path to passage is likely to be smoother. Bipartisan support on the Public Works Committee signals other members that there are no obvious partisan or policy reasons to oppose the committee's leaders; giving projects to those members is a way for leaders to secure their support for that purpose. Leaders also have the ability to signal members about acceptable votes, and in the case of chamber leaders, to clear the path to passage through favorable procedures; other key committee leaders can make life easier or more difficult for the Public Works Committee by virtue of their control of important aspects of the highway program. Thus, the Big Four are likely to try to secure their support by giving them projects as well.

"Donor" is a dummy variable that, when it takes the value 1, indicates that the member represents a state that contributed more to the Highway Trust Fund in gas taxes than it got back in federal highway spending; Donor = 0 for members representing donee states, those that received at least as much in spending as they contributed in taxes.[3] The likely impact of this variable is not obvious. Leaders have reason to give projects to legislators from donor states, who have a policy reason to oppose the highway program because of its funding formulas. However, donor state members might be less likely than others even to request a project, because they must oppose the bill due to funding inequities. On the other hand, a project might be especially valuable for representatives of donor states: They see their states as underfunded, and a demonstration project guarantees their districts a greater share of a limited resource. If that is

[3] The calculation of donor versus donee states is based on data from the Federal Highway Administration (http://www.fhwa.dot.gov/ohim/donor) for the years encompassed by the previous program authorization, the 1982 Surface Transportation Assistance Act; the relevant years are 1982–1986. I counted a state as a donor if it paid more to the Highway Trust Fund than it received in apportionments from the highway account in more than one year of that five-year authorization or if it was a donor in one year and was on the FHWA's list of long-term donor states from 1957 to 1997. Four of the seventeen donor states fall into the latter category. I included them as donors because their long-standing donor status is assumed to influence their positions on the 1987 bill. I followed a similar procedure, using the same data source, for the years prior to the 1991 bill, 1987–1990. During that period, the number of donor states grew from seventeen to twenty-two. The donor states for the 1987 bill were as follows: Arkansas, California, Florida, Georgia, Indiana, Maine, Michigan, Mississippi, Missouri, North Carolina, New Jersey, Ohio, Oklahoma, South Carolina, Tennessee, Texas, and Wisconsin. For the 1991 bill, the donor states were Alabama, Arkansas, Arizona, California, Florida, Georgia, Indiana, Kansas, Kentucky, Maine, Michigan, Mississippi, Missouri, North Carolina, Ohio, Oklahoma, Oregon, South Carolina, Tennessee, Texas, Virginia, and Wisconsin.

the case, donor state members might be especially susceptible to trading their vote for a project, and leaders might then give them one.

Additionally, the member's level of electoral need was measured as the percentage of the vote received by the incumbent in the previous election. Such members might be particularly attracted by such benefits and therefore receptive to the vote-buying strategy. Thus, the closer the member's last election contest, the more likely it is that the leaders inserted a project into the bill for that member to help with the next electoral battle.

Similarly, although we expect the distribution process to be bipartisan, as leaders wish to gain the votes of members of both parties, the possibility of a partisan distribution process must be examined. If partisan theories are correct in their analysis of the uses of pork (especially Cox and McCubbins 1993, pp. 123–125), projects should go only to Democrats.

TABLE 3.2 *Determinants of Project Allocation: Dichotomous Project Variable*

Variable	1986–1987 bill	1991 bill
Expected Committee Support	0.029[b]	0.017
	(.013)	(.011)
Public Works	0.581	1.497[a]
	(.429)	(.353)
Leader	0.740[b]	−0.031
	(.331)	(.322)
Donor	0.062	0.053
	(.170)	(.133)
Previous election percentage	−0.004	−0.011[a]
	(.006)	(.004)
Democrat	−0.320	−0.620
	(.329)	(.578)
CS Residual	−0.011	0.005
	(.013)	(.011)
Intercept	−2.872[a]	0.046
	(.961)	(.585)
Pseudo R^2	.199	.128
N	381	429

[a] $p \leq .01$.
[b] $p \leq .05$.
Note: Cell entries are unstandardized regression coefficients. Numbers in parentheses are standard errors. Significance tests are one-tailed. In 1986–1987, only members who served in both the 99th and 100th Congresses were included; hence, N = 381. In 1991, N reflects a number of vacant seats. See Appendix for explanation of CS Residual.

TABLE 3.3 *Determinants of the Number of Projects Received*

Variable	1986–87 bill	1991 bill
Committee Support	0.001	0.010
	(.005)	(.013)
Public Works	0.710[a]	2.311[a]
	(.179)	(.255)
Leader	0.451[a]	0.654[b]
	(.129)	(.332)
Donor	−0.050	−0.254
	(.055)	(.163)
Previous election percentage	−0.002	−0.001
	(.002)	(.005)
Democrat	0.092	−0.266
	(.130)	(.644)
Intercept	0.259	0.480
	(.371)	(.638)
R^2	.196	.274
N	381	429

[a] $p \leq .01$.
[b] $p \leq .05$.
Note: Cell entries are unstandardized regression coefficients. Numbers in parentheses are standard errors. Significance tests are one-tailed. In 1986–1987, only members who served in both the 99th and 100th Congresses were included; hence, N = 381. In 1991, N reflects a number of vacant seats.

Thus, a dummy variable, Democrat, is included for that purpose. It takes a value of 1 for members who are Democrats, 0 for Republicans.

To estimate members' likely support for the committee leaders on these bills (Committee Support), I used their actual votes (the estimation technique for Expected Committee Support is described in the Appendix). For the 1986–1987 bill, I pooled data from the 99th and 100th Congresses, as the legislation was voted on in both congresses and members of both received projects. The data set consists of the 381 members who served in both congresses. For the 1991 bill, the data set potentially consists of all 435 members; however, six seats were vacant during this time; those districts were not included.

The results appear in Tables 3.2 and 3.3. Table 3.2 reports the results of probit analyses for the dichotomous dependent variable, which measures whether the member received a project at all. In 1986–1987, the more support the member could be expected to provide the committee, the more likely the committee leaders were to give him or her a project; by contrast, in 1991, expected support had no effect on whether or not leaders gave members a project. These results support the argument made in Chapter 2 that, on the first bill, leaders were able to discover rank-and-file members' voting intentions because members had not yet realized that they could benefit from concealing those intentions. Thus, leaders gave out demonstration projects in accordance with members' expected loyalty. However, in 1991, they did not distribute projects in accordance with members' expected support for leaders' positions on the bill. That finding supports the argument that in 1991, members concealed their true degree of support for the leaders, who, in response, gave out projects (and many more of them) to anyone who asked. The interviews certainly support the inference that in 1991, leaders gave projects to anyone who could provide a reasonable rationale.

The possibility that the Big Four employed a precisely targeted, efficient strategy of project distribution, most likely giving to members who were undecided about the highway bill (suggesting a curvilinear relationship between Expected Committee Support and receipt of a project), was tested with the addition of a quadratic term for the committee support variable. However, that variable was not significant; moreover, the pseudo R^2 was lower for 1986 and unchanged for 1991. Therefore, that term was omitted. Other nonlinear specifications were tested with similar results. Thus, the linear relationship is reported here, as it is significant in 1986.

In other respects, the pattern was different for the two bills as well. Members of the Public Works and Transportation Committee were not especially favored in 1986, but leaders were more likely to get projects. In 1991, committee members were especially favored, and leaders were not. In both years the distribution process was bipartisan, as previous scholarship on distributive politics leads us to expect. Donor states were neither favored nor disfavored. Additionally, in 1991 only, there appeared to be an effort to use projects to protect incumbents; the lower members' 1990 election percentage, the more likely they were to receive at least one demonstration project. This strategy, however, was not partisan; an interactive term for party and prior election percentage was not significant, an additional indication of the bipartisan tradition of this committee. The last variable, "CS Residual," was included as part of the two-stage estimation procedure; its interpretation is provided in the Appendix.

The results discussed above are for a model of whether a member received a project at all; the dependent variable is, therefore, dichotomous.

Table 3.3 presents the results of an analysis of the *number* of projects that members received in each bill; for this, OLS regression was used.[4] In this analysis, the member's likely support for the bill in the absence of a project is irrelevant; the coefficient for Committee Support is not significant for either bill. Once again, tests for nonlinear relationship were not significant, and adjusted R^2s were lower.

However, in both years, members of the Public Works Committee and leaders were likely to get more projects than others. The most dramatic effect is for members of the Public Works committee in 1991; such members received 2.31 more projects than noncommittee members. Additionally, a comparison of the 1991 coefficient estimates for the leadership variable in the two models shows that while nonleaders were just as likely to get a project as leaders (Table 3.2), leaders did get more projects than other members (Table 3.3). Thus, especially in 1991, leadership status and membership on the Public Works Committee determined how much of the largesse one received (Table 3.3). Again, however, the process was bipartisan; moreover, in neither year did a member's prior election percentage have an impact on the number of projects received. In 1991, it was evidently important only that less safe members bring home some pork (Table 3.2), not the whole barrel (Table 3.3).

Summary of Statistical Findings

We expected that the first time that leaders used this technique for forming a supporting coalition for their version of the bill, they would be able to use an efficient, targeted approach to support buying. That turns out not to be the case, as fence-sitters did not do better than more certain supporters. Nevertheless, leaders evidently did award projects in the 1986–1987 bill according to members' likely support, as Table 3.2 shows. As expected, that variable was significant in 1986–1987. But the second time around, in 1991, leaders were not significantly more likely to give to

[4] A third possible measure of the degree to which a member was favored by the Big Four is the dollar value of his or her projects. However, as Stein and Bickers (1995, p. 135) note, constituents are more likely to respond to "the occurrence of an award, not its dollar size." "Each award provides an opportunity for a legislator to demonstrate his or her efficacy," and the more awards there are, the more segments of a constituency can be visibly helped (Stein and Bickers 1994a, p. 380). What counts politically is the announcement of the award, along with the additional credit the member can claim when the project is completed. Constituents are unlikely to retain dollar amounts. Indeed, for both years, equations modeling the dollar value of members' projects performed much worse than those reported in Table 3.3, which model the number of projects.

more supportive members or fence-sitters. Rather than targeting project awards in this way, the leaders of Public Works and Transportation appear to have followed a purely reactive strategy as they determined who would receive a project once they had given to members of their own committee and to leaders. Although they were explicit about expecting the loyalty of those they favored with projects, they evidently were not particular about who received them. The burden thus was on project recipients to make sure they could fulfill the expected commitment before they requested a project, or risk retaliation later. Staff members who were interviewed on both bills alluded guardedly to such retaliation in a few cases.

The fact that leaders targeted projects to members of their own committee, leaders of other key committees, and floor leaders does suggest a strategy of vote buying. If the strategy were successful, the support of all of those people could only help the legislation on the floor of the House. Giving to committee members is a way to ensure that the committee will present a solid front to both Republicans and Democrats looking for cues as to how to vote on the floor. Giving projects to other key leaders is designed either to ensure their support or at least to minimize their opposition, again reducing any negative cues that might diminish support on the floor.

CONCLUSIONS

Who controls the project allocation process? If committee leaders were fully in control, as we expected them to be on the first bill when members had less chance to behave strategically, we would see projects go to only a minority of members of the House and to be targeted according to members' likely support for the leaders' positions. We found evidence of both. Only seventy-six members received projects, and for the dichotomous project variable, members' likely support for the leaders' wishes significantly affected their chances of getting a project.

On the second bill in the sequence, again as expected, there is evidence that leaders gave up control of the project distribution process. First, the number of projects grew massively from one bill to the next. Second, the interview evidence indicates that committee leaders' decision to give demonstration projects to a supermajority of members in 1991 was a result of their use of projects in 1986–1987, when they first revealed that they were willing to buy votes. Third, the statistical analysis shows that members' expected support for the leaders' positions did not have an impact on project distribution. The committee leaders took advantage of

TABLE 3.4 *Numbers and Cost of Highway Demonstration Projects in Reauthorization Legislation, 1973–1998*

Year	1973	1978	1982	1987	1991	1998
Number of projects	14	8	10	152	538	1,850
Cost in millions	N.A.	N.A.	$426	$1,400	$5,171	$6,516

Note: Data for 1973–1987 are from the Federal Highway Administration; data for 1991 are from the Congressional Research Service (Hornbeck 1994); data for 1998 are from *1998 CQ Almanac*. Project costs (including those for 1982) are presented in 1987 dollars.

the expansion of member expectations for projects between the first and second bills; in 1991, they advertised the availability of projects and demanded project recipients' support for their policy priorities in return. In effect, the leaders treated the increased demand for projects as an opportunity to secure their own version of the legislation, worrying little about the policy implications of the rapidly expanding number of projects. It is therefore reasonable to expect that the demand for projects would continue to grow over time. That has indeed been the case. The five-year reauthorization subsequent to that passed in 1991 was the 1998 Transportation Equity Act for the 21st Century (TEA-21). The number of demonstration projects in the final legislation again increased dramatically, from 538 to 1,850. Table 3.4 reproduces Table 3.1, with the addition of the number and cost of projects in TEA-21. The costs of the projects in the 1991 and 1998 bills are adjusted for inflation and presented in 1987 dollars.

As this table shows, in 1998 the number of projects once again increased more than three-fold over the previous reauthorization, although between 1991 and 1998 the cost increased at a much lower rate, by about 26 percent, than between 1987 and 1991, when the increase was 369 percent. Figure 3.1 shows graphically the relative growth of demonstration projects in numbers and cost for the years in which the cost was available. It appears that as the consensus that formerly supported the highway program diminished (primarily as a result of the virtual completion of the Interstate Highway System, the major broad-based, general interest portion of the program), the purely distributive component of federal highway legislation increased. Moreover, there is no apparent end in sight. As federal highway policy became more controversial, the utility of demonstration projects increased. By distributing them, leaders hoped to secure members' loyalty for the floor fights to come. The next chapter examines the extent to which they succeeded in doing so.

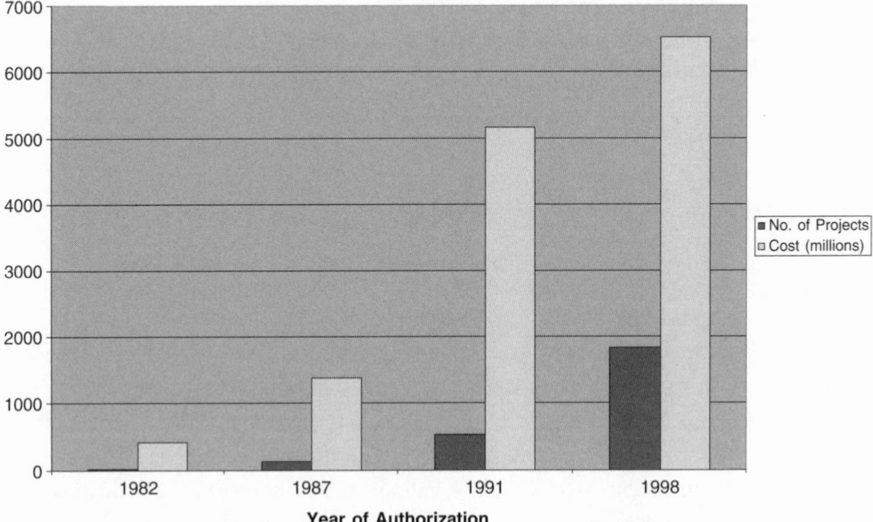

FIGURE 3.1. Growth of demonstration projects, 1982–1998.

APPENDIX: COMMITTEE SUPPORT

In both models of the way in which projects were allocated (see Tables 3.2 and 3.3), members' likely support for the committee leaders' position is treated as an endogenous variable, necessitating two-stage estimation procedures. That is because the only available measure of how likely members were to support the bill without a project is how they actually voted on the bill, with the impact on their votes of receiving a project removed. A member's support for the previous highway bill would be a preferable measure of their likely support for the current one, but the issues may change from one bill to the next. More important, the program is reauthorized only once every five or six years, so the number of current members who have a relevant voting record is considerably reduced. As a result of using members' actual votes on the bill as an explanatory variable in the project distribution model, there are in effect two endogenous variables: projects received and expected support for the leadership position. Therefore, two-stage estimation techniques are both statistically necessary and best simulate what committee leaders do as they decide to whom to award projects.

The member's expected support for the committee position (Expected Committee Support) on each of the highway bills was estimated as follows: For each member, I calculated the percentage of recorded votes on which the member supported the position of the Public Works Committee leaders. The votes used as the basis for that calculation were those on which the four committee leaders took a unified position, as indicated by their recorded votes. Given their reputation for working out differences among themselves and the fact that final project distribution decisions were made by the Big Four working together, it is reasonable to assume that the leaders called in their debts only on those issues on which they were unanimous. The results of the first-stage estimates are not of particular interest here and are therefore only summarized at the end of this section. From those first-stage results, each member's probability of supporting the leadership without a project was calculated. The point of the first stage procedure was to develop an appropriate Expected Committee Support variable to use in the equations that are really of interest here, the ones that estimate the impact of likely support on the distribution of projects.

For the model of the dichotomous project variable reported in Table 3.2, I used a two-stage OLS-probit procedure developed by Rivers and Vuong (1988). Although the first-stage equation, the estimation of Expected Committee Support, was estimated using OLS regression, the Rivers and Vuong technique differs from the usual two stage least squares (2SLS) procedure in its second-stage equation, which is necessarily estimated using probit analysis, as it models a dichotomous dependent variable. Specifically, their technique does not require an instrument for the endogenous variable that appears on the right-hand side of the equation (Expected Committee Support). Rather, the second-stage model uses the member's actual committee support scores as the Expected Committee Support variable and includes the residuals (CS Residual in Table 3.2) from the first-stage model. The latter variable accounts for the variance in Committee Support that was not explained by the exogenous variables; such variance potentially includes the impact of receiving a demonstration project, hence an instrument for the Committee Support variable is not needed. Significance for the residual variable indicates endogeneity in the second stage, and in that case the t-statistics for the other parameter estimates must be evaluated more conservatively than usual.[5] Looking at Table 3.2 once again, it is clear that endogeneity is not a problem in either equation: CS Residual does not even approach significance. Therefore, the standard errors can be taken at face value.

[5] Rivers and Vuong 1988; and Rivers, personal communication.

The models of the total number of projects that members received, whose second-stage estimates were reported in Table 3.3, were estimated using conventional 2SLS regression, in which both equations are estimated using OLS regression. Here, Expected Committee Support in Table 3.3 is an instrumental variable calculated from the estimated parameters in the first-stage equation, which modeled members' actual votes on each bill, omitting the influence of receiving a project.

The first stage equations, which model Expected Committee Support, are the same for both sets of models, although the results are used differently. For those equations, the exogenous variables expected to have an impact on members' degree of support for the leadership position on these bills are those usually employed in models of roll call voting. Also included in the first-stage equations are those exogenous variables expected to influence a member's chances of receiving a project. The variables employed to explain members' support for the leadership are as follows: party (Republican = 1 and Democrat = 0); the member's 1985 or 1992 Conservative Coalition score (a measure of the liberalism of the member's voting record), which did not include votes taken on these bills; and the dummy variables described earlier for holding a seat on Public Works and a leadership position. Also included was the donor state dummy variable.

Additionally, for the 1987 bill several political action committee (PAC) variables and two district variables were relevant. One amendment restricted the use of imported cement; thus the summed contributions of three cement industry PACs were included.[6] Another amendment would have reduced compensation to billboard owners for removal of their billboards from federal highways; thus contributions from the Outdoor Advertising Association were included. As both votes were taken in 1986, contributions for the 1984 election were used. With respect to district variables, two issues were relevant. Three votes dealt with the 55 mph speed limit; as there was pressure from western states to raise it, a dummy variable was included for states in the West.[7] If a member was from one of those states, that variable took a value of 1; it was set at 0 otherwise. Additionally, two amendments would have stopped construction of the Los Angeles Metrorail system pending completion of a supplemental

[6] Included were contributions from the National Ready Mixed Concrete Association, the National Concrete Masonry Association, and the Portland Cement Association.

[7] The states designated as western include all the West Coast states, the mountain states of Arizona, Colorado, Idaho, Montana, Nevada, New Mexico, Utah, and Wyoming, as well as Iowa, Kansas, Minnesota, Missouri, Nebraska, North Dakota, and South Dakota. Alternative measures were tried in the model, but this worked best.

environmental impact statement; thus a dummy variable was included for those members who represented the Los Angeles metropolitan area.

The OLS estimates of Expected Committee Support produced adjusted R^2s of .353 for 1986–1987 and .50 for 1991. Significant variables in both equations (1986–1987 and 1991) include party, membership on the Public Works Committee, and seniority. The dummy variable for donor state was significant in 1991.

4

Highway Demonstration Projects and Voting on the Federal Highway Program

The previous chapter examined how Public Works and Transportation Committee leaders distributed highway demonstration projects, with a focus on which members they targeted with projects in their efforts to influence those members' votes later, when the highway bills came to the floor of the House. In statistical terms, the dependent variable was project awards to members. We established that leaders distributed projects strategically in an effort to secure the votes not only of rank-and-file members, but also members whose support would be especially valuable: their own committee members and other leaders.

This chapter assesses the effectiveness of leaders' attempts to influence members with pork barrel benefits. It addresses the following questions: Did members who received projects then respond as the leaders hoped, voting to support the leaders' positions? Did the leaders who used this strategy succeed in undermining the cohesion of the opposing party? This chapter answers those questions for highway demonstration projects. Chapter 5 answers them for the president's efforts to get congressional approval of NAFTA in the House; and Chapter 6 examines the Senate's use of appropriations earmarks to win votes for Appropriations subcommittee chairs' versions of particular appropriations bills. In all of those analyses, the dependent variable is the member's roll call vote.

While it seems obvious that project recipients would vote for final passage of a bill that provides them with benefits, controversial legislation must typically overcome numerous obstacles before the final vote. Specifically, rank-and-file members might not support the leaders' position on amendments and other votes that do not affect their pork barrel benefits. This chapter concentrates on the question of whether leaders can actually buy loyalty with demonstration projects on all of the votes that they care about in addition to the vote on final passage. An examination of the 1987 and 1991 highway reauthorization bills shows whether leaders' efforts were effective at influencing members' roll call votes. If they were successful on the first bill, when they gave out projects somewhat sparingly, targeted on the basis of members' likely support, were they equally successful when they gave out projects rather indiscriminately, as they did in 1991? If, as Chapter 2 argues, many more potential supporters in 1991 bargained for projects in return for votes that they would have cast for the leaders anyway, the effect of projects that year might have diminished, at least for those members. Looking at the two highway bills in sequence allows us to assess the dynamic effect of introducing this coalition-building technique into a policy area that previously had not needed it.

"Demos arise from a desire to forge a bill that has the support of the House and to make good national policy," said a committee staff member about the leaders' use of demonstration projects in the 1987 highway reauthorization bill. In fact, it was generally accepted among those who worked on the 1987 and 1991 highway bills that the leaders of the Public Works and Transportation Committee gave out highway projects to influence members' votes on both bills. High on the list of specific policies for which leaders wished to trade projects were the 55 mph speed limit in 1987 and an increase in the federal gasoline tax in 1991. More broadly, the fundamental policy changes required by the completion of interstate highway construction made demonstration projects seem particularly useful to leaders who wanted to put their own marks on the future of federal surface transportation policy.

The last chapter showed that the Big Four leaders of the Public Works and Transportation Committee and its Surface Transportation Subcommittee began adding demonstration projects to their highway bills as the construction of that gargantuan public works project, the Interstate and Defense Highway System, drew to a close. As a consequence, members of Congress, especially in the House, found less and less for which they could take credit in the formula-based program and began to seek individual highway projects from the massive revenue source of the Highway Trust Fund. They were obliged in their efforts by the men who chaired Public Works in the late 1980s and early 1990s – James Howard (D-N.J.), Glenn Anderson (D-Calif.), and Robert Roe (D-N.J.) – and the other committee and subcommittee leaders.

Consistent with earlier accounts of policy making on the Public Works Committee (Murphy 1974), those leaders had strong policy commitments, some of which responded to constituent needs and some of which clearly reflected their own visions of good public policy. A few issues on which they held strong views came to a vote on the floor of the House, but most did not, despite the scope and complexity of these bills. Moreover, very few issues came to a vote in subcommittee or full committee. Much of the credit for keeping things quiet goes to the bipartisan unity among the Big Four leaders of the committee and subcommittee. Additionally, to a degree that cannot be determined empirically, it is possible that some issues never came to the floor due to the existence of demonstration projects in the bills.

Central to the legislative process on those bills was negotiation among the committee's four key leaders; thus, the account of each bill begins with a description of the committee leaders' policy commitments. It is on those matters that the Big Four were most likely to trade projects for support, whether or not those issues ever came to a floor vote. The following pages provide an account of those priorities based on interviews with staff members who worked on both bills; the interviews are supplemented by printed sources. Following that is a discussion of the issues that did come to the floor of the House for roll call votes, along with an account of where the leaders stood on them. The impact of highway demonstration projects on members' votes is assessed by means of statistical analysis of the roll call votes taken on each of the two highway bills.

THE 1986–1987 HIGHWAY BILL

Leaders' Policy Priorities

A number of issues were especially important to the leaders of Public Works as they negotiated the shape of the 1986–1987 reauthorization bill. But by all accounts, the policy commitments that counted the most were those held by James Howard, the committee chair. As a staff member said, "Howard really controlled the [Surface Transportation] subcommittee. He deployed his staff heavily there," using five of his own staff members on that panel, while subcommittee chairman Anderson and ranking minority member Shuster had only one staffer each.[1] Thus, although the Big Four

[1] In fact, Howard had once attempted to consolidate his power over surface transportation by seeking the chairmanship of the subcommittee along with his full committee post, but the Democratic caucus on the full committee "pressured him out of it," according to a staff member.

strove for policy consensus, "the others generally deferred to Howard on things he felt strongly about."

True to committee tradition, Howard's top priority was highway construction, especially the completion of the interstate highway system. On interstate completion, there was broad agreement not only in the committee but in the House as a whole. Because this was not and never had been a controversial issue in the House, however (or in the Senate, for that matter), Howard had little need of demonstration projects in order to achieve it.

Beyond this consensus issue, Howard's two top priorities were preservation of the 55 mph speed limit and urban mass transit. The speed limit came to a vote on the floor repeatedly, and thus we can expect Howard to have used demonstration projects to gain members' votes. Mass transit, however, caused only a minor detour on the floor and is discussed only briefly here.

Mass transit was first folded into the highway bill in the 1970s in a policy trade-off between transit-dependent cities and the rest of the country, an arrangement designed to strengthen support for mass transit. As one staffer said, "transit by itself couldn't pass. It needed the weight of the highway lobby groups." Howard's interest stemmed in part from the fact that in his district was a commuter rail line into New York City. For him, the major transit policy issue concerned the preservation of operating assistance for urban mass transit systems. Although such aid was strongly opposed by market-oriented Republicans, it never came to a vote in any venue, an indication of the power of the logrolling coalition that supported it.

Howard's commitment to the 55 mph speed limit was more personal. He was convinced that the low speed limit, imposed as a conservation measure during the energy crisis of the early 1970s, had proved crucial in saving lives on the highways. That view was reflected, not surprisingly, in the committee report on the highway bill, which noted that the Transportation Research Board had estimated that overall, the lower speed limit saved between 2,000 and 4,000 lives annually. Further, it judged that on rural interstates, where speed limits would have been raised to 65 mph under the most popular pending proposal, 500 additional lives would be lost annually due to increased speeds (U.S. House, Report 99-665, pp. 51–52). Those figures so haunted Howard that a lobbyist said that he had told her of having a nightmare in which he saw people dying in highway crashes. A staff member said, "Howard wouldn't relent; it was his main issue, and he was held in such high regard, the committee wouldn't stick it to him on something so important to him."

Nevertheless, there was considerable opposition in Congress to the 55 mph speed limit. Members from sparsely populated districts, particularly in the West, were clamoring for an increase, as was the Senate, with its disproportionate representation of large, low-population states. Indeed, there was disagreement among the Big Four. As one staffer said, "[Subcommittee chairman] Anderson was getting killed in California on [the 55 mph limit], but he went along." The subcommittee's ranking minority member, Bud Shuster, also wanted an increase to 65 mph, with a concurrent mandatory seat-belt law. (Although one might think that a conservative Republican would oppose such a mandate, Shuster's outer office was graced by a framed fragment of a seat belt with a plaque that credited it with saving his life.) However, like Anderson, Shuster went along with Howard's stance on the lower speed limit. This issue did come to the floor, and eventually, Howard lost, but he held the line through the entire 99th Congress, scuttling the House-Senate conference over that issue, in part. As the statistical analysis of the roll call votes will show, this was a prime issue on which Howard called in the debts owed him by those to whom he gave demonstration projects.

An additional controversial matter, known euphemistically as highway beautification, concerned billboards, particularly the conditions for their removal. The position of the Big Four, driven by Howard and Shuster, was for full compensation of billboard owners by states that removed signs that failed to comply with federal law. In vehement opposition, E. Clay Shaw (R-Fla.) offered an amendment both in committee and on the floor that would have eliminated the full compensation requirement and allowed states to devise their own plans for billboard removal. This, despite the fact that, as one staffer said, Shaw "was tilting at windmills; the committee was tight on this, except for him." This was another issue on which the leaders failed to defuse opposition in committee and later on the floor; therefore, it was one on which demonstration projects could be expected to prove useful.

Additionally, the leadership of the Public Works Committee wanted to exempt the Highway Trust Fund from Gramm-Rudman-Hollings rules designed to limit spending and reduce the deficit. They argued that because revenues from the trust fund legally could be spent only on highways and mass transit, it made no sense to count that money toward overall federal revenues. Doing so made it politically impossible to spend all the available money in the trust fund for the purposes for which it was intended, as unspent balances in the trust fund made the deficit appear smaller. However, opponents of taking the trust fund "off-budget," as it was called, argued that doing so would require cuts in other areas.

This short list of issues does not exhaust all of the points in contention on the massive transportation bill, but they were the ones that reflected the highest policy priorities of the committee leadership, especially Chairman Howard. However, the overall problem for committee leaders, as the last chapter made clear, was the fact that the interstate highway system already was substantially complete, and the coalition that had supported the program when highway construction was its main expenditure was beginning to break up over issues now coming to the fore. Among the latter were such matters as the size of the guaranteed minimum allocation of highway funds to be given to donor states (i.e., the percentage of donor states' total contribution to the Highway Trust Fund that they were to receive back in federal highway funds), the amount of money to go to the rehabilitation of existing roads (a priority for many state departments of transportation) versus new construction, and how much flexibility states would be allowed in moving money among funding categories.

The following section describes the course of the bill in the Public Works and Transportation Committee markup and on the floor of the House, concentrating on the issues that came up for recorded votes on the floor. Many of those votes concerned the leadership priorities just described; some of them are general interest issues, such as the speed limit, and some, like the billboard compensation issue, are not. As noted in Chapter 2, pork barrel projects can be used for leverage on any type of measure, and highway legislation illustrates both general and particularized uses for pork barrel benefits. In the next section, following the description of the issues that came to recorded votes, I note the likely expectations of committee leaders if they called in the debts owed them by the members to whom they gave demonstration projects, indicating how those members would have voted if they were repaying the leaders for their projects.

The 1986–1987 Bill in Committee and on the Floor of the House

In 1986, the Public Works and Transportation Committee unanimously reported the Surface Transportation and Uniform Relocation Assistance Act, H.R. 3129, to the House. However, as indicated above, this apparent harmony masked some dissension in both the full committee and the Surface Transportation Subcommittee: A number of amendments opposed by committee leaders were offered in both panels' markups. They covered such areas as treatment of labor on federal construction projects (Tom DeLay, R-Tex., offered two antilabor amendments), two amendments to increase monies available to donor states, and a number of amendments by E. Clay Shaw (R-Fla.) to make it easier for states to remove illegal billboards. However, in an indication of the leadership's sway over committee members, all the amendments that they opposed were defeated; indeed, the few that came up for recorded votes lost by overwhelming margins. Despite that fact and the committee's unanimous report to the House, the illusion of unity was not fully maintained on the floor, as Shaw again offered one of his billboard amendments and another committee member split the Big Four over an amendment to expand a "buy America" provision already in the bill.

Debate on the bill on the floor of the House occurred over several days between August 6 and 15, 1986. A number of amendments were offered and accepted by committee leaders. A few, which were opposed by those leaders, were withdrawn following the leaders' promises that they would deal with those issues in the House-Senate conference on the bill. Nevertheless, recorded votes were taken on six amendments.

The very first vote was a direct challenge to Howard's most cherished policy commitment – an amendment offered by David McCurdy (D-Okla.) to establish a five-year test program to allow states to raise the speed limit to 65 mph on rural portions of the interstate system. Debate was extensive, with many members staking out their positions, but only a few themes were struck throughout. Proponents of the increase argued that the 55 mph limit was not necessary for safety in rural areas and, in any case, was not observed anywhere in the country. Dick Cheney's (R-Wyo.) argument was typical:

> In Wyoming we have half a million people living in an area of almost 98,000 square miles where we are approximately the size of the Federal Republic of Germany. The notion that somehow we should operate the same way on our Interstate System that states do in far more congested areas, it seems to me, is extremely unwise. . . . I can assure you on stretches of interstate that were built for 75 or 80 miles an hour, where it is 100 miles between towns and it is a straight shot, that 55 miles an hour is not often observed. (U.S. Congress, *Cong. Record*, Aug. 6, 1986, daily ed., H5598)

On the other side, despite differences in constituency interest, the Big Four stuck together in vigorous opposition to the amendment. The subcommittee's ranking minority member, Bud Shuster (R-Penn.), said,

> I was one of the Members of this body who originally was opposed to the 55-mile-an-hour speed limit. Mr. Chairman, I was wrong. I was dead wrong because the evidence is overwhelming. The 55-mile-an-hour speed limit saves lives. . . . The so-called rural remote areas of our Interstate System that our friend refers to represent 95 percent of our Interstate System. So this is a backdoor way to eliminate 55. (U.S. Congress, *Cong. Record*, Aug. 6, 1986, daily ed., H5595)

The proposal to raise the speed limit was defeated on a vote of 198 to 218; if only eleven of the opponents had switched to vote for the amendment, it would have passed. Because the committee's leaders were unified in opposition, and especially because it was one of Howard's highest priorities, if they expected anything at all in return for a demonstration project, they expected it on this amendment. The statistical analysis to follow will show whether project recipients opposed the increase in the speed limit.

Immediately following the speed limit amendment was a vote on the only amendment on which the Big Four failed to stick together. Offered by Helen Bentley (R-Md.), the amendment barred all foreign cement from federally funded transportation projects. The bill already specifically excluded Canadian and Mexican cement as part of its broader "Buy America" provisions; the Bentley amendment would make the ban universal. The subcommittee's ranking minority member Shuster spoke strongly in support of it, and both full committee chair Howard and ranking member Snyder voted for it. However, subcommittee chair Anderson opposed it, arguing that domestic supply was already insufficient to meet demand and that prices would therefore inevitably increase, a consequence that was no doubt intended by the amendment's supporters (U.S. Congress, *Cong. Record*, Aug 6, 1986, daily ed., H5606–5607). The amendment passed by a vote of 300 to 102. Given the Big Four's norm of consensus and their ability to maintain it on virtually every vote, this unusual public split indicates that there was no leadership position to enforce on this issue. Thus, demonstration projects probably had no impact on members' votes on this amendment.

On the second day of debate, August 7, Shaw offered one of his billboard amendments after consistently failing to make any headway in the committee, which had sided resolutely with its leaders and the billboard industry. His amendment proposed to ban new billboards on rural federal-aid highways, to prohibit cutting trees on public land to expose billboards on private land, and to allow states to amortize the value of billboards over their useful life so that they could remove them without federal funds. The law then required the use of federal funds to remove billboards, but due to chronic federal deficits, such funds were rarely available for that purpose. Thus, billboards were seldom, if ever, removed. Shaw argued that the status quo amounted to billboard industry protectionism.

Shuster countered with a substitute amendment backed by the Big Four. That measure made one concession to the proponents of highway beautification: The number of billboards on federal highways would be frozen. However, contrary to the Shaw amendment, owners would continue to received full federal reimbursement for signs that were removed (assuming, of course, that funds were available, which was not assured by the substitute amendment). Essentially, the Shuster substitute, while giving up ground on net new billboard construction, would allow billboards currently standing to remain unless their removal were fully compensated; compared with the Shaw amendment, the Shuster substitute continued federal protection of the billboard industry. The Shuster substitute passed handily on a vote of 251 to 159. Because the Big Four were so adamantly in favor of a pro-billboard industry policy, they probably expected members who received projects to vote with them on the Shuster substitute.

Given the tendency of members of Congress vociferously to defend construction projects in their own districts, one amendment comes as something of a surprise. That was a measure offered by Henry Waxman (D-Calif.) to eliminate funds for the construction of a subway, the Los Angeles Metrorail system, much of which was slated to be located in his district. His move was prompted by an underground explosion in a methane gas pocket in an area through which the tunnel had been planned. Although the Urban Mass Transit Administration (UMTA) had already rerouted the tunnel, Waxman noted that the new route would go through other methane gas pockets and earthquake faults. The amendment would have delayed construction pending an environmental impact statement and a subsequent separate authorization for the system by Congress.

The explosion had clearly aroused the ire of Waxman's constituents, but they opposed the system on additional grounds. As Waxman said:

> The people in my district are telling me: "Do not do it. Do not start it." They do not have confidence in the RTD and they do not have confidence in this metro system itself. They do not want to have the communities and neighborhoods disrupted and they are urging me to urge the Members not to start something until we know it makes sense to go forward and finish. (U.S. Congress, *Cong. Record*, Aug. 7, 1986, daily ed., H5653)

Waxman argued, as did Bobbi Fiedler (R-Calif.), that it was unsafe, too expensive, and ill-conceived, given that UMTA and Congress wanted to begin building it without even having settled on the system's terminal point.

Other members of the Los Angeles delegation supported construction of the system, as did subcommittee chairman Glenn Anderson of Long Beach. Anderson also had a district-related interest in the system, as it was planned to connect to a light rail system that would begin in his district and provide mass transit from Long Beach into Los Angeles. For a commuter in his district, that same trip by car was long and miserable. Anderson cited support for the system by California Governor George Deukmejian and most of the state's congressional delegation. Additionally, he argued that there was no documented evidence that the route through Waxman's district posed any of the risks that he had cited; moreover, he argued that "Los Angeles is the only city of its size in the world that does not have a rail transit system. Yet this city has a demonstrated need for efficient rail transit" (U.S. Congress, *Cong. Record*, Aug. 7, 1986, daily ed., H5653).

In an unusual defeat for the committee leadership, which was unified in opposition to Waxman's amendment, the measure passed on a vote of 210 to 201. However, Waxman's victory was short-lived. The committee applied pressure to enough members to snatch victory from the jaws of defeat a week later, when on reconsideration, the amendment went down to defeat, 153 to 201. On both votes, we can expect that members who received a project were more likely to vote with committee leaders.

The final effort to alter the bill in 1986 came on a procedural maneuver by Public Works Committee member Bob McEwen (R-Ohio) to take the Highway Trust Fund (HTF) off-budget, that is, to exempt the HTF from the limits imposed by Gramm-Rudman-Hollings.[2] This measure was strongly supported by the committee leaders. As noted above, it would allow the unspent balance in the trust fund to be expended, as that excess would no longer be reserved to reduce the apparent size of the federal budget deficit. To individualize the argument for their colleagues, the committee presented a table showing the tens of millions of dollars that would be available for each state to spend from the HTF if the budget process did not prohibit the obligation of those funds.

[2] Indeed, the Big Four had originally requested that the rule under which the bill came to the floor allow an amendment to take the HTF off-budget. However, the Rules Committee denied that request; in fact, that amendment was the only one prohibited by an otherwise open rule. McEwen's motion would have recommitted the bill to committee with instructions to return it to the floor with that provision attached. If this effort had succeeded, it would have eviscerated the rule.

Dan Rostenkowski (D-Ill.), chairman of the Ways and Means Committee, and members of the Budget and Appropriations committees opposed the motion, arguing that the committee's real motive was to exempt highway program funds from the possibility of sequestration (mandatory withholding) under Gramm-Rudman-Hollings, thus exposing other programs to larger reductions. More generally, opponents argued that taking the trust fund off-budget was unjustifiable special treatment that would make deficit reduction more difficult. McEwen's motion failed, 171 to 214. Because the Big Four were strongly behind the motion, we expect legislators who received a demonstration project to be more likely to vote for it. Once McEwen's attempt to make an end run around the budget rules failed, the bill itself passed, 345 to 34.

Despite agreement in the House, considerable friction between the House and Senate ultimately defeated the conference committee's efforts to report a compromise bill to the House and Senate before the end of the 99th Congress in 1986. That failure is particularly remarkable in view of the fact that the states' authority to spend federal highway money ran out in September of that year. All members of the conference committee were under strong pressure to resolve their differences, and their failure to do so indicates just how powerful were the policy disagreements between the two bodies. One of the most prominent was a dispute over highway demonstration projects. Other disagreements included the 65 mph speed limit, which the Senate wanted to implement on rural portions of the interstate highway system. Billboard removal was another contentious issue; the Senate's position was consistent with that of the unsuccessful Shaw amendment, which would have eliminated required federal compensation for billboard removal and established a moratorium on the construction of new ones. In addition, the Senate opposed the House's insistence that interstate construction remain a separate funding category; it preferred that interstate monies be folded into a new program that would fund the construction of other roads along with interstate repair and rehabilitation ("Highway Reauthorization Dies," p. 284). (The latter issue was a foreshadowing of the path that highway legislation would take in the future, as Congress adapted to the completion of the interstate highway system.)

However, the failure of the conference in 1986 came down to two of those issues: demonstration projects and the speed limit. The Senate opposed demonstration projects for both political and practical reasons. Politically, their opposition to projects was evidently designed to help them to win an increase in the speed limit. Staff members indicated that Senate conferees calculated that House leaders were by then so committed to demonstration projects that they would give in on the speed limit if the Senate forced the choice, despite the fact that the projects had originally been added to protect the lower speed limit.

In practical terms, senators had less reason to cherish demonstration projects than House members. As a Senate staffer said, "House members take a more parochial view. It's harder for a senator to help a state this way; they can't meet the potential demand." That is because most states are so much larger than a congressional district that senators would need many more projects than House members to make a real difference to their reelection chances, and the demand, especially in the larger states, might become unmanageable once they opened the door to such requests. Far more important to senators were the formulas by which overall highway funds were allocated, as formulas more favorable to a senator's state meant more money for the whole state, not just a small portion. As one staffer said, "Formulas are the Senate's pork."

Despite these disavowals of interest in demonstration projects, senators did some earmarking of their own in the highway bill. However, they did not grant demonstration projects; rather, they designated "priority projects," which would come out of a state's normal funding allocation and would be built only if the state decided to do so. The major funding concession was that states would be able to move funds from other categories to build priority projects, an option that they normally did not enjoy. In the end, the Senate's objection to the House's demonstration projects appeared to be based primarily on their expense, not on any principled opposition to earmarking. Senators especially disliked the fact that the projects were fully funded by federal monies over and above a state's normal allocation.

Although the conference committee made progress on some of the key issues at the end of the 99th Congress, it failed to resolve the impasse over the speed limit and funding of demonstration projects ("Highway Reauthorization Dies," pp. 284 and 286). Thus, the bill had to be introduced anew as H.R. 2 in the 100th Congress in January 1987. The House bill was virtually identical to H.R. 3129, the one that passed in the previous Congress; it came to the floor immediately in late January without further committee action. This time the speed limit was the major bone of contention. Although the bill had come to the floor in 1986 with a modified open rule, which prohibited only one specific amendment, in 1987 it came to the floor under a closed rule, which prohibited any amendments at all. Both Howard and House Speaker Jim Wright (D-Tex.) favored the 55 mph speed limit and sought the closed rule to block a vote on the

65 mph limit, which clearly was gaining ground in the House. Opposing the proposed rule, James Hansen (R-Utah) and Dave McCurdy (D-Okla.), among others, urged the House to amend it to allow a vote to increase the speed limit. However, the leadership of the House and the Public Works Committee continued to support the rule, and the subcommittee's ranking minority member Shuster tried to win over some supporters of 65 mph by promising to support in conference a 65 mph speed limit tied to state laws requiring seat belts. In the end, there was never a vote on amending the rule, and the key vote was on a motion by Rules Committee member Joe Moakley (D-Mass.) to end debate on the rule. The motion passed, 331 to 88, and the rule then passed on a voice vote (U.S. Congress, *Cong. Record*, Jan. 21, 1987, daily ed., H281-288). The 55 mph speed limit was intact for the moment. On this vote, once again, we expect members who received a project to support the leadership by voting to end debate on the rule and proceed to a vote on the rule.

The second conference committee finally resolved the differences between the two bodies on demonstration projects and the speed limit. In the end, the conferees agreed to reduce Highway Trust Fund monies available for demonstration projects and introduce a state matching requirement of 20 percent of the projects' cost. The Senate added its own demonstration projects to the bill, resulting in a final total of 152 projects, with funding approximately equally divided between the House and Senate. In addition, Howard reluctantly gave in on the speed limit, agreeing to a separate vote in the House on the 65 mph rural speed limit, which had already passed the Senate. This clearly was a capitulation on his part, designed primarily to protect demonstration projects.

The House passed the conference report nearly unanimously (407 to 17) on March 18 and proceeded to a vote on a concurrent resolution to amend the bill to adopt the Senate's provision for a 65 mph speed limit on rural interstates. Howard's cherished 55 mph speed limit crashed and burned on a 217-206 vote. By agreeing in conference to a vote on this issue, the Big Four effectively consented to let the Senate position win; therefore, it is expected that members who had received projects were not strongly inclined to support the leaders on this issue. Moreover, because the vote occurred after the conference committee had finished modifying the bill, the leaders' last opportunity to punish members for defying them had passed. Thus, receipt of a project is not expected to affect members' votes this time.

The battle for the highway bill was not won, however. In fact, demonstration projects continued to cause trouble. President Reagan vetoed the bill; his veto message to Congress blamed the demonstration projects, along with the level of funding for mass transit programs ("Highway Bill Passes, p. 332). In his March 28 radio address to the nation, Reagan justified his veto in colorful terms:

Only this week, the Congress sent me a highway construction bill that was loaded with pork barrel projects. I haven't seen so much lard since I handed out blue ribbons at the Iowa State Fair. ("President Reagan's Radio Address")

Ironically, House and committee leaders were counting on the lard to help them to override the president's veto. Although a definitive answer as to whether it did so will await the statistical analysis of the vote, the veto was overridden on a massive, bipartisan 350-73 vote. In an extraordinary turn of events, even the House Republican leader, Robert Michel (R-Ill.), voted to override his own president, despite the fact that he normally would have been expected to be the president's chief water-carrier in the House in the effort to sustain the veto. In his remarks, Michel made it crystal clear that he would vote to override in order to protect his demonstration project:

The legislative branch of Government was created in part to ensure that the legitimate local needs of the people are recognized and that there is a guard at the door against complete subjugation of local needs and concerns. No one else in the other two branches of Government is really charged with that responsibility to represent, defend, and promote local public interests. That is why I have made the very difficult decision for the first time in the Reagan Presidency to vote against the President's recommendations on a major piece of legislation. . . . This bill contains funding for $27 million in improvement and widening of U.S. Route 121, which will connect Interstate 74 on the north with Interstate 55 on the south in my home State of Illinois. My constituents have strong feelings about that road, and my area's economic development badly needs it. I am here to represent those feelings and try to help meet those needs. But there is another side of the coin as well. The President doesn't see Route 121 as I do. In some respects, the President sees this bill as a budget buster. It is. He sees it as yet another dangerous precedent for big, huge, omnibus bills. He's right there, too. He's looking at programs and projects in this bill that are not essential, that could be delayed or terminated. I am looking at central Illinois, and a road that kills and injures. I am looking at economic development in a hard hit region of the rust belt, one of the hardest hit areas of the country. The President is right, but so am I. The Washington Post is right, when it called this bill "Pork on Wheels," but so was the Escondido, CA, Times-Advocate in Ron Packard's district when it said, "Build the roads, Jack." I will vote to override this veto, because the U.S. 121 project in this bill and a good many others in Illinois are badly needed and could surely stand on their own before this House. As is the case in many other States. (U.S. Congress, *Cong. Record*, March. 31, 1987, daily ed., H1635)

Another Republican, Arthur Ravenel (R-S.C.), was a bit more vivid in expressing his determination to vote to override his own party's president in order to preserve a bridge for his district: "You can bet your spring petunias that this Congressman is going to vote to override and save that $15,230,000. President Reagan? He ain't gonna be runnin' in 1988, but I am" (U.S. Congress, *Cong. Record*, March 31, 1987, daily ed., H1632).

As was the case with these Republicans, on this vote we expect that legislators who received demonstration projects were likely to vote to override the veto. Of course, one might think that the very nature of the bill without demonstration projects would be sufficient to induce members to vote to override. If that were so, it should have been the case in the Senate as well as the House. Yet the Senate just barely mustered enough votes to override, and then only after first voting to sustain the veto. In fact, the second effort to override succeeded only after freshman senator Terry Sanford (D-N.C.) changed his vote from "nay" on override to "yea" after being heavily pressured by Senate Democratic leaders, House Democrats from North Carolina, and state officials (Ehrenhalt 1987, p. 1110; "Highway Bill Passes," p. 333).

The Impact of Demonstration Projects on Roll Call Voting on the 1986–1987 Highway Bill

Over the two congresses during which the House considered this bill, there were nine recorded votes decided by a greater than 90–10 percent division. The question is whether on these votes members who received a demonstration project were more likely to support the positions of the Big Four committee leaders than were other members. To determine that, the conditions must be specified under which these leaders were likely to have called in the debts owed by project recipients. Two closely related conditions both must hold in order for projects to influence members' votes: First, there must be a unified, thus clear committee leadership position on the issue at hand. Second, the leadership must have demanded loyalty from project recipients on the vote.

The first condition derives from the Public Works committee leaders' widely known practice of forming a consensus behind closed doors through a process of vigorous horse trading. Failure to achieve such a consensus on a particular issue means that there was no leadership position on an issue, and therefore no quid pro quo would have been demanded in return for a project. Consequently, there is no expectation that receipt of a project influenced the member's vote on that issue. This condition, a clear leadership position on an issue, is assumed to have been met when the Big Four voted together on a measure on the floor, displaying the unity forged in private. With respect to the second condition, that the leaders demanded loyalty on the vote, firsthand information is not available. Hence, I assume that the leaders demanded loyalty unless they themselves were split on the vote (i.e., when the first condition is not met) or there is evidence that, even if they were unified, they did *not* demand loyalty of project recipients for other reasons.

There were only two votes on which one of the two conditions was not met: the vote on excluding foreign cement from federal construction projects, a vote on which the leaders split; and the second, post conference vote on the speed limit. The leaders stuck together on the floor in opposition to the speed limit increase before the second conference committee. However, during the 1987 floor debate prior to conference, there was one sign of a crack in the armor: The subcommittee's ranking minority member Shuster stated a willingness to support an increase in the speed limit in conference, but only if it were accompanied by a requirement for the use of seat belts. Yet the Big Four clearly had struck a bargain with the Senate to stop defending the 55 mph speed limit; thus, they most likely did not hold project recipients to loyalty on this issue. With the exception of these two votes, the receipt of a demonstration project is expected to influence members to vote in support of the leadership position.

A first cut into the data is provided by a simple table that shows how those who did and did not receive one or more projects voted on each of these recorded votes. The votes are presented in the chronological order in which they were taken. Table 4.1 names the vote and how project recipients are expected to vote, consistent with leadership expectations, if any, for that vote. The second and third columns of the table show how members voted depending on their receipt of at least one project. Here, for simplicity of presentation, the project variable is dichotomous; a member either received one or more projects or got nothing.

On many of these votes, there is a dramatic difference between project recipients and nonrecipients in levels of support for the leadership position, especially on those votes for which leaders would have expected the beneficiaries' support. In all cases except cement protection, where the leaders were split, we see that project recipients were more likely than nonrecipients to support the leaders' position; in all cases where a significant relationship was expected between receipt of a project and a member's vote, such a relationship occurred. At the same time, we see that projects are not associated with universal compliance with leaders' wishes.

TABLE 4.1 *Percentage of Members Voting Yes by Receipt of a Demonstration Project, 1986–1987 Bill*

Vote	Expected vote	Member of Congress did not receive project	Member of Congress received project
Speed Limit I[a]	No	51.5	30.6
Cement Protection	–	74.3	76.5
Billboards[a]	Yes	56.5	82.9
L.A. Metrorail I[a]	No	57.9	18.3
L.A. Metrorail II[a]	No	45.3	14.7
HTF off-budget[a]	Yes	38.8	72.1
Rule[a]	Yes	76.9	88.9
Speed Limit II	–	53.0	44.3
Veto Override[a]	Yes	81.0	89.2

[a] Chi-square $p \leq .05$.

For that to have occurred, we would have had to see 100 percent support for the leadership position among project recipients. Clearly, and unsurprisingly, other variables had an important influence on members' votes.

To determine the impact of projects on members' votes relative to other considerations that commonly weigh on their voting decisions, I estimated the following model, using logit analysis, for each recorded vote. The first four explanatory variables were included in all models; the last two were included where appropriate.

Member's vote = fn(Demo Project, Public Works, Republican, Conservatism, Donor, district interest, PAC contributions)

Descriptions of all of the variables in the model follow. Unless otherwise specified, variables are dichotomous, or dummy variables, that take the value of 1 if the condition described obtains and 0 if it does not.

Demo Project: The key explanatory variable is a member's receipt of a demonstration project in the 1986 version of the highway bill, H.R. 3129, or in the 1987 conference committee version of H.R. 2, depending on the year in which the vote was taken. The allocation of projects was virtually identical in both versions of the bill. This variable takes a value of 1 if the member received one or more projects and a value of 0 if they did not receive even one.[3] If members received one or more projects, they are expected to vote in support of the leaders' position.

[3] There are other ways to measure this variable; of course. One could use the total dollar value of a member's projects or the number of projects. Both were tried, and total dollar

Public Works: The Public Works Committee enjoyed a long-standing bipartisan policy consensus that was painstakingly cultivated by the leaders in 1986 and 1987; thus a dichotomous variable was included for membership on that committee. Committee members are expected to support their leaders' positions.

Republican: This variable takes a value of 1 for Republicans and 0 for Democrats. Republicans are expected to support President Reagan's position against the bill.

Conservatism: The conservatism of the member's voting record is measured by the member's Conservative Coalition support score for 1985 in the 99th Congress and 1988 in the 100th Congress. The range of scores is 0 to 100.[4]

Donor: It is necessary to take account of a potentially important district-based reason for opposing the leaders. Here the discontent of representatives of the seventeen donor states comes into play. We expect members from those states to be less inclined than members from donee states to support the leaders' version of the bill. Thus, a dummy variable was included to indicate that a member came from a donor state, one that received less income from the federal highway program than it contributed to its revenues through the gas tax. To the extent that leaders did not satisfy donor state representatives with this bill, Donor is expected to be negatively related to support for the leadership position on the bill and amendments. (This variable is described on p. 79, note 3.)

Other constituency factors came into play on votes on the speed limit and the Los Angeles Metrorail system.

West: For the three votes relevant to the speed limit, this variable denotes members who represented a western state. The large, less densely populated western states were the source of most of the pressure to raise the

value performed no better than the dichotomous measure, and the number of projects performed considerably less well. For further discussion, see note 4 in Chapter 3.

4 Scores for 1985 were used for the 99th Congress to avoid including in the score votes which were taken on H.R. 3129 in 1986; the same rationale applies to use of the 1988 scores in the 100th Congress. There is little cost to this device; the correlations between members' scores in the two years of one Congress are .95 or higher. The scores are calculated so that abstentions do not affect the score; that is, a member's failure to vote does not lower the support score.

TABLE 4.2 *Demonstration Projects and Voting on the 1986–87 Highway Bill (recorded votes)*

Explanatory Variables	Speed Limit I	Cement Protection	Billboard	L.A. Metrorail	L.A. Metrorail II	HTF	Rule	Speed Limit II	Veto Override
Demo Project	−0.716[b]	−0.137	0.954[a]	−1.701[a]	−1.159[a]	1.271[a]	1.363[a]	−0.411[c]	1.051[b]
	(.351)	(.340)	(.370)	(.360)	(.383)	(.396)	(.510)	(.324)	(.486)
Public Works	−1.767[a]	0.572	0.982[b]	−0.946[b]	−1.460[a]	4.734[a]	2.956[a]	−1.157[a]	1.265[b]
	(.481)	(.441)	(.504)	(.427)	(.512)	(1.058)	(1.052)	(.377)	(.623)
Republican	0.134	−0.902[a]	−1.576[a]	0.927[a]	0.776[a]	0.576[b]	−2.813[a]	−0.031	−3.321[a]
	(.307)	(.356)	(.363)	(.302)	(.308)	(.322)	(.568)	(.308)	(.756)
Conservatism	0.035[a]	0.012[b]	0.033[a]	0.010[b]	0.001	0.290[a]	−0.061[a]	0.037[a]	−0.071[a]
	(.005)	(.005)	(.005)	(.004)	(.005)	(.006)	(.016)	(.005)	(.020)
Donor	0.126	0.243	−0.187	−0.552[a]	−0.280	0.003	0.137	0.003	−0.770[b]
	(.242)	(.239)	(.229)	(.229)	(.227)	(.259)	(.348)	(.237)	(.337)
West	1.333[a]	–	–	–	–	–	−1.004[a]	1.321[a]	–
	(.288)						(.384)	(.291)	
L.A.	–	–	–	−0.787[b]	−0.350	–	–	–	–
				(.417)	(.404)				
Cement PAC	–	0.001	–	–	–	–	–	–	–
		(.001)							

Billboard PAC	–	–	0.002[a] (.001)	–	–	–	–	–	–
Intercept	−2.325[a] (.317)	0.588[b] (.255)	−0.971[a] (.254)	−0.211 (.239)	−0.361 (.249)	−2.769[a] (.369)	8.008[a] (1.347)	−2.277[a] (.322)	10.097[a] (1.865)
Model chi-square	144.64[a]	13.20[b]	85.33[a]	96.90[a]	51.22[a]	157.59[a]	215.23[a]	141.45[a]	175.90[a]
Pseudo R^2	.251	.029	.156	.169	.100	.298	.501	.241	.445
Cases correctly classified (%)	74.28	74.38	70.24	70.46	66.32	76.62	88.70	73.11	88.44
Percentage reduction of error	46.00	0	23.26	39.60	15.46	47.37	46.19	44.78	33.02

[a] $p \leq .01$.
[b] $p \leq .05$.
[c] $p \leq .10$.

Note: For each vote the expected direction of the Demo Project coefficient is as follows: Speed Limit I, negative; Cement, no effect; Billboard, positive; Metrorail I and II, negative; HTF and Rule, positive; Speed Limit II, no effect; and Veto Override, positive. The number in parentheses beneath each coefficient is the standard error. The model chi-square statistic tests the hypothesis that all coefficients in the equation equal 0. Significance for this statistic allows the rejection of that hypothesis. The percentage reduction of error statistic (ROE) indicates the extent to which the model's predictions improve on predicting that everyone will fall into the modal category of the dependent variable. %ROE = 100 × (% correctly classified −% in modal category)/(100% −% in modal category).

speed limit, according to staff members, and are expected to oppose the leadership on this.[5]

L.A.: For the amendment to stall the Los Angeles Metrorail system, a dummy variable was included for representatives from the L.A. metropolitan area, as that system was linked to plans for a wider-ranging light rail system. It is expected that most Angelenos (Waxman excluded) supported the system and opposed the amendment.

Two amendments targeted specific economic interests: the billboard industry and the cement industry. Political action committees for both industries made campaign contributions in the elections preceding the Congress during which the votes were taken. The potential impact of those contributions on members' voting was accounted for by including the dollar amount given to each member by the PACs sponsored by the businesses affected. In both cases, PAC contributions, if they have any impact, are likely to be associated with support for the amendments to assist the respective industries. The variables follow.

Billboard PAC: In the case of the billboard amendment, contributions came from the Outdoor Advertising Association.

Cement PAC: For the cement amendment the variable consists of the summed contributions of three cement industry association PACs.

In all equations, a "yes" vote was given a value of 1; a "no" vote took a value of 0. The expected direction of the Demo Project coefficient is determined by the committee leaders' position and noted for each equation in a footnote to the table.

Table 4.2 reports the results of the statistical analysis. On all votes but two, the receipt of a demonstration project had a significant effect on members' votes at or beyond the traditional .05 level of confidence. Moreover, the exceptions occurred on the two votes on which projects were not expected to have an impact: the votes on the protectionist cement amendment, on which the leadership was split, and the final vote on the speed limit (Speed Limit II), an issue on which Chairman Howard

[5] The states designated as western include all the West Coast states, including Alaska, the mountain states of Arizona, Colorado, Idaho, Montana, Nevada, New Mexico, Utah and Wyoming, as well as Iowa, Kansas, Minnesota, Missouri, Nebraska, North Dakota, and South Dakota. Other measures of the wide-open-spaces concept, such as the percentage of a district's population living in rural areas, did not fare as well as this variable in the statistical analysis.

surrendered in conference committee. However, even on the final vote on the speed limit, projects had some impact on the vote: Although the coefficient falls short of the .05 level of confidence, it is significant at the .10 level. Thus, even when defeat appeared inevitable, Howard was able to elicit some loyalty from project recipients. Overall, therefore, it is clear that House members who received a demonstration project were significantly more likely to support the committee leaders' position on the votes on which they were expected to do so.

Additionally, members of the Public Works and Transportation committee displayed a high degree of loyalty to their leaders' positions; on every vote but Cement Protection, where there was no leadership position, committee members were significantly more likely to vote as their leaders wished.

However bipartisan the committee itself may have been, party did have an impact on other House members' voting on most of these issues, with Republicans opposing the bipartisan committee leadership on most of the votes.

Donor state members were not significantly more likely than members from donee states to oppose the leadership position except on the veto override vote, their best chance to kill the bill.

Other constituency variables were relevant for four votes. For all three votes involving the speed limit, western members were indeed more likely to vote for an increase and to oppose the rule that was intended to block a vote on it in 1987 (recall that the leadership supported a closed rule in 1987 in order to prevent a vote on the speed limit). Additionally, for the first vote to stop construction of the L.A. Metrorail system, representatives from Los Angeles and environs were significantly more likely to favor continued development of the system; but by the time they voted on it a second time, after committee leaders built support for the system, they were not more likely to support it than other members.

With respect to the impact of PAC contributions on the two votes for which they were relevant, the results are consistent with the assertions of Senate staffers and lobbyists that billboard owners had influence with committee leaders: Their PAC contributions had a significant impact on voting for the billboard amendment that promised to benefit them. With respect to the second issue on which PAC contributions might have been relevant, Cement Protection, the money had no impact. Such conflicting results are common in the analysis of the impact of PAC contributions (Conway 1991; Evans 1996).

A major advantage of the technique of using pork barrel benefits to influence members' votes is the potential to overcome partisan opposition to policy coalition leaders. Normally, those in the best position to give pork barrel benefits are leaders in the majority party. The question is, are those leaders able to buy the votes of members of the minority party, votes that they otherwise would not have received, by giving them distributive benefits? One way to address this question is to calculate for each issue the probability that a member of the minority party would have supported the leadership without receiving a project and compare it to the probability that he or she would have done so with one. Given that members' partisanship affected most of these votes and that Republicans tended to oppose the committee overall, this question is particularly interesting. If projects help policy coalition leaders to breach the partisan walls, members of the minority party who receive projects should be at least as strongly influenced as members of the majority. In some cases, they may be more so, if members of the majority are already inclined to vote with their leaders on the basis of partisanship, ideology, or issue agreement. It is also worth asking whether members of the majority party are affected by receiving a project, as the leaders may also want them to vote contrary to their partisan or policy inclinations on some issues.

For this analysis I used the coefficients estimated for the equations reported in Table 4.2 to calculate the probability that a Republican or a Democrat would vote in support of the committee leaders, first without and then with a demonstration project. To describe the method in nonmathematical terms, I assumed that the hypothetical Republican or Democrat whose probability I was calculating was not a member of the Public Works and Transportation Committee, had the mean conservatism score for his or her party (Republicans' scores averaged 83.9; Democrats' scores averaged 38.2), and did not represent a donor state. Where other variables were important for a particular vote, I assumed that the member was from the West for the votes on the speed limit, as leaders especially wanted to convert them to support for the 55 mph speed limit. I also assumed that members received no PAC contributions, as the typical member did not receive money from the groups considered here. The method for calculating the probabilities from the logit coefficients was taken from Menard (1995, pp. 43–44).[6]

Table 4.3 displays the results. The entries consist of the probabilities that the typical Republican or Democrat would have supported the position favored by the Big Four for the seven votes on which the leaders

[6] The method for each equation reported in Table 4.3 is to multiply each estimated coefficient by a specific value (described in the text) of the variable with which it is associated and sum all of the products, as in any linear regression analysis. The resulting number is the logit; the probability is calculated as follows: $P(y = 1) = e^{logit}/(1 + e^{logit})$.

TABLE 4.3 *Probability That a Member Supported Committee Leaders by Receipt of a Project, 1986–1987 Bill*

Vote	Republican without a a Project	Republican with a Project	Change in probability	Democrat without a Project	Democrat with a Project	Change in probability
Speed Limit I	.120	.218	.098	.424	.601	.177
Billboard	.555	.764	.209	.572	.776	.204
L.A. Metrorail I	.174	.536	.362	.457	.822	.365
L.A. Metrorail II	.378	.659	.281	.582	.815	.233
HTF	.559	.819	.260	.159	.403	.244
Rule	.285	.609	.324	.991	.998	.007
Veto	.695	.867	.172	.999	.999	0

Note: Calculations are done assuming that members are not on the Public Works Committee, or from a donor state, that they are from the West, that they are not from Los Angeles, and that they received no campaign contributions from cement PACs or the Outdoor Advertising Association. Members are assumed to be at the mean conservatism score for their party; for Republicans, that is 83.9; for Democrats, it is 38.2.

took a position and expected support from project recipients. Looking at the third and sixth columns first, we see that on five of the seven votes, the magnitude of the effect of receiving a project was greater on Republicans than on Democrats. Those votes were Billboard, L.A. Metro II, HTF (Highway Trust Fund), Rule, and Veto. Two of those, Rule and Veto, were straight party votes for Democrats, as the table shows, so there was no need for leaders to try to call in the chits with them.

Another way to look at the probabilities is to ask whether there were issues on which the typical Democrat or Republican actually changed his or her vote as a result of receiving a project. That is the case when the member's probability of voting with the leaders without a project was below .5 and increased to above .5 with the receipt of a demonstration project. There were four votes on which such a member was swayed by receiving a project. For Democrats it was the first speed limit vote and the first vote on the L.A. Metrorail system. The typical Republican was swayed on the first and second votes on L.A. Metrorail and on Rule. Additionally, of course, some members' votes could have been changed on other issues as well. That could be the case when a member was already more inclined to vote with the leaders than the typical (or mean) member of his or her party, but was still below a probability of .5 of voting with the leaders. For some of those members, projects could also have made the critical difference.

What is the partisan significance of these results? Looking at the fourth column in Table 4.3, we see that on four of the seven votes, Democrats were already inclined to support the Big Four. On two of the remaining three votes, projects made the difference. On only one vote did Democrats hold firm against the wishes of the Big Four. That was the vote to take the Highway Trust Fund off-budget; Republicans, by contrast, supported that effort. That is likely because the effect of the HTF amendment, as the chairman of the Ways and Means Committee, Dan Rostenkowski, warned, would probably be cuts in other programs, something that Democrats are more likely to oppose than Republicans. In summary, there were three votes on which the leaders needed to influence Democrats; they were successful on two of them.

Republicans, on the other hand, were already inclined to support the leaders on HTF, perhaps for the same reason that Democrats opposed them; on Billboard, a vote that favored private business over government; and Veto Override, despite the fact that the veto was by a president of their own party. There were thus four remaining votes on which leaders hoped to influence them. On three of them, L.A. Metro I and II and Rule, they were evidently successful.

Finally, the table shows that there were only two votes on which both Democrats and Republicans were already inclined to support the leaders: Billboard and Veto Override. On all but one of the other five votes, demonstration projects evidently changed the vote of the mean member of the party that was not otherwise inclined to support the Big Four. Thus, the evidence is that the committee leaders successfully used the projects that they gave out to win the votes that they needed to protect their version of the 1986–1987 highway reauthorization; they succeeded not only with members of the majority party, but also with members of the minority.

There is one aspect of this case that foreshadows changes in the process of passing the 1991 reauthorization, changes that stemmed from adding demonstration projects to the bill. Recall that in the 1987 conference committee, the Big Four gave in on the speed limit in order to protect the demonstration projects in the bill. Their reordering of priorities was ironic indeed. The projects originally were added by the committee leaders in order to allow them a free hand in devising the substance of the bill; Chairman Howard particularly cherished the 55 mph speed limit. Yet in the end, the projects drove out the speed limit, as the committee's leaders not only found it impossible to sacrifice demonstration projects, which the Senate initially demanded, but in fact found themselves in the position of sacrificing one of the major policies that they had hoped to use the projects to protect and did so in order to protect the projects! Thus, by the end of the road in 1987, demonstration projects were already beginning to rival in importance key aspects of the bill to which they were attached, a change that only accelerated in subsequent reauthorizations. The important question here is whether the projects retained any power to protect the leaders' version of the bill. That question is answered with an examination of the next reauthorization, which occurred in 1991.

THE 1991 BILL

As noted in the previous chapter, the number of demonstration projects, already high at 100 projects for 76 members in the 1987 bill, skyrocketed to 489 projects for 262 members in the 1991 highway bill. Chapter 3 shows that leaders evidently gave out projects much more indiscriminately in 1991 than in 1986–1987. We saw that they gave to members regardless of their initial inclination to support the bill. That being the case, did projects then affect those members' votes? On one hand, members have reason not to betray their benefactors, as they might lose their projects if they do. However, some legislators could be under such strong pressure to oppose the leaders on some issues that a project would not deter them from doing so. By not carefully distributing projects, leaders may give to those who must oppose them, thus increasing the chance of defections compared with the first time they gave projects. On the other hand, some of the members who receive projects the second time are probably supporters of the bill who nevertheless bargained for a benefit, perhaps by strategically concealing their true preferences. In their case, other factors, such as party, already incline them to support the leaders, so their projects may not substantially increase the probability that they will do so. This section helps to resolve the question of whether the impact of projects changes the second time they are used to buy votes. First is a discussion of the leaders' policy priorities; second, I describe the 1991 highway bill's debate and passage on the floor of the House. Finally, I model the voting statistically to discover whether leaders successfully influenced members' votes on the 1991 highway reauthorization, as they did on the earlier bill, and calculate separate probabilities for Democrats and Republicans of supporting the leaders with and without a project.

Leaders' Policy Priorities

Between 1987 and 1991, the cast of characters that comprised the Big Four changed considerably, as noted in Chapter 3. James Howard died of a heart attack in 1988 and was replaced as Public Works chairman by Glenn Anderson (D-Calif.), who was replaced by Robert Roe (D-N.J.) in 1990. Roe did not rise to his new post by the traditional route of chairmanship of the Surface Transportation Subcommittee, but from the Water Resources Subcommittee, which he had previously chaired, and from the chairmanship of the Science, Space, and Technology Committee. Pork barrel projects had already proved very useful to Roe. Of his contest with Norman Mineta (D-Calif.) for the chairmanship of Public Works, he said, "Everybody I looked at [for support], I think either had a bridge or a highway or a railroad or something we worked with them on" (Barone and Ujifusa 1992, p. 794). The clear implication of that remark is that those members' votes for chairman were influenced by the pork barrel projects that Roe had given them in the past; it was to be expected that he would continue to ply his colleagues with favors from his new position.

Other members of the Big Four had changed as well. The ranking minority member of the full committee was now John Paul Hammerschmidt (R-Ark.). The subcommittee chairman was Norman Mineta, while the one holdover from the Big Four in 1987 was the subcommittee's ranking minority member, Bud Shuster (who rose to chair the full committee in the 104th Congress). Even in 1986–1987, Shuster played a major role in managing the highway bill on the floor of the House, speaking more than any of the other Big Four, despite Howard's reported dominance of the committee behind the scenes. Regardless of the change in the cast of characters, committee staff members indicated that the norm of private, bipartisan consensus building among the Big Four continued, with Chairman Roe dominating the process as Howard had done before him.

Chapter 3 described the Senate version of the 1991 bill, Senator Moynihan's strongly policy-oriented draft of the ISTEA. In contrast, Roe displayed the traditional orientation toward pouring asphalt through formula funding and special projects. His strategy for financing those commitments was to pass an increase in the federal gas tax. As one staffer said, "Roe had a strong belief that projects are good; he thought that's why members are sent here." Therefore, the increased pressure from members to provide more and more demonstration projects was perfectly consistent with the new chairman's view that the committee ought to hand out projects and build more highways, however it funded them.

To say that Roe wanted to build highways is not to say that he did not wish to use the projects for leverage. After all, he won the committee chairmanship partly on the basis of the leverage that such projects had given him in the past. By all accounts, the particular policy for which he most wished to use projects was the increase in the gas tax.

This time, several things were different from the case in 1986; chief among them was the committee's active marketing of demonstration projects, compared with the more passive approach adopted by the committee on the earlier bill. In 1986, as a staffer noted, "The committee [didn't] go out and say it's having a sale of demos; *you* go to the committee; it says jump through these hoops, and you get it." In the 102nd Congress, by contrast, the committee *did* have "a sale of demos"; that year, another staffer said, the committee "put out the word" early in the process that it would be giving out demonstration projects. And early on, it was made very clear, very publicly, that the price of a project was support for the gas tax increase.

Despite his commitment to highway building, Roe had other interests as well. In particular, mass transit policy was important to his metropolitan New Jersey district. Thus, Roe favored Moynihan's plan to fund linkages among different modes of transportation and to increase states' ability to transfer funds from one mode of transportation to another, especially from highways to urban mass transit. In addition, Roe and the rest of the Big Four were committed to the establishment of a new funding category for highways, the National Highway System. This system was to encompass interstate highways but would also include primary roads linked to them. Roe especially liked the system (requested by the Bush administration) because it offered a means to justify more highway construction and the money to fund it.

Trouble was brewing, however. Despite the potential for more highway building in the new bill, donor states were at least as discontented as they had been in 1986–1987, if not more so. With the interstate highway system now essentially complete, the national purpose of highway legislation had, in their view, been accomplished, and they saw no reason why they should endure the funding inequities any longer. Given that demonstration projects provided them with no special funding advantage, as they were included under donor states' overall spending limits, the committee had little leverage over them. Their crumbling support for federal highway policy compelled the Big Four to offer them more policy concessions than they had in the past. Most important, the leaders increased the minimum allocation guarantee to each donor state from 85 percent (the minimum established in 1982) to 90 percent in an attempt to quell their opposition ("Highways, Mass Transit Funded," p. 142).

The following section describes the course of the 1991 bill in committee and on the floor of the House, with a stress on the issues that came up for recorded votes on the floor. I also specify how members who received demonstration projects could be expected to cast their votes if those projects influenced them.

The 1991 Bill in Committee and on the Floor of the House

By 1991, the deterioration of support for the federal highway program was in evidence even in the Public Works and Transportation Committee. Although some amendments to the leaders' bill had been offered in committee in 1986, they were easily defeated. By contrast, in 1991, the subcommittee and full committee markups offered the spectacle not only of a split between the subcommittee's chairman Mineta and ranking minority member Shuster, but also of the defeat of an amendment offered by Mineta. That amendment, cosponsored by Gus Savage (D-Ill.), would have expanded the Disadvantaged Business Enterprise (DBE), or minority set-aside program, which required that 10 percent of state highway money go to minority or (since 1987) women contractors. Mineta and Savage argued that the result of adding women contractors to what originally had been a pure minority group set-aside had damaged minority businesses. Their amendment would have retained the 10 percent minority requirement and added a 5 percent set-aside for women-owned businesses. Shuster opposed the amendment in subcommittee and full committee, and Mineta suffered defeats in both, even losing twelve of his own Democrats in full committee ("Highways, Mass Transit Funded," p. 143). Any leverage offered by demonstration projects apparently was not available to Mineta. On the other hand, by offering his amendment publicly rather than working out a Big Four consensus in private, he violated the leaders' norm of unity and could hardly have been expected to prevail, given the control traditionally held over projects by the committee chair. Once that amendment was disposed of, however, the full Public Works Committee reported the bill with a nearly unanimous 53-3 vote.

The increase in the gas tax remained an issue, however, especially given the fact that the Public Works Committee lacked the jurisdiction to raise it. Instead, that right belonged to the Ways and Means Committee. Chairman Dan Rostenkowski (D-Ill.) favored the increase, as did House Speaker Tom Foley (D-Wash.). Indeed, there was considerable agreement that such an increase would be needed to pay for the highway bill in order to comply with 1990 budget rules that required that new spending be paid for by new taxes or cuts in already-mandated spending programs. Despite that, many members were leery of voting for a tax increase, especially given that there remained a surplus in the Highway Trust Fund (Cloud 1991, p. 1881). Moreover, Transportation Secretary Samuel K. Skinner reminded the House of President Bush's pledge to veto the bill if it was accompanied by the tax increase. Finally, many members were embarrassed by the well-publicized trade-off between demonstration projects and the tax increase, a combination that could be politically toxic, especially if the president chose to use it to justify a veto. As Ways and Means Democrat Byron Dorgan (N.D.) said, "Why would we want to be pushing for a relatively regressive tax that the president is insisting he would veto?" ("Highways, Mass Transit Funded," p. 143). In the end, the rank-and-file rebellion killed the gas tax increase. Yet the Public Works Committee got a smaller increase through the back door: Half of the nickel increase in the gas tax that had been enacted as part of a 1990 budget deal was extended for an additional four years to help pay for the highway program, including demonstration projects. Thus, the death of the additional nickel in the gas tax did not doom demonstration projects, despite the initial link between them. As a committee staffer said, once the committee leaders solicited and granted projects, they were not in a position to remove them from the bill just because the tax increase failed. So once again, demonstration projects had a life of their own.

On the floor of the House, one of the biggest issues was the rule under which the bill was to be considered. Despite bitter objections from Republicans, the Rules Committee's proposal allowed only twelve amendments, eight of them by Democrats, out of fifty-three that had been proposed. Those that the Rules Committee refused to allow included some of the controversial matters that had bedeviled highway legislation in the past: a limit on the construction of new billboards, repeal of a national speed limit, stronger drunk-driving legislation, and cuts in funding for mass transit and demonstration projects. That it was a highly partisan rule was indicated by the complaint of the ranking minority member of the Rules Committee, Gerald Solomon (R-N.Y.): "This rule is truly unprecedented, unjustified, and unfair. What is this House coming to when a committee's bill is treated as almost sacrosanct, beyond the reach of members on this floor?" (U.S. Congress, *Cong. Record*, Oct. 23, 1991, daily ed., H8202). Republican opponents of the rule complained bitterly on the floor until the previous question was ordered by roll call vote. The motion on the previous question (which is a motion to proceed to a vote) passed on a 319-102 vote. The vote on the rule itself passed by a nearly identical 323-102 vote, and the motion to table the motion to reconsider the vote on the rule passed similarly by 319 to 89. Despite the opposition of many Republicans to the rule, the Big Four were unified in favor of it; a committee staffer conceded that demonstration projects probably helped to pass it. Thus, we expect that the statistical analysis of these votes will show that demonstration projects influenced members' votes.

There was another attempt to expand the minority set-aside, or DBE, program to 10 percent for minorities and an additional 5 percent for women. This time the amendment was offered by Delegate Eleanor Holmes Norton (D-D.C.), who argued that the program had pitted women and minorities against each other and had resulted in fewer contracts for minority-owned businesses. Opponents, led by Public Works Committee ranking minority member Hammerschmidt, argued that it had been impossible to meet the 10 percent goal with minority businesses alone, thus he had in 1987 proposed the floor amendment that added women to the 10 percent set-aside. The Big Four split on party lines on this vote, with Democrats Roe and Mineta voting for it and Republicans Hammerschmidt and Shuster in opposition. The amendment failed on a 133-295 vote. Because the Big Four split, the expectation here is that demonstration projects did not influence members' votes.

Another amendment, one that would permit states to require contractors to guarantee their work, passed by an overwhelming 400-26 margin. It was interesting only because subcommittee chairman Mineta opposed it, arguing that there were implications for the insurance industry and that he would prefer to hold hearings before legislating such guarantees. Once again, he lost. Because the vote was so close to unanimity, it is not included in the statistical analysis in the next section.

The final amendment that came to a recorded vote, offered by Robert Walker (R-Penn.), would have removed from the bill a provision that would establish an office to promote "intermodalism," or coordination among different modes of transportation. Those who opposed the establishment of this office interpreted it as a means to undermine automobiles and highways and promote alternative forms of transportation. As John Kyl (R-Ariz.) said,

> The idea of the office of intermodalism . . . is to try to figure out ways to get people out of their cars so that they will move around by means other than the automobile. As has been pointed out here earlier, one-seventh of the jobs in this country are either already or indirectly related to the automobile industry. So, if my colleagues want a job-killing provision of a bill, I think this office . . . is exactly that. (U.S. Congress, *Cong. Record*, Oct. 23, 1991, daily ed., H8356)

Despite Kyl's attempt to appeal to fears of job losses, the Big Four opposed the amendment. Their commitment to highways was in fact hard to dispute, and the amendment failed by a whopping 69-348 vote. Thus, members who received demonstration projects are expected to oppose this amendment.

In what was arguably the most colorful moment in the debate over the bill, Walker, a persistent critic of demonstration projects, questioned a provision in the bill that not only gave New Jersey (Chairman Roe's state) a particular project, but granted the governor of New Jersey the right to waive any and all federal requirements related to it. After listing the kinds of federal laws that might be violated by such a provision, Walker said,

> Well, I will tell you, it is a little disturbing, because that kind of language is totally contrary to all kinds of federal practice. You cannot designate essentially a special project and then suggest that federal law of no kind applies to it, and yet no one on the committee can explain to me what the language really means?

Roe, outraged almost beyond the ability to articulate, responded,

> Where does anybody have the right – and I will not yield – where does anybody have the right to get up on this floor and suggest that the governor of the state of New Jersey, because this language, which they do not understand and will not

listen to and really do not care about – I am from New Jersey, and I am chairman of the committee – what they are trying to do is to belittle so and run people down in some surreptitious way. I do not know what you gain by that. I do not know what you have achieved.

You could not hurt me if you hit me with a baseball bat because you people are princes of darkness, princes of darkness is what you are.

Shuster, defending the provision a bit more specifically, said,

. . . if [the governor] were to somehow destroy the environmental laws or the civil rights laws, he would be hauled into court in a lawsuit faster than you could say "Jack Robinson."

"Or princes of darkness," added Roe. (U.S. Congress, *Cong. Record*, Oct. 23, 1991, daily ed., H8329)

Despite the heated debate on the rule, the bill in general, and some of the amendments, the bill as amended passed easily on a recorded vote of 343 to 83. The question remains as to whether the 489 projects for 262 members contained in the bill induced members to vote to support the positions of the leaders who bestowed them.

The Impact of Demonstration Projects on Roll Call Voting on the 1991 Highway Bill

In Chapter 3, I argued that on the committee's second go-round of project distribution, members who otherwise would have voted for its bill have an incentive to bargain for a project, reasoning that if other, less committed members received a project in return for their support, they should, too. However, if those members already have adequate reason to support the leaders, then receiving a project may not have any impact on their votes. Projects should still affect some members' votes, but given the dilution of the pool of recipients with larger numbers of supporters, the overall impact might, on the second bill, be weaker than on the first.

However, I also argued that projects are designed not only to get support for the leaders' version of the bill, but for all kinds of amendments on which supporters of the bill itself might be inclined to stray from the leadership position. If the strategy of buying unconditional support on all issues related to the bill is successful, projects would have an impact on voting on amendments, notwithstanding a dilution of the recipient pool relative to support for the bill itself. Moreover, there is another reason to expect projects to have an impact on voting on the 1991 highway bill: Given the increasing controversy surrounding highway policy and the diminished incentive for the average member to support the bill, projects were widely acknowledged to be the cement holding the program together. If that were the case, projects would have an impact not just on voting on amendments but on the rule that lays out the terms for consideration of the bill and on final passage itself. On balance, it is reasonable to expect projects to continue to have an impact on support for the highway bill.

Once again, the issues on which projects are expected to have an impact are those on which the Big Four were unified. Those were the votes on the rule, which the leaders favored, the Walker amendment to delete the Office of Intermodalism, which they opposed, and the final vote on the bill, which they favored, of course. The Big Four split on two amendments: the one that would expand the DBE program, which divided the leaders along party lines, and the nearly unanimous vote to let states require contractors to guarantee their work, which Mineta opposed; the latter is not included in this analysis. Projects are not expected to have an impact on the DBE vote, because there was no leadership position. Table 4.4 summarizes the votes expected of project recipients. The first three call for a bit of explanation. The first, "Rule: Previous Question," is the vote to order the previous question on the rule, that is, to end debate and vote on the rule. "Rule" is the actual vote on the rule, and "Rule: Table Reconsideration" is the vote to table a motion to reconsider the vote on the rule. It is a procedural vote that ensures that the vote on the rule is final and cannot be reconsidered later and possibly overturned.

Table 4.4 provides a first look at the relationship between members' votes and whether or not they received a project. With respect to these bivariate relationships, we see that once again, on those votes on which

TABLE 4.4 *Percentage of Members Voting Yes by Receipt of a Demonstration Project, 1991 Bill*

Vote	Expected vote	Member of Congress did not receive project	Member of Congress received project
Rule: Previous Question[a]	Yes	64.5	82.4
Rule[a]	Yes	64.7	83.3
Rule: Table Reconsideration[a]	Yes	67.7	85.0
DBE	–	28.0	31.9
Intermodalism[a]	No	25.2	11.0
Bill[a]	Yes	69.0	88.0

[a] Chi-square $p \leq .05$.

members are expected to vote with the committee leaders, they in fact do so. Moreover, the relationships are statistically significant.

The question is whether these relationships hold up in mulitvariate analysis. The model for the 1991 bill is essentially the same as that for the 1987 legislation, with appropriate adaptations. The conservatism measure is a member's conservative coalition support score for 1992.[7] The donor state variable now includes twenty-two states, up from the seventeen states that experienced a net revenue loss from the program in 1986–1987. That figure alone indicates the increasing difficulty of building support for the program.

Table 4.5 displays the results of the logit analysis of the six nonunanimous recorded votes taken on the 1991 highway bill. Once again, a yes vote is coded 1; no is coded 0. As before, demonstration projects are measured as a dichotomous variable, where a value of 1 indicates that a member received a project. Table 4.5 shows that the impact of a demonstration project on members' votes remained strong in 1991. On the five votes on which projects were expected to influence members to support the Big Four, they did so.

Other variables were also important. This time, donor state representatives were even more likely to oppose the committee than in 1986–1987; in 1991, they were significantly more likely to do so on four of the five votes on which leaders were unified. Additionally, once other variables are accounted for, members of the Public Works and Transportation Committee were not more loyal than other members. The suggestions in the narrative above of a new partisanship on the committee may help to account for that: the coefficients for party and ideology are indeed significant, with Republicans and conservatives more likely to oppose the committee than Democrats and liberals. That was true on the previous bill as well; what is different here is that Public Works Committee members were likely to be loyal on far fewer votes than they were in 1986–1987. On the earlier bill, they were more likely to be loyal than other members on eight of the nine votes. In 1991, that was true (at the normal .05 level of confidence) on only two of the five votes on which the committee leaders agreed on a position. Thus, it appears that other considerations, partisanship among them, overshadowed the tradition of committee loyalty.

[7] The correlation between the 1991 and 1992 conservative coalition support scores is .955. The 1992 score is preferable, because the 1991 score includes one of the votes analyzed here. The score is calculated so that abstentions do not affect the score; that is, failure to vote does not lower the support score.

TABLE 4.5 *Demonstration Projects and Voting on the 1991 Highway Bill (recorded votes)*

Explanatory Variables	Rule: Previous Qestion	Rule	Rule: Table Reconsideration	DBE	Intermodal	Bill
Demo Project	0.932[a]	1.132[a]	1.365[a]	−0.094	−1.037[a]	1.124[a]
	(.355)	(.344)	(.379)	(.319)	(.357)	(.288)
Public Works	1.681[a]	1.140[b]	0.878[c]	0.364	−0.391	0.292
	(.580)	(.556)	(.567)	(.446)	(.562)	(.500)
Republican	−4.642[a]	−4.454[a]	−5.363[a]	−2.000[a]	4.282[a]	−1.360[a]
	(.694)	(.669)	(1.087)	(.778)	(.863)	(.400)
Conservatism	−0.008	−0.003	−0.028[b]	−0.057[a]	0.012	−0.013[b]
	(.012)	(.011)	(.016)	(.007)	(.014)	(.007)
Donor	−0.804[b]	−0.717[b]	−0.909[a]	0.469	1.204[a]	0.146
	(.364)	(.349)	(.377)	(.310)	(.371)	(.294)
Intercept	4.545[a]	3.911[a]	7.079	2.032[a]	−5.765[a]	2.324[a]
	(.817)	(.714)	(1.435)	(.370)	(1.073)	(.443)
Model chi-square	245.90[a]	225.13[a]	233.34[a]	232.72[a]	160.23[a]	77.68[a]
Pseudo R^2	.522	.481	.546	.443	.428	.185
Cases correctly Classified (%)	88.39	87.74	88.45	83.64	86.81	81.69
Percentage reduction of error	52.79	48.92	47.04	47.34	20.30	6.00

[a] $p \leq .01$.
[b] $p \leq .05$.
[c] $p \leq .10$.

Note: For each vote the expected direction of the Demo Project coefficient is as follows: Rule: Previous Question, Rule, and Rule: Table Reconsideration, positive; DBE, no effect; Intermodalism, negative; Bill, positive. The number in parentheses beneath each coefficient is the standard error. The model chi-square statistic tests the hypothesis that all coefficients in the equation equal 0. Significance for this statistic allows the rejection of that hypothesis. The percentage reduction of error statistic (ROE) indicates the extent to which the model's predictions improve on predicting that everyone will fall into the modal category of the dependent variable. %ROE = 100 × (% correctly classified −% in modal category)/(100% −% in modal category).

TABLE 4.6 *Probability That a Member Supported Committee Leaders by Receipt of a Project, 1991 Bill*

Vote	Republican without a project	Republican with a project	Change in probability	Democrat without a project	Democrat with a project	Change in Probability
Rule: Previous Question	.313	.536	.223	.985	.994	.009
Rule	.310	.582	.272	.978	.993	.015
Rule: Table Reconsideration	.333	.662	.329	.997	.999	.002
Intermodal	.610	.815	.305	.995	.998	.003
Bill	.462	.726	.264	.855	.948	.093

Note: Calculations are done assuming that members are not on the Public Works Committee and not from a donor state and that they are at the mean conservatism score for their party; for Republicans, that is 86.15; for Democrats, it is 42.37.

Table 4.6 takes a closer look at the effect of demonstration projects on the behavior of Democrats compared with Republicans. This table, like Table 4.3, presents separately for Democrats and Republicans the probabilities that they voted with the committee leaders on the five votes on which the leaders took a unified position. The first and fourth columns consist of the probabilities that members supported the leaders without receiving a project; the second and fifth columns contain the probabilities that those who received projects did so, with other variables held constant. The values of the other variables for purposes of these calculations were as follows: members were assigned the mean conservatism score for their party; for Republicans, that was 86.15; for Democrats it was 42.37. They were also treated as if they were not members of Public Works and were not from donor states.

Again, the partisan effects are much more dramatic here than on the earlier bill. Looking at the third and sixth columns first, we see that on every vote, the magnitude of the effect on Republicans was greater than on Democrats. In fact, the Democrats, unlike the Republicans, were tightly unified on these votes, regardless of whether they received projects; they overwhelmingly supported committee leaders on every vote. The real impact of demonstration projects on this bill was to pull Republicans away from their own partisan inclinations. On each of the four votes on which Republicans without projects were unlikely to support the leadership, those with projects did support them. Thus, projects evidently did buy the votes of Republicans.

As in 1986–1987, the evidence is that the committee leaders successfully used highway demonstration projects to win members' votes for their version of the 1991 highway reauthorization; because Democrats were so unified, the main effect of demonstration projects was on the behavior of Republicans.

CONCLUSIONS

It is time to consider the combined implications of the findings of this chapter and the previous one in terms of the expectations expressed in Chapter 2. The expectation was that the first time a committee's leaders used pork barrel benefits to build support for their preferred policies, they would give out benefits to a minority of members, as other members would support the bill on its own merits. Because the projects were intended to swing the votes of those who might be undecided either on the bill or amendments to it, on this first round of project distribution, leaders would give projects to members on the basis of their likely support for the leaders. The evidence in Chapter 3 shows that to have been the case on the first highway bill on which leaders gave out demonstration projects. Subsequently, we expected that members who received projects would make good on their obligations, voting in support of the leaders who bestowed them. The evidence in this chapter supports that hypothesis as well: House members who received projects were significantly more likely to support committee leaders on all votes on which the Big Four took a unified position on the 1986–1987 bill.

On the second go-round for the committee, that is, on the second bill on which the leaders use this strategy to win members' support, things start getting a bit more complicated. Members see that they could have bargained for a project the first time around and decide not to give away their votes this time. So the demand for projects skyrockets, as it did on the second highway bill. Moreover, because leaders find it more difficult to ascertain members' true intentions, they give up and distribute projects indiscriminately, without regard to members' likely support for the bill ex ante. In the case of the 1991 highway bill, this tendency was aided by the committee chair's enthusiasm for giving projects and his prior experience of winning loyalty with them on other subcommittees. Accordingly, we found no relationship between a member's expected support of the leadership and his or her receipt of a project on the 1991 highway bill. However, once members accept a project, they also accept the obligation to be loyal to those who gave it. Clearly, on the 1991 highway bill, members honored their bargains: Those who received projects were more likely to support committee leaders on the five votes on which there was a leadership position.

Thus, between 1987 and 1991, although the number of demonstration projects grew dramatically, projects lost none of their importance as inducements to vote with the leaders who bestowed them, despite the fact that committee leaders awarded them less selectively in 1991. Even if members behaved strategically in asking for projects in 1991, concealing their true support for the legislation, the impact of the projects overall was undiminished. However, one of the most important findings here is the differential impact of projects on members of the two parties. In the case of both bills, on most votes projects had a greater impact on members of the party that was otherwise least inclined to support the committee leaders. While projects influenced the votes of members of both parties, on the 1991 bill in particular, projects were most likely to change the voting intentions of Republicans. Democrats, on the other hand, were already inclined to support the leaders. Combining these results with those of Chapter 3, we see that committee leaders used an even less efficient distribution strategy in 1991 than in 1986–1987. They gave to likely supporters, who did in fact vote for the leaders' positions, as this chapter shows, and to possible opponents as well, unlike in 1986–1987. But when it was time for members to pay their debts, this chapter shows that many who otherwise would have voted against the Big Four in fact supported them if they had been awarded a project. In 1991, most of those who paid up were Republicans.

These two bills show that if policy coalition leaders cannot get the votes they want any other way for broad-based legislation, they can buy them with pork barrel projects. Moreover, the 1991 bill is a particularly dramatic example of the use of pork barrel projects to drive a wedge into the minority party on general interest measures. The rule under which that bill was considered on the House floor prohibited members from voting on amendments that would have made the bill more congenial to Republican philosophy, such as a repeal of the national speed limit and cuts in operating subsidies for urban mass transit. But regardless of whether the measure being voted on was particularized or broad-based, pork barrel projects split the Republicans (and in 1986–1987, the Democrats) and bought votes. This chapter shows that demonstration projects influenced the votes of members of both parties, at least in 1986–1987, when on some amendments the votes of Democrats as well as Republicans were uncertain. As the chapters that follow show, there are times that pork indeed has more impact on Democrats' votes. Ultimately, we see that although pork barrel bargaining is most useful to the majority party leadership (simply because it is normally more available to them), the lure and impact of pork on its recipients is bipartisan.[8]

[8] It is quite possible, as Bickers and Stein (2000) find, that some kinds of distributive benefits are in fact more appealing to Republicans, while others appeal to Democrats. If that were the case here, it could be an alternative explanation for the seemingly greater impact of projects on Republicans, although only in 1991. Specifically, Bickers and Stein find that Democrats are more likely to favor entitlements aimed at their political base, while Republicans favor contingent liability programs, in which the government underwrites the risk of private business and individuals, paying only when those businesses incur a loss or fail to meet a financial obligation. However, highway demonstration projects fall into neither category, but they have some of the appeal of both. To put it in terms of the archetypal images of each party, demonstration projects' appeal to Republicans might well lie in the fact that they bring contracts to businesses in their districts. For Democrats, the projects create blue-collar jobs, as those same businesses hire workers and abide by the federal requirement that they pay the "prevailing wage" for such work. For both parties, such projects are seen as stimulative to local economies through their multiplier effect.

Thus far, we have devoted two chapters to examining the House Public Works and Transportation Committee's use of pork barrel projects in two successive reauthorization bills. Those bills deserved such generous attention because they offered a rare opportunity to examine the dynamics of project distribution and its impact over time. Although other committees, especially the appropriations committees, distribute such benefits year after year, on these highway bills we have an example of the first use of such projects to buy large numbers of votes and the second such use by the same committee. That has allowed an assessment of how the process begins and how it changes over time. As these chapters show, most of the change was in the process of awarding projects. Even though the committee leaders were quite willing to give out much larger numbers of projects in 1991, we have seen that they would have found it difficult to avoid doing so, as many more members demanded them. Yet the projects lost none of their impact on members' behavior, provided that the representatives' votes were in question in the first place.

Chapter 5 continues the examination of efforts to buy votes with distributive benefits, this time for the North American Free Trade Agreement. That case provides a different kind of example of the strategy, with a concentration on the role of the president as policy coalition leader. In this case, the president's own party was reluctant to support NAFTA. Therefore, the president and his allies in Congress worked to split the members of the president's own party, the majority party Democrats, and add some of their votes to those already pledged by Republicans.

5

Presidential Bargaining with Congress: The NAFTA Bazaar

Anyone with adequate political resources can be a policy coalition leader, as Chapter 2 explains. Among those people are committee and party leaders in each house of Congress. Some of those leaders have access to distributive benefits to trade for votes on general interest legislation. So does the president, who can, for example, influence the allocation of some of the massive amounts of money distributed on a discretionary basis by the bureaucracy, as candidates who challenge his reelection often discover to their dismay. This chapter provides an account and systematic analysis of President Clinton's use of distributive benefits to persuade the House of Representatives to pass legislation to implement the North American Free Trade Agreement (NAFTA) in 1993. He did so in concert with the leadership of the House Republicans, not his own majority-party Democrats. Thus we move from a focus in Chapters 3 and 4 on the use of distributive benefits by committee leaders in the House to a focus on the president and minority party leaders in that same body.

On November 17, 1993, the House of Representatives approved NAFTA by passing H.R. 3450, a bill to provide for implementation of the terms of that agreement. The Clinton administration's victory on the 234-200 vote had been in doubt until only a week earlier. By all accounts, the administration prevailed in the end only with a series of concessions to members of Congress representing a long list of local interests that felt threatened by NAFTA's liberalization of trade with Mexico and Canada. Interest groups that opposed the pact and editorial writers who generally favored it all condemned what they characterized as the blatant and very public vote buying that secured NAFTA's victory in the House.

However, no long-term observer of the presidency could have been surprised by Clinton's attempts to win votes by offering something in return; he merely followed the example set by many of his predecessors. Presidential historian Richard Neustadt made that point with an example in an op-ed article that appeared in *Newsday* a month after the vote:

> Frederick Lawton, Harry S. Truman's last budget director, who had been for decades a career official at the Office of Management and Budget (as it now is called), once told me of a summons to Franklin Roosevelt's office in 1938, when the last big piece of New Deal legislation ever passed, the Fair Labor Standards Act, was teetering before the House of Representatives. "Fred," President Roosevelt said, as I heard the story, "I want you to go across the street (to the then State Department, now the Executive Office Building), find a vacant office with a desk, two chairs and a telephone, take a copy of the Budget Document with you, call me and give me the room number and then wait there all day. From time to time, members of Congress, sent by me, one by one, will knock on your door. And when they do, Fred, let them in, shut the door, open the Budget, and give them whatever they ask." (Neustadt 1993)

Similarly, Ronald Reagan's budget director, David Stockman, recounted numerous instances of vote buying by the president and his staff as they attempted to cut both taxes and the domestic budget. Ironically, the cost of Reagan's deals often vitiated the budget-cutting impact of the very legislation that they were meant to help pass (Stockman 1986, pp. 264–265). Of the conservative coalition of Republicans and Southern Democrats that Reagan relied on for his legislative victories, Stockman said,

> The latent GOP-Boll Weevil parliamentary majority, in terms of gross vote numbers, was nearly meaningless. An actual majority for any specific bill had to be reconstructed from scratch every time. It had to be cobbled out of a patchwork of raw, parochial deals that set off a political billiard game of counterreactions and corresponding demands. The last 10 or 20 percent of the votes needed for a majority of both houses had to be bought, period. (Stockman 1986, pp. 250–251)[1]

[1] There are a good many accounts of presidential bargaining in the literature on particular presidents and the presidency in general (e.g., Dahl and Lindblom 1953; Kearns 1976, p. 236; Edwards 1980, 128–30; Carter 1982, pp. 78–84; Neustadt 1990; Jones 1995, p. 132). Richard Neustadt traces its prevalence to the president's weakness relative to Congress, weakness that was designed into the Constitution. As a result of that imbalance of power, even when members of Congress agree with the president on the public policy at issue, they frequently ask for a quid pro quo in return for their support (Neustadt 1990, 40).

President Jimmy Carter's rocky relationship with Congress can be traced in part to his unwillingness to curry favor with its members by responding to their desire for district-level benefits. In his own memoir, Carter admits, "I had several serious disagreements with Congress, but the issue of water projects was the one that caused the deepest breach between me and the Democratic leadership" (Carter 1982, p. 78). Carter's opposition to pork barrel projects and his unwillingness to trade projects for national policy, according to then-representative Norman Mineta, made his relations with his own party's majority quite difficult (Jacobson 1997, p. 193).

President Clinton was not so constrained by scruples about pork barrel projects; in fact, he faced the opposite problem when one of his first legislative priorities, an economic stimulus bill, failed despite the favors it bestowed on individual members of the House. In the president's judgment, that bill was so full of pork that it would have failed to provide the stimulus that he sought in the first place (Woodward 1994, p. 174), an example of vote buying run amok. As explained in Chapter 2, the process of vote buying can rapidly escape the control of the leaders who started it, with escalating demands for pork from members who threaten to withhold their votes without it.

As the fate of the stimulus bill suggests, Clinton set precedents that produced heightened expectations of payoffs among representatives long before the November 17 vote on NAFTA. To gain passage of his economic plan (separate from the stimulus bill mentioned above) early in his first year in office, Clinton made a number of deals with members of Congress, winning passage of the plan in the House by a scant one-vote margin (Woodward 1994, pp. 300–302). And there were other examples of Clinton's willingness to deal. A congressional staffer also cited the fact that in the first months of his administration, Clinton backed down, at the demand of western cattlemen, on his plan to increase grazing fees for federal land holdings, a plan proposed by his own Secretary of the Interior. That, the staffer said, was the signal that this was the way to do business with this president. More generally, she noted that "some people just hold out as a rule," even if they support what the president wants, "especially if it's a tough vote. They can say 'not only did I think it was right, but I also made them come to me.'" Thus, Clinton's prior deals created clear expectations among members of Congress that the president also would buy votes on NAFTA (and anything else he really wanted, for that matter). Specifically, moderate and conservative Democrats, whose votes were most likely to be available on NAFTA, saw that if they held out, they could get something in return. As this staffer said, by bargaining in this way on his economic plan, Clinton in effect "opened the flood gates" to similar requests on other matters.

To learn how such deal making fits into the battle over NAFTA in the House, where, unlike the Senate, passage was by no means assured, I conducted interviews with a number of people involved in the process, including those for and against the bill. Respondents included House staffers, Clinton administration officials, and public and private interest group lobbyists. In the next section I draw on those interviews as well as published sources to describe how the president and his allies in the House used particularized benefits to buy votes for NAFTA. In the section following that account, I analyze statistically the effectiveness of the strategy with a model of the vote in the House, a model that includes as its key independent variable a House member's receipt of a particularized benefit. As in Chapter 4, I also examine the impact of the deal making separately on the votes of Republicans and Democrats to determine the partisan impact of the president's attempts at vote buying.

THE CAMPAIGN FOR NAFTA

The ground for the November 17, 1993, House vote was prepared more than two years earlier on May 23, 1991, when Congress voted to extend for two years the "fast track" process for considering trade legislation. That procedure, designed to facilitate the president's ability to negotiate trade agreements without a great deal of second-guessing from Congress, required a straight up-or-down vote on trade agreement legislation. No amendments were allowed, and committees could not block the path to the floor by refusing to report the legislation. The fast track procedure also required a floor vote on the legislation in each house of Congress within ninety days of its introduction. Short-term extensions of fast track authority, in this case for two years, were designed to give the president an incentive to keep Congress involved as he negotiated trade agreements.

The vote on the fast track procedure was controversial, a prelude to the conflict that would surround NAFTA; indeed, the interest group coalition that would be active against NAFTA emerged during the fast track debate. Members of that coalition saw the campaign against fast track authority as a way to begin to mobilize for the vote on NAFTA as well as upcoming votes relating to the General Agreement on Tariffs and Trade (GATT), which also would liberalize international trade. The core of the fair trade coalition, as it called itself, consisted of labor unions and environmental groups. Ralph Nader's Public Citizen, a proconsumer interest group, organized the Citizens' Trade Watch Campaign, which was cited by a number of interviewees as being particularly central to the coalition. Labor unions were concerned about the negative impact of lower trade barriers on the wages of U.S. workers; the lower the trade barriers, they argued, the easier and more tempting it would be for U.S. manufacturers to join the waxing tide of manufacturing operations flowing to other, lower-wage, nations, especially Mexico. Unions were already feeling pressure to agree to lower wages for U.S. workers as a price for limiting the movement of manufacturing jobs out of the United States; with NAFTA, they expected that pressure to increase.

For environmentalists, the concerns revolved around the impact of lower or nonexistent pollution controls in the countries to which manufacturing was flowing; in particular, they worried about the massive pollution on the U.S.-Mexican border caused by the Mexican "maquiladoras," manufacturing plants mostly owned by U.S. corporations. They also feared that certain provisions in international trade agreements could result in U.S. environmental laws being branded as unfair trading practices by international trade organizations, which might then compel a loosening of U.S. environmental laws.

The advance organization of the fair trade coalition combined with the electoral clout of organized labor set up the hurdle that a Democratic president ultimately would have to overcome. That he chose to do so with special benefits to many of his own party members, who were most vulnerable to pressure from the coalition, is not surprising.

However, NAFTA did not originate with Clinton; in fact, it was a Republican initiative. President George H.W. Bush completed the NAFTA agreement near the end of his term in office and initialed it along with President Salinas of Mexico on August 12, 1992. It was left to newly elected President Clinton to gain congressional approval of the pact. Pressed during the 1992 campaign for his views on NAFTA, candidate Clinton, who was supported by both environmental and labor groups, promised to negotiate a set of "side agreements" to NAFTA that would be designed to address many of those groups' concerns.

Once elected, Clinton was faced with the daunting task of assembling a majority coalition for NAFTA, a particularly difficult challenge in the House, which harbored more suspicion of liberalized trade than the Senate. On the surface, Republican support would seem to have been assured, as Republicans normally support free trade and the agreement itself was negotiated by a president of their own party. Had NAFTA come before the 102nd Congress when Bush was still president, Republican votes for NAFTA probably would largely have been guaranteed. However, attaining final approval and implementation was left to a Democratic president, one who had defeated the Republican incumbent. Minority Whip Newt Gingrich, who led the House Republican effort, initially withheld his support, which the president badly needed; Democratic and Republican House staffers alike said that Gingrich had sixty to 100 Republican votes in his pocket. The question was, how would he use them? Gingrich was said by congressional staffers to have weighed the cost of handing a major victory to the Democratic president against the benefits that might flow from showing both that Clinton needed Republicans to pass his legislative program and that, under the right conditions, they would work with him on a bipartisan basis. However, there was much pressure within both his own party and the business community to support NAFTA, and Gingrich eventually delivered the votes.

Clinton's own party clearly would pose serious problems, given the fervent opposition of groups in the Democrats' electoral base. The rift over NAFTA between Democratic liberals and moderates even split the Democratic leadership in the House. Although Speaker Tom Foley (D-Wash.) was a loyal supporter of the president and NAFTA, Majority Leader Richard Gephardt (D-Mo.) deferred his support while Clinton negotiated the side agreements that he had promised during the campaign (Audley 1997, p. 74).

Worse for Clinton was the fervent opposition of pro-labor Democratic Whip David Bonior (D-Mich.). Bonior said, "With or without the side agreement, NAFTA rolls out the red carpet for more multinationals to close their plants in the U.S. and open them up in Mexico instead, leaving hundreds of thousands of American workers without jobs" ("Congress OKs North American Trade Pact," p. 176). In a letter cosigned by more than 100 members of the House, Bonior asked Clinton to delay the vote on NAFTA until 1994, and, in a thinly veiled threat to Clinton's most treasured policy initiative, suggested that forcing consideration in the fall of 1993 might put at risk Clinton's health care reform proposal (Sawyer 1993). Thus, it was clear early on that Clinton would have to try to pass NAFTA despite both a split in the House Democratic leadership and a Republican Party that had no love for him and no wish to help him win a big victory on turf that they felt was rightfully their own. The incentive for the president to begin handing out particularized benefits in order to win votes was strong.

First, however, Clinton made good on his promise to add side agreements to try to ameliorate aspects of the agreement that were most objectionable to his supporters. Three side agreements were signed at a White House ceremony on September 14. Two of them were designed to ensure that both the United States and Mexico would adhere to their own environmental and labor laws; the third was intended to protect U.S. businesses from surges in exports from Mexico and Canada ("Congress OKs North American Trade Pact," p. 173).

The administration effort suffered yet another blow when, within hours of the September 14 signing ceremony, Gephardt declared that the side agreements were "not supportable." On September 21, he announced that he would not vote for NAFTA. With Bonior already working hard against the pact, using his leadership office in the Capitol building as the staging ground for the anti-NAFTA campaign, Speaker Foley bowed to the inevitable. Seeking to avoid intraparty bloodshed, he freed Democrats from any fear of reprisal for an anti-NAFTA vote, saying that people would be allowed the latitude to follow their consciences (Cohen 1993b; "Congress OKs North American Trade Pact," p. 176). Presumably, they were also free to make deals with the president for their votes.

Outside Congress, the side agreements split the environmental community; some environmental groups were won over by the agreement on environmental law, while others opposed it. However, labor unions remained unified; they were entirely dissatisfied with the labor agreement and broke with the administration over its weakness. As one labor lobbyist said in an interview, "We were marginally hopeful that the side agreement could be done to mitigate the harm of NAFTA. We made a serious effort to discuss the details, but they came up empty; worker rights – the freedom to organize and bargain [in Mexico] – were taken off the table." The *New York Times* reported that AFL-CIO president Lane Kirkland said he had asked the administration, including the president, to "insist on strict enforcement against built-in Mexican competition-killers. [Kirkland] said he wanted no more than the enforcement NAFTA gives against violations of intellectual property – patents, royalties and so on.... Only when [the administration] failed to come through, he says, did labor go into the field against NAFTA." With evident bitterness, Kirkland asserted, "Mr. Clinton's 'victory' forced into opposition millions of working people who had voted for him. They (and I) would have supported NAFTA, if they had been given the safeguards granted to Americans who produce 'intellectual property'" (Rosenthal 1993). Reinforcing this view of the inadequacy of the side agreements on labor matters, a

House Democratic staffer said, "The side agreements were a fig leaf for the Democrats. Republicans didn't like them," and the administration kept them weak to avoid alienating the Republican supporters that he clearly needed.

Although NAFTA supporters complained that Clinton was slow to turn his attention to the campaign to pass it, by mid-October, his team was in gear. The president began meeting with several undecided House members twice weekly and telephoning three of them each day; cabinet members were given the names of representatives to lobby and told to give interviews on local talk shows in key members' districts (Stokes 1993).

In the meantime, votes were being counted by participants and observers alike; the tallies varied, but in late September and early October it was clear that the president was falling short. On October 1, the *Washington Post* reported that NAFTA would have been defeated had it been brought to a vote that day. An AFL-CIO vote tally taken just a few days earlier (September 27) (supplied to me by a union official) showed that 233 members were either committed to vote no or were leaning against NAFTA. That left only 202 House members to be counted as potential supporters. The union's count included thirty-seven members leaning against NAFTA; clearly, the administration would be compelled to turn some of the latter its way. The vote-winning potential of the side agreements regarding labor and the environment had already been exploited, mostly unsuccessfully.

Given that the schism among environmental groups formed early in the process and labor was a lost cause, it became essential for NAFTA supporters to look to other member concerns for potential votes. How was the administration to gain the needed votes, given the opposition? The answer, by all accounts, was to buy them.

A major opportunity to barter for members' votes was provided by worries about NAFTA's impact on agriculture, particularly agricultural imports from Mexico, but also the impact of durum wheat from Canada on farmers in the upper Midwest. In October, efforts to win the votes of members with district agricultural interests began in earnest. On October 1, more than half of the Florida House delegation was thought to be opposed to NAFTA on the basis of its likely impact on local agricultural interests (Shanahan 1993). Thus, even as the *Christian Science Monitor* was reporting, on October 12, that Republicans were complaining that Clinton had put too little pressure on Democrats to support NAFTA (Dillin 1993), the office of the U.S. Trade Representative (USTR) was cutting deals for agricultural interests.

During that process, the House Agriculture Committee made a play for influence over the administration's deal making. In a "mock markup" on October 26 (remember that fast track rules prohibited amendments to trade accords), that committee approved a draft of NAFTA's agriculture provisions; however, it also proposed amendments to protect crops in many committee members' districts, including peanuts, sugar, fruit, vegetables, and fresh-cut flowers ("Congress OKs North American Trade Pact," p. 176). Because amendments could not be added to the trade accord itself, the committee's clear intent was to signal the administration about the deals that would be needed to win those members' support. Not that Agriculture Committee Chairman Kika de la Garza (D-Tex.) was himself unsupportive of NAFTA. With a district positioned on the Mexican border, de la Garza was a strong supporter of closer ties with Mexico, a popular stance with his heavily Mexican-American constituents, many of whom depended on trade with Mexico. It was, therefore, in his interest to encourage deal making that would win his committee members' votes. To that end, de la Garza worked with the administration to gain various concessions.

As an official of the office of the USTR said in an interview, the geographic concentration of agricultural interests, compared with the dispersion of environmental and labor groups, made it worthwhile to focus on the former. Such a focus is not surprising: Serving particular, concentrated interests lies at the heart of pork barrel politics; individual members can take deals home for their farmers and believably claim credit for them. Therefore, a number of bargains were made with agricultural interests across the country, but Florida, with its large House delegation, was a particularly tempting target. USTR officials and their congressional supporters believed that with the right inducements, they could win over most of that twenty-three-member delegation. Thus, the USTR, in conjunction with the Agriculture Department, worked to sway the undecided Floridians, especially as support began to build among other members and Florida's block of votes increasingly appeared to hold the key to victory.

Within Florida, demands for concessions came from groups representing sugar cane, citrus fruits, tomatoes, and winter vegetables. However, administration negotiators said in interviews that it appeared to them that much of the trouble with these groups stemmed more from one-upmanship than from genuine opposition to NAFTA. In particular, once the agreement was substantially negotiated by the Bush administration in the early fall of 1991, Florida fruit and vegetable interests reportedly breathed a collective sigh of relief over its provisions. But sugar interests were unhappy and vowed to force changes; the groups representing fruit and vegetable interests, not to be outdone, began to make additional demands as well. As one executive branch participant said, the fruit and vegetable groups "had to look like they had 'political pop' too." Sugar interests had a long wish list on which they lobbied both the Clinton administration and Congress. When administration negotiators granted them something, the fruit and vegetable groups made an additional demand as well; one frustrated negotiator asserted that the latter, in their effort to keep up, often had trouble even identifying what they wanted.

Despite deals given to Florida's sugar and citrus industries, as of November 6, most members of the Florida delegation continued strategically to withhold their votes. Some interviewees commented on that strategy; one said that "many refrained from taking a position or opposed the agreement in order to wring [more] concessions out of the administration for the state's citrus, sugar and vegetable growers." However, the administration countered this intransigence with some hardball of its own, asserting that "the citrus and sugar deals came with an unwritten understanding – the arrangements could be nullified if half of Florida's delegation [did not] turn around and support NAFTA" (Dahl 1993).

Florida's representatives finally blinked. On November 16, in a meeting with their state's agriculture lobbyists, the Florida delegation was read a letter from Clinton with one last promise to strengthen safeguards for tomato growers. At that point, Tom Lewis (R-Fla.), a high-ranking member of the Agriculture Committee, argued that the delegation had received almost everything they had asked for and that it was time to "declare victory." His switch from opposition to support for NAFTA reportedly brought on board nine other members of the delegation ("Congress OKs North American Trade Pact," p. 176). In the end, thirteen of the twenty-three Florida representatives voted for the pact, just barely meeting the minimum level of support that the administration said that it required to make good on the deals for agriculture.

The deals for Florida were the most widely noticed, but the administration reportedly made dozens of other expensive trades of special benefits for the votes of members from all around the country. A high-profile example concerned funding for the North American Development Bank (NADBank), a benefit promised by Treasury Secretary Lloyd Bentsen to members of the Congressional Hispanic Caucus from U.S.-Mexican border districts. This deal was intended to allay Latino constituents' fears of job losses to Mexico. NADBank was to receive $450 million over four years, 50 percent of which was to be contributed by the United States and

50 percent by Mexico. The money was to be used mostly for environmental cleanup, but 10 percent of the funds were designated for distribution to U.S. communities that were adversely affected by NAFTA ("Congress OKs North American Trade Pact," p. 178). The deal was requested by Esteban Torres (D-Calif.), who was expected to deliver the votes of eight other Hispanic members; however, when Bentsen announced the development bank, only Torres announced his support for NAFTA (Mintz 1993).

Additionally, in a bid for one more Sunbelt vote, the administration announced support for the acquisition of six C-17 cargo planes, two more than the president had originally requested in his budget. The target was Eddie Bernice Johnson (D-Tex.), whose district was home to the cargo plane's builder. Immediately following that announcement, Johnson declared her support for NAFTA. However, unlike some members, Johnson was unwilling publicly to link her vote to the deal:

> The *Journal of Commerce* broke the story that Johnson agreed to support NAFTA after an unnamed administration official promised that the Pentagon would purchase two additional C-17 cargo planes – at a cost of $1.4 billion – from the Vought Aircraft factory in her south Dallas district. The controversial military transport plane has an impressive history of technical failures. Johnson claims she was misquoted. Her decision to support NAFTA, she says, was based on the "broad needs" of her constituents; the *Journal of Commerce* reporter stands by his story. (Lewis 1993)

Other deals were intended to protect myriad industries in particular members' districts: "formal 'Executive Letter of Agreement' tariff agreements were made on sugar and syrup goods, wine and brandy, flat glass, home appliances and bedding components such as springs, iron rails and wooden parts, to name a few" (Lewis 1993).

Although the pro-NAFTA campaign was far from being exclusively an inside game played between Congress and the Clinton administration, the massive outside lobbying campaign mounted by business was organized very late compared with the two-year anti-NAFTA campaign conducted by labor and environmental interests. The business coalition did not even begin its work until after the side agreements were completed in August, and for a long time thereafter, they were outflanked by the anti-NAFTA lobby. Consequently, as the vote on NAFTA approached, the pro-NAFTA business coalition worried about its own ability to sway enough members to turn the tide in its favor, even with the president's efforts. On November 12, only five days before the House vote, the *New York Times* noted,

> Sputtering for months, the business community's lobbying campaign is now running wide open, producing mailings, telephone calls, newspaper advertisements

> and speeches on behalf of the North American Free Trade Agreement. Hundreds of business executives are spending more time on Capitol Hill than at home, and hundreds of factory workers are being pulled off the line to visit members of Congress. "I think we've done more on NAFTA than on any legislative issue in history," said Lawrence A. Bossidy, the chairman of Allied Signal Inc. and the head of USA-NAFTA, an umbrella coalition of thousands of companies and trade organizations backing the pact. But it is far from certain whether the lobbying will put votes in the pact's corner when the House of Representatives squares off on Wednesday. "We have not converted many members," said Ron E. Brower, A.T.& T.'s government relations official in Florida and head of USA-NAFTA's campaign there, after traveling to Washington with 100 executives last week. (Mills 1993)

The ultimate effectiveness of the business campaign is doubtful. Instead, observers and participants in the fray stressed the importance of the administration's deals with House members. One of the leaders of the anti-NAFTA labor-environmentalist coalition put it baldly, "[W]e didn't start losing people until the president started buying them." She argued that representatives initially opposed to NAFTA "were not peeled off by corporations sitting on them; [members] could not overcome the fact that we had their voters. The question was, could members get something more valuable" in the form of an appealing pork barrel deal; if so, then, and only then, did they change their positions.

The legislation to approve and implement NAFTA, H.R. 3450, was introduced in the House on November 4, 1993, and scheduled for a vote on November 17. NAFTA's support was bipartisan, despite the fact that the key Democratic floor leaders opposed it. The pro-NAFTA forces in the House were led by a coalition consisting of Democrats Bill Richardson (N.M.), the only one of the Democrats' four chief deputy whips to support the pact, and Robert Matsui (Calif.) and by Republicans Jim Kolbe (Ariz.) and David Dreier (Calif.). In the weeks leading up to the vote, the Democrats worked with administration representative George Stephanopoulos; according to one staff participant, a major subject of their meetings concerned what members needed to receive in order to vote for NAFTA. In addition, coalition leaders scoured legislators' campaign contribution lists and asked their pro-NAFTA business contributors to call and ask them to support the legislation.

On the other side, the bipartisan anti-NAFTA coalition led in part by Majority Whip Bonior tried, generally unsuccessfully, to prevent the fence-sitters from being picked off by the White House. Their tactics were hardball: One staff member for this effort said that committee chairs who opposed NAFTA told members who had received promises of special benefits that they would not get the necessary authorizations or appropriations. Nevertheless, the coalition found it difficult to counter the president, especially with freshmen, when Clinton not only offered many of them deals, but also argued that they would be responsible for the success or failure of his presidency.[2]

Additionally, the administration decided that it was necessary to try to defuse Ross Perot's very public anti-NAFTA campaign by challenging him to a televised debate with Vice President Al Gore. A staff member for a leading NAFTA opponent in the House offered the cynical view that the White House used the Perot gambit because the press favored NAFTA and hated Perot; they knew the press would declare Gore the winner, almost no matter what happened. However, others argued that the strategy carried risks, as Gore's vice presidential campaign debate with Dan Quayle had been widely rated as a draw, despite Gore's command of public policy details and Quayle's reputation for a lack thereof (Komarow 1993).

The strategy paid off. Following a vituperative debate on November 9, opinion polls showed that the majority of Americans believed that Gore bested Perot. The administration crowed. "Paul Begala, Clinton's political adviser, put it... bluntly: 'As we say in Texas, Gore beat him like a bad piece of meat. He's ready for chili now.' Clinton said, 'I honestly believe we're going to win it now, and that's not just political puff.... I'd be surprised if we don't'" (Lee 1993).

Nevertheless, three days before NAFTA was to come up on the floor of the House, the administration was still scrambling for votes. On November 14, U.S. Trade Representative Mickey Kantor, appearing on NBC's *Meet the Press*, said that the administration was still a dozen votes shy of the 218 needed; but he asserted that "we have enough right now to put us within striking distance. We probably have as many as the other side... but by Wednesday we'll have it." However, appearing on the same program, David Bonior claimed that opponents had 222 anti-NAFTA votes and were on track to win. He said, "We think we're going to hold our vote because I think the American people are calling their members of Congress and telling them that this is a job-loss bill." Between them, Kantor and Bonior claimed 428 out of 435 possible votes, yet an

[2] The anti-NAFTA forces in the House might have tried to outbid the president with promises of pork barrel benefits in return for votes against the accord; however, there was no evidence from interviews or published accounts that they made such an attempt.

Associated Press poll of the House counted fifty-one members as undecided (Nichols 1993).

Although Kantor denied that Clinton was buying votes with projects, saying, "There's no 'for sale' sign above the White House," Treasury Secretary Lloyd Bentsen said that the deals to help protect sugar, citrus, and vegetable farmers would strengthen NAFTA (Dutt 1993). In a final measure of the administration's desperation, President Clinton promised a reward of great partisan (or bipartisan) significance: He pledged on November 13 that, as repayment to NAFTA supporters, he would protect Republicans as well as Democrats in the 1994 congressional elections against opponents who tried to use their pro-NAFTA votes against them (Dutt 1993). A day later, the Associated Press's survey had the number of undecided votes down to thirty-nine, a number still insufficient to give victory to either side. The administration had little choice but to buy votes up until the last minute, including those of at least four farm state representatives who were won over when Clinton agreed to block imports of Canada's subsidized durum wheat (Lee and Nichols 1993). Additionally, the following day, only one day before the vote,

> The White House picked up three Democrats from textile states with a pledge to increase by $15 million the budget for Customs agents to enforce trade laws on textiles and apparel and an agreement to negotiate in the upcoming round of global trade talks for a 15-year phase-out in textile quotas rather than a 10-year phase-out. The three Democrats are Reps. John M. Spratt Jr. (S.C.), W. G. "Bill" Hefner (N.C.) and Nathan Deal (Ga.). (Devroy and Cooper 1993)

The eleven-hour debate on the floor of the House on November 17 involved numerous variations on a few arguments. Those against NAFTA argued that it would cost U.S. jobs; and where it did not, it would drive down salaries and dilute health and safety standards in a race to the bottom with Mexican industry. Secondarily, opponents argued that it would do nothing to raise the wages of Mexican workers so that they would better be able to purchase American products. Moreover, they argued that it would worsen pollution on the U.S.-Mexican border. Finally, there was concern, mostly among conservatives, that international governing bodies would undermine U.S. sovereignty. A few examples of those arguments follow. According to Butler Derrick (D-S.C.):

> Let me say that there is a lot of misinformation that has gone out on both sides of this argument, but one thing that is true as I stand here this morning and speak to the Members is the fact that if we pass NAFTA, Americans are going to lose

jobs. The Members should not take my word for it. The *Wall Street Journal* did a survey in which some 500 executives throughout this country were asked what they would do if NAFTA passed; 55 percent of them responded that if NAFTA passed, they would give serious consideration to moving part of their operations to Mexico. (U.S. Congress, *Cong. Record*, Nov. 17, 1993, daily ed., H9876)

The sovereignty argument was made by, among others, Gerald Solomon (R-N.Y.). Referring to such bodies as NADBank and the Border Environment Cooperation Commission, both of which would be established by NAFTA, he said:

Take the time to read this pact. These unelected, unaccountable tribunals will effectively usurp the legitimate authority of this U.S. Congress. They will usurp and abrogate States' rights. Members' own State laws dealing with the environment and labor. And they will override our own U.S. Federal Court System. (U.S. Congress, *Cong. Record*, Nov. 17, 1993, daily ed., H9877)

With respect to pollution on the Mexican border from the *maquiladoras*, Bob Filner (D-Calif.) said, "Today – and every day – 50 million gallons of raw sewage flow through my district from Tijuana. With NAFTA, we see that getting twice as bad" (U.S. Congress, *Cong. Record*, Nov. 17, 1993, daily ed., H9966).

Arguments for NAFTA were phrased in terms of the general interest. Those arguments consisted of denials that the dire predictions would materialize and assertions that NAFTA was necessary to keep the U.S. competitive in the new world economy. For example, Dan Rostenkowski (D-Ill.), who as chairman of the Ways and Means Committee introduced H.R. 3450, argued,

I fear that both sides have been guilty of grossly overstating the impact it will have in the days and weeks ahead. We will not experience a hemispheric boom or burst in January because we approve this agreement in November. Nor will we see a burst of job gains – or job losses – in the first quarter of next year because we approved NAFTA in the last quarter of this year. Today's jobless will not suddenly find work because there's a NAFTA. And those workers whose jobs are in jeopardy today will not be any safer if NAFTA fails. (U.S. Congress, *Cong. Record*, Nov. 17, 1993, daily ed., H9875)

More generally, David Levy (D-N.Y.) argued that NAFTA was essential to American economic leadership:

Mr. Chairman, outside this Chamber, the anti-NAFTA forces are hearing this debate and they are in an absolute panic. And, as the hours go by, they are becoming more and more creative. Earlier, they tried telling us that NAFTA causes cancer. That was disproved and now – on my way over here – I was lobbied against

NAFTA on the ground that – get this – NAFTA's passage will lead to the drainage of all the water from the Great Lakes. I am still working on that one. Let us stop the nonsense – the scare tactics and the misinformation.

It all boils down to these questions: Does the United States want to take part in the new world financial order or retreat from it? Do we want to unite with our hemispheric partners to compete with Japan and Germany or maintain barriers between this country and our most obvious trading partners? The United States has traditionally been a world leader in the area of international trade. By defeating NAFTA we will be signaling to the world that we can no longer compete, that we support protectionism instead of free trade. We will be telling our neighbors "Look elsewhere, not to us, for an industrial power from which to purchase goods and services free of tariffs that inflate prices artificially." (U.S. Congress, *Cong. Record*, Nov. 17, 1993, daily ed., H9996)

Despite the general-interest justifications for NAFTA, the president's vote-buying campaign did not go unremarked. Numerous NAFTA opponents objected to it. An example is this statement by Jim Bunning (R-Ky.):

We just don't know the costs of all the promises that are being made in the back rooms at the White House and on Capitol Hill. The American people should be outraged at the way this treaty has been bought – vote by vote – with wheeling and dealing that would make a rug merchant blush. If we tried this kind of vote buying in Kentucky, there would be a grand jury looking into it. In fact, we do try it in Kentucky and there is a grand jury looking into it. (U.S. Congress, *Cong. Record*, Nov. 17, 1993, daily ed., H10016)

In the end, the strategy that outraged NAFTA opponents appeared to have been successful. The implementing legislation passed on a vote of 234 to 200 on the evening of November 17. Fewer than half of the Democrats, 102 of 258, voted in favor of the pact, while a majority of Republicans, 132 of 175, did so. Three days later, the Senate quietly passed the legislation on a filibuster-proof vote of 61 to 38.

Chapter 2 described the incentive for members to conceal their voting intentions once they learn that policy coalition leaders are buying votes. Those strategic incentives made a big impression on members, particularly more junior ones:

Those dewy-eyed freshmen who raised their right hands, swore to uphold and defend the Constitution and joined the Congress of the United States last January now have learned one basic fact of congressional life: If you came to Congress with anything less than the loftiest of motives, on any close issue it doesn't pay to make up your mind early. Or, if the issue seems so clear you can't help making up your mind early, you don't tell anyone. It pays to be counted as an "undecided." (Pike 1993)

The day after the vote, Louise M. Slaughter (D-N.Y.), a NAFTA opponent, said, "'I can't tell you how many people I've talked to who have said, 'Now I know the game. You don't commit on your vote until you see what you can get for it.' I think it's going to be harder to pass health care. . . . Buying votes every time we put something up here is not a good idea in my opinion." Indeed, according to the same newspaper account that quoted Slaughter,

> some pro-NAFTA lawmakers were wishing they had held out for some pork cutlets of their own. Rep. Dana Rohrabacher (R-Calif.), a NAFTA supporter, spotted [Treasury Secretary] Bentsen eating a hot Reuben sandwich in the House members' dining room along with Richardson. "Mr. Secretary, Bill has promised me I'd get that bridge between L.A. and Catalina," Rohrabacher joked. "No problem," Bentsen said, playing along. (Merida and Kenworthy 1993)

As noted in Chapter 2, once a leader reveals a willingness to buy votes, members have every incentive to conceal their true preferences in order to extract a distributive benefit on each subsequent bill; the leader thus faces the need to give out an ever-increasing number of benefits. Unsurprisingly, observers of the NAFTA campaign concluded that the strategy of vote buying may have had lasting effects on Clinton's legislative strategies. A journalist commented:

> [I]f there's one thing congressional Democrats have learned, it's that Clinton rewards disloyalty. During the congressional battles over Clinton's first economic package and NAFTA, Democrats discovered that if they held out, a very conciliatory president eventually would be on the other end of the line. (Kosova 1994)

Among the losers, there was considerable bitterness about the way they lost. An official of the AFL-CIO who lobbied against the pact lamented their defeat in an interview: "This issue was framed better from our perspective than it ever will be again – evil polluters, job loss – and we still lost. That's what discourages me the most." One of his colleagues, who was also active in the anti-NAFTA campaign, explained Clinton's successful lobbying campaign succinctly: "He did it the old-fashioned way. He bought it."

The following section tests systematically the hypothesis, stated by many observers as fact, that Clinton bought his narrow, last-minute victory on NAFTA with the distributive benefits that his administration and his congressional allies offered members of the House. It also examines the impact of his deal making on Democrats and Republicans separately. I noted in previous chapters that vote buying was mainly a technique of the majority party, as they have better access to such benefits through their control of the legislative body and its committees. As this case study shows, the minority party was able to play this game as well, working in concert with the president to use his access to such benefits to create a majority coalition, giving distributive benefits to members of both parties.

THE IMPACT OF DISTRICT BENEFITS ON VOTING FOR NAFTA

The descriptions given by the press and my own interview subjects of the process leading to the House vote on NAFTA leave little room for doubt that President Clinton attempted to trade benefits to various members' districts for their support for NAFTA. Moreover, those who participated in the process attributed the support of late-deciding members to deals that many of them made with the president. However, the question is whether those members would probably have voted for NAFTA in any case and merely behaved strategically by withholding their support until they received a deal. Clinton's previous deals on issues such as his economic package, advertised for all to see on national television by beneficiaries such as Senator Bob Kerrey (D-Neb.), set the stage for members to hold out and try to extract a particularized benefit for their votes on NAFTA. By demonstrating his willingness to buy votes so publicly in the past, Clinton set up the expectation that he would do so on any policy that mattered to him.

Thus, the question is whether the deals Clinton made with members actually influenced their votes or whether they were already inclined to vote for or against NAFTA by other factors. To put it in terms of the model to be estimated here, did those who received a benefit behave differently from similarly situated members who did not?[3]

The key variable consists of the district benefits given by the Clinton administration to members of the House in return for their votes. The data on benefits were provided by the public interest group Public Citizen, which organized the Citizens Trade Watch coalition that helped to lead the campaign against NAFTA. They compiled the data from press

[3] Other scholars have modeled the NAFTA vote, mostly in terms of the usual variables that affect roll call voting, with a focus on district characteristics, which they found to have an impact on members' voting (Kahane 1996 Wink, Livingston, and Garand 1996; Box-Steffensmeier, Arnold, and Zorn 1997). These studies do not add the distributive benefits given by the president. Another study adds to the usual variables in roll call models the impact of presidential contact with members (which includes more than specific trades) on their NAFTA votes, finding a significant impact for the contact variable (Palazzolo and Swinford 1994).

reports collected by their local coalition members and grass-roots activists nationwide. In an effort to embarrass the deal-making members into opposing NAFTA, Public Citizen published the data shortly before the NAFTA vote ("NAFTA's Bizarre Bazaar"; "Public Citizen Launches"). While it is possible that some bargains went undetected, their total of benefits to seventy-six House members far exceeds estimates from some Hill staffers that only about thirty people made deals with the White House. Thus, the data are likely to be as complete as is feasible, given that some bargains might have been secret. However, a note about the definition of a district benefit is in order. I count something as a benefit if it was promised to the member, as promises clearly were the currency used; fulfillment of those promises often was to be carried out well into the future. Some would not be executed at all unless Mexico engaged in damaging trading practices. For example, Florida tomato and pepper growers were promised that imports of those commodities would be monitored by the International Trade Commission, so that if Mexico suddenly flooded the U.S. market, duties or quotas could be reimposed quickly.

The examples of district benefits cited in this chapter may raise a question as to whether these benefits are truly distributive. Many of them clearly are different from the traditional pork barrel project, which normally involves building something in the district. Nevertheless, most of them satisfy the components of the definition of distributive benefits as laid out in Chapter 1: They are disaggregable benefits for interests within members' districts; their costs are spread throughout the country; and one benefit can be eliminated without affecting other members' benefits. Thus, although most of them are not projects, they are nevertheless distributive benefits for identifiable interests within members' districts. Moreover, those interests, such as the Florida tomato and pepper growers cited above, are politically important to the legislators who represent them; hence the advantage to members of favoring them with targeted government benefits.

Table 5.1 presents a first look at the data. If these results could be taken as a definitive indication of cause and effect, one could say without question that receipt of a district benefit influenced members' votes. Only about 16 percent of the members who received one (twelve out of seventy-six benefits recipients) voted against NAFTA, while nearly 53 percent of those who did not receive one did so. Moreover, there is reason to speculate that some of those who received benefits but voted no might have supported NAFTA had their votes been critical. The day

TABLE 5.1 *NAFTA Vote by Receipt of a Benefit*

Vote on NAFTA	Members did not receive benefit	Members received benefit
Yes	47.5	84.2
No	52.5	15.8
Total	100.0	100.0

Note: Numbers in cells are the percentages of members voting for or against NAFTA. Chi-square $p \leq .001$.

before the vote one newspaper indicated that White House sources had acknowledged that they had obtained enough private promises of support to win and were currently making decisions about which members would be released from their promises to support NAFTA (Lee and Nichols 1993), presumably on the basis of those members' electoral needs. Therefore, some representatives who appear to have reneged may secretly have been excused at the last minute from their obligations. The "benefit" variable in Table 5.1 is dichotomous. That is, it indicates whether a member received one or more deals from the administration or nothing at all. It is worth noting, however, that the data document a total of 186 district benefits to the seventy-six members who received them. Most members (forty-five) received only one deal from the White House, but four members received six, the maximum number to any member. Moreover, nineteen, including members of the Florida delegation, received at least five benefits as a result of the bargains over sugar, fruits, and vegetables. Finally, five members received two benefits each and four members received three benefits each. A model of the allocation of benefits (i.e., which members were most likely to receive them) showed no clear pattern; the only significant variable was the percentage of union members in a member's district, and that was negatively related to receipt of a benefit. That is, the more union members in a district, the less likely the representative was to receive a benefit. That finding points again to vociferous union opposition to NAFTA and indicates that many members in highly unionized districts could not afford to sell their votes for NAFTA at any price. The results for the allocation model appear in the Appendix to this chapter.

To draw more accurate inferences about the impact of benefits given by the president on the NAFTA vote, I estimated a multivariate logit model. The dependent variable is the vote taken on NAFTA on November 17; it is a dummy variable which takes a value of 1 if the member voted for the

NAFTA legislation and 0 if the member voted no. The model and variable descriptions follow:

Member's vote = fn (District Benefit, Democrat, COPE Score, Business PAC Contributions, Labor PAC Contributions, Percent Union, Median Income, Percent Farm, Mexican Border)

District Benefit: This is a dichotomous variable that takes a value of 1 if the member received one or more particularized benefits from the White House and a value of 0 otherwise. It is expected that members who received such benefits were more likely to vote for NAFTA than those who did not.

Democrat: This is a dichotomous variable that takes a value of 1 for Democrats and 0 for Republicans. According to interviewees, some Democrats were inclined to support NAFTA by their free-trade views, and others wanted to support the first Democratic president in twelve years on an issue on which he had publicly staked his prestige. However, labor's adamant opposition to NAFTA produced cross-pressures for many Democrats and seemed more than anything else to account for the split in the leadership. Republicans were also split internally. On one hand, there were reasons for them to support the pact: It had been negotiated by a Republican president and was changed only at the margins by his Democratic successor; moreover, Republicans are generally committed to a free-trade position. On the other hand, some farm state Republicans were concerned about the impact of NAFTA on their constituents, and others, generally more conservative Republicans, were worried that the pact might damage U.S. sovereignty. Given this background, the expectation is that party is not significantly related to support for NAFTA.

COPE Score: Because Democrats in particular were cross-pressured on this vote and the jobs issue was central to the debate, it is necessary to include in the model a measure of members' prolabor voting predispositions. Here I include members' 1993 COPE (Committee on Political Education) score, the AFL-CIO's rating of members' voting on issues of interest to the union. In 1993, COPE scores for House members were based on members' votes on twelve issues, of which NAFTA, predictably, was one. It thus was necessary to purge members' COPE scores of this vote, recalculating the scores on the basis of eleven votes. It is expected that the higher a member's COPE score, the lower the probability that he or she voted for NAFTA.

Business PAC and Labor PAC Contributions: Inclusion of variables for campaign contributions takes account of two possible forces: first, the possibility that members were influenced by their contributors, repaying prior contributions with votes. During the fight over NAFTA, a large business coalition conducted a massive pro-NAFTA campaign; likewise, big labor waged a vigorous fight against the pact. The possible effects of those efforts are taken into account by contribution variables for those two coalitions, using data from the Federal Election Commission on contributions to candidates for the House during the election cycle preceding the vote on NAFTA (1991–1992). The variable, Business PAC Contributions, consists of the summed contributions in thousands of dollars received by a member from business, trade, association, and health PACs.[4] The Labor PAC Contributions variable consists of the total contributions given to a member by labor unions. Business contributions are expected to be positively related to a vote for NAFTA, and labor contributions are expected to be negatively related to the member's vote. Both variables are measured in thousands of dollars.

The remainder of the variables in the model are connected to members' districts. These variables measure characteristics of members' constituencies that could reasonably be expected to influence their decisions on NAFTA. They are as follows.

Percent Union: The anti-NAFTA campaign appealed to the fears of union members that their jobs would literally go south as a result of the passage of the pact, a fear fanned by labor unions at both the national and local levels. Thus, it is necessary to capture the effect of unionization in members' districts on their votes. This variable consists of the percentage of private sector workers who belonged to a union in a member's district in 1991–1992.[5] Two other variables, COPE Score and Labor PAC

4 The last three groups, generally classified as business PACs, are lumped into one category by the Federal Election Commission.

5 The data on percent union were created and described by Box-Steffensmeier et al. 1997. The variable was obtained from the Interuniversity Consortium for Political and Social Research, study no. 1126. Additional assistance was kindly provided by two of the authors of that study, Janet Box-Steffensmeier and Christopher Zorn.

Contributions, also incorporate some of the impact of the labor campaign; however, both of those reflect pressures that go beyond the district, such as the member's ideology, party pressures, and contributions from national unions. Percent Union, on the other hand, captures effects that are specific to members' districts, in particular, the degree of pressure from local union members. This variable is expected to be negatively associated with a vote for NAFTA.

Median Income: Many who felt that their livelihoods were threatened probably were not union members, especially given the well-known decline in the percentage of the work force that is unionized. More generally, constituents of lower socioeconomic status would probably be fearful about a further worsening of their economic condition as a result of NAFTA. Conversely, higher income constituents, more secure about their own status, more confident of the benefits of the global economy, and less tied to labor unions and their world-view, would be more likely to exert pro-NAFTA pressure. Hence, the median family income (in thousands of dollars) in the district is expected to be positively associated with a vote for NAFTA.

Percent Farm: Many of the worries about NAFTA concerned its impact on farmers. Thus, a variable was included to account for the effect of the district farm population on the NAFTA vote. This variable is simply the percentage of people in the district who live on farms, taken from 1990 Census data. The expected impact of this variable is uncertain. If Clinton satisfied all of the farm groups that were concerned about NAFTA, something that cannot be known with certainty, a positive relationship could be expected. If he satisfied only a minority, this variable would be negatively related. If he satisfied some and not others, there might be no relationship, as the effects would cancel each other out.

Mexican Border: The major concerns about NAFTA related to Mexico. In particular, residents of states along the U.S.-Mexican border expected that they would be affected by the passage of the agreement. Although that well-known Texan Ross Perot vociferously opposed NAFTA, members from states on the Mexican border, such as Representative Kika de la Garza, chairman of the House Agriculture Committee, had reason strongly to favor NAFTA because of its expected stimulus to cross-border trade. A dummy variable was included for region, with states along the U.S.-Mexican border expected especially to favor NAFTA for

TABLE 5.2 *Deals and Voting on NAFTA*

Explanatory variables	Logit coefficient	Standard error
District Benefit	1.742[a]	0.383
Democrat	0.247	0.544
COPE Score	−0.013[c]	0.007
Business PAC	0.003[a]	0.001
Labor PAC	−0.012[a]	0.003
Percent Union	−0.050[b]	0.024
Percent Farm	0.319	0.248
Median Income	0.049[a]	0.017
Mexican Border	0.592[c]	0.308
Constant	−0.496	0.696
Model chi square	157.57	
Pseudo R^2	0.263	
Cases correctly classified (%)	77.88	
Percentage reduction of error	55.00	

[a] $p \leq .01$.
[b] $p \leq .05$.
[c] $p \leq .10$.
Note: The model chi-square statistic tests the hypothesis that all coefficients in the equation equal 0. Significance for this statistic allows the rejection of that hypothesis. The percentage reduction of error statistic (ROE) indicates the extent to which the model's predictions improve on predicting that each will fall into the modal category of the dependent variable. %ROE = 100 × (% correctly classified − % in modal category)/(100% − % in modal category).

its positive impact on cross-border trade. Those states are Texas, New Mexico, Arizona, and California.

The results of the logit analysis are presented in Table 5.2. As the interviews and press coverage indicate, even accounting for the effects of all of the additional variables, it is the case that representatives who received a district benefit from the president were more likely to vote for NAFTA.

The dependent variable here is dichotomous; an alternate measure of district benefits is the *number* of benefits members received from the White House. The model was also estimated using that variable. Those results are not reproduced here, but they were the same as those in Table 5.2 for all but the benefit variable. Unlike the dichotomous benefit variable, the number of benefits received did not have a significant impact on members' support for NAFTA. At first glance, this is an odd result: If getting one or more benefits influenced members' votes, should that same result not emerge when we examine the impact of the actual number of benefits received? That is, we would expect to see at least as many of those who received five concessions supporting NAFTA as those who received only one, if not an increasing effect with an increasing number of benefits. However, a closer look at the data shines an interesting light on the limits of persuasion. Most members received only one benefit in return for their vote, although nine received two or three benefits. However, as the interviews with negotiators from the office of the U.S. Trade Representative indicated, the entire Florida House delegation was the target of five or six benefits in an effort to get the approval of the key agricultural commodity groups, which presumably then would give members the green light to vote for NAFTA. Yet ten of the twenty-three House members from Florida voted against the pact anyway. In fact, they were almost the only members who received benefits who did vote against NAFTA; only two other representatives did so. In the end, the administration realized that it would still not get the entire delegation's votes, so it imposed the requirement that half of the delegation vote for NAFTA, and only just over that proportion did so. Thus, the key to winning support seemed to be for the administration to give in not to multiple requests, but rather to the right requests, tailoring them to the concerns of individual representatives rather than whole delegations, some of whose members' votes could never be won.

Most other variables also had the expected effects. The party variable was not significant, as expected, reflecting the split in both parties. However, members' connections to labor unions, which worked so hard at both the national and local levels to defeat NAFTA, clearly had an impact on their votes. As indicated by the significant, negative effect of members' COPE scores, the more prolabor members' voting overall records were, the less likely they were to vote for NAFTA.[6] Consistent with the results for COPE scores, PAC contributions from labor unions are significantly and negatively related to a vote for NAFTA. On the other hand, business-oriented PAC contributions are positively related to the vote. Whatever the mechanism by which agreement between members and their contributors

[6] However, the COPE score and the dummy variable for party are correlated at .88; therefore, I estimated the model with alternative specifications, omitting, in turn, party and COPE score. The results were essentially the same for each variable. In the end, I included party in the final model because of its importance in a fully specified roll call model and its minimal impact on the coefficients and standard errors of the other variables despite its high collinearity with COPE score.

was achieved, on this bill, House members tended to vote with their contributors' positions.

In addition, the district-based measure of members' responsiveness to labor, the percentage of constituents belonging to labor unions, shows yet another source of labor's influence on support for NAFTA. The higher the percentage of members' constituents belonging to unions, the less likely they were to support NAFTA. On the other hand, the percentage of the district involved in farming did not have an impact on how members voted. That may be because the many benefits given to agricultural districts allayed farmers' concerns about the impact of NAFTA on their livelihoods. However, the regional variable did have an impact: Members from the four states bordering Mexico were significantly more likely than members from other regions to support NAFTA.

For a look at the substantive impact of district benefits on Democrats and Republicans, I used the coefficients estimated for the equations reported in Table 5.2 to calculate the probability that a Republican or a Democrat would vote for NAFTA, first without, and then with a benefit. The method is described in more detail in Chapter 4, note 6. Table 5.3 displays the results. The calculations involve two sets of conditions. For the first row in the table, labeled NAFTA (a), I calculated probabilities of voting for NAFTA for the mean member of the House by party: for members with the mean percentage of farming in their districts, the mean PAC contributions, and so on. The only exception was for COPE scores;

TABLE 5.3 *Probability That a Member Supported Committee Leaders by Receipt of a Benefit*

Vote	Democrat without a project	Democrat with a project	Change in probability	Republican without a project	Republican with a project	Change in probability
NAFTA(a)	.373	.772	.399	.532	.867	.335
NAFTA(b)	.275	.684	.409	.688	.927	.239

Note: For NAFTA(a): Probabilities are calculated for the typical member, except for COPE score: Members received the mean contribution from labor union and business PACs; their districts were at the mean income, mean percent union, and mean percent in farming; they were not from Mexican border states. They were at the mean COPE score for Democrats (90.77) or Republicans (21.83). For NAFTA(b): Probabilities are calculated for the typical Republican or Democrat: Members are set at the mean for their party for labor PAC contributions, district income, and COPE scores. They were set at the overall mean for corporate PAC contributions, mean percent in farming, and mean percent union, as there was no significant difference between the parties on the latter variables.

there I used the mean COPE score for the member's party (the mean Republican score was 21.83; the mean Democratic score was 90.77). However, Republican and Democratic districts differed significantly on two other explanatory variables: income and labor PAC contributions. Thus, for the second row, NAFTA (b), I calculated the probabilities using each party's mean COPE score, as before, and mean district income and labor PAC contributions for each party. Corporate PAC contributions did not differ significantly between the two parties for the 1991–1992 election cycle; that variable and Percent Farm were set to their means. For all calculations, members were assumed not to be from a state on the Mexican border.

Under both sets of assumptions, getting a benefit from the president had a substantial impact on members of both parties. However, the votes of Democrats were more likely to be changed; that was true under both sets of conditions. For the typical Democrat, making a deal with the president more than doubled the probability that he or she would vote for NAFTA, switching them from no votes to yes votes. This table shows that the typical Republican under either set of conditions was already inclined to vote for NAFTA, yet even Republicans showed substantially increased probabilities of supporting it with a project. In this case, the president and his congressional allies used projects to firm up support for his position in the both the majority and minority parties, both of which were split on this issue.

CONCLUSIONS

Many members of the House, Democrats and Republicans alike, were under strong pressure from constituency interests to oppose a trade pact that, some argued, would lower the American standard of living and damage the environment. So why did some of them trade their votes, despite that opposition? In some cases, the answer is obvious. The deals Clinton made altered the implementation of the policy in certain, often minor, specifics that would protect district interests, particularly in agriculture. Accepting a deal in return for supporting NAFTA allowed those members to take a position that many wanted to take either as a result of their commitment to free trade or out of a sense of loyalty to their own party's president. The district benefit served as political cover, providing a justification for supporting the pact. One House staff member who worked on NAFTA confirmed this interpretation. Comparing House members' public handling of their NAFTA deals with highway demonstration projects, he noted that while they announced highway projects at home, they often publicized their NAFTA deals in press conferences with the national media in attendance. The national approach was designed, he said, to allow members to justify their votes not only to their constituents but, in the Democrats' case, to the national labor unions that had vowed to defeat Democrats who voted for NAFTA.

Table 5.1 shows that the great majority of House members who received a special benefit from the administration then supported it on NAFTA, a result that withstands multivariate analysis. Although vote buying is popularly associated with PAC contributions, here the evidence is far more direct for vote buying with district benefits. Certainly, PAC contributions had a significant effect on the vote. However, PAC contributions are often associated with lobbying effort and may to some extent be a proxy for them (Herndon 1982; Langbein 1986; Wright 1990). In this case, the members who received contributions from business or labor interests were probably also lobbied intensively by those same interests, and it is possible that the apparent effect of contributions is really an effect of lobbying.

However, that is not likely to be true for members' responses to the benefits offered by the administration in return for voting for NAFTA. If lobbying alone had been sufficient to change members' minds, the administration would not still have been short of commitments as little as two weeks before the vote, and it would not have had to engage in frantic last-minute deal making with members it had already lobbied. Therefore, the special deals themselves, while no doubt given to those whom the administration lobbied, evidently influenced recipients' votes, especially on the Democratic side of the aisle.

In the weeks following the vote, opinion writers had a field day condemning the wheeling and dealing that led to the passage of NAFTA. However, presidential historian Richard Neustadt, in his op-ed piece for Long Island *Newsday*, expressed surprise that anyone was shocked at the bargaining that won the last few votes on NAFTA:

> trading of that sort has characterized the fight for almost every major, controversial measure of domestic legislation in the last half century . . . the teasing out of bare majorities by promises to marginal members of Congress of either party . . . is as traditional as apple pie. Why then does it surprise and even shock contemporary journalists? Worse, from my standpoint, they now are mostly college graduates. So what fantasies have we in colleges been teaching them? Or is it just that they were inattentive, sleeping through poli. sci.?

Either way, it's not something to make academics proud. Or editors. (Neustadt 1993)

In this chapter and the previous one, we have seen that efforts at vote buying with distributive benefits were successful in three major instances in the House of Representatives. On the highway bills, the provisions for which votes were bought encompassed both general interest and more particularized measures. The NAFTA battle was a case of a general interest bill against more particular interests (although at least one of the opposing interests, concerning the environment, fits the definition in Chapter 1 of the general interest.) In this case, district benefits appear to have been essential to gaining House approval of this general interest bill. Moreover, benefits had the most effect on the votes of Democrats, the party with the strongest anti-NAFTA coalition among its core supporters.

We have examined this vote-buying technique in the hands of committee leaders and the president; it worked for all of them. On the two highway reauthorization bills and NAFTA, policy coalition leaders evidently succeeded in changing members' voting intentions by giving them distributive benefits for their districts. Those benefits affect the votes of members of the party that initially was least likely to vote as the policy coalition leaders wished.

Thus far, we have considered vote buying with distributive benefits exclusively in the House of Representatives during the era when Democrats held the majority. That raises two additional questions. First, does vote buying with distributive benefits work in the Senate as well as the House? Senate staffers who were interviewed about the highway bills asserted that the Senate was not as interested in pork as the House because for most senators, such benefits would help a far smaller proportion of their constituents; therefore, pork barrel projects are not a practical way to provide benefits for their constituents. Notwithstanding that argument, senators did add their own highway projects to both highway bills in the conference committees, suggesting that local benefits are not unattractive to them. If that is true, pork barrel benefits might serve as a source of leverage for policy coalition leaders in the Senate as well.

Second, do Republicans use this technique as enthusiastically and effectively as Democrats? Participants in the 1993 NAFTA battle indicated that House Republicans helped with the vote-buying effort. Yet there was a good deal of anti-pork rhetoric from Republicans during the 1994 election campaigns. Thus, there is reason to ask whether they stuck to their principles once they gained the majority in Congress in 1995 or whether they operated like Democrats, using distributive benefits to get their way on broad-based legislation. Chapter 6 addresses both of those questions through an examination of earmarking by the Senate Appropriations Committee during years of both Democratic and Republican control.

APPENDIX

A logit model of a member's receipt of a deal from those seeking support for NAFTA was estimated using both member and district characteristics. The dependent variable is the member's receipt of a deal from the administration. The model is as follows:

District Benefit = fn (Democrat, COPE Score, Median Income, Percent Union, Percent Farm, Mexican Border, Ways and Means, Trade Subcommittee, Seniority, Vote 92)

Most of the variables are described in the section of this chapter that reports the results of the model of the NAFTA vote. There are a few additional variables, however.

Ways and Means: a dummy variable that takes the value of 1 if the member served on the Ways and Means Committee, which had jurisdiction over NAFTA.

Trade Subcommittee: a dummy variable that takes the value of 1 if the member served on the Ways and Means Committee's Subcommittee on Trade.

Seniority: the number of years that the member had served as of 1993, the year of the vote.

These three variables were included to test for the possibilities that members of the committee and subcommittee and more senior members used their positions to try to extract extra benefits for themselves or that their support was particularly valuable for the signals it would send to other members.

Vote92: The member's percentage of the vote in the 1992 election. This variable tests the hypothesis that members who won less comfortably were more likely to request a district benefit, which might serve as an

TABLE 5.4 *The Allocation of District Benefits for NAFTA*

Explanatory variables	Logit coefficient	Standard error
Democrat	0.284	0.620
COPE Score	−0.002	0.007
Median Income	−0.000	0.000
Percent Union	−20.589[a]	3.326
Percent Farm	−0.447	0.295
Mexican Border	−0.002	0.320
Ways and Means Committee	0.584	0.569
Trade Subcommittee	−0.303	0.884
Seniority	−0.018	0.018
Vote 92	0.011	0.013
Constant	−0.034	1.137
Model chi square	62.97[a]	
Pseudo R^2	0.156	
Cases correctly classified (%)	83.22	
Percentage reduction of error	3.95	

[a] $p \leq .01$.

extra measure of protection in the 1994 election, in return for their votes.

The results are presented in Table 5.4. The only significant variable is the percentage of the district's private sector employees who belonged to unions. The more union members were in a representative's district, the less likely that member was to receive a deal designed to win his or her vote for NAFTA. Members in more highly unionized districts were probably considered lost causes, as they could not use district benefits to compensate their constituents for a vote that might cost significant numbers of them their jobs. The deal would not be worth the cost for such members. Additionally, given that party is not significant, these findings support accounts of the deal making that stress the bipartisan nature of the effort.

6

Pork Barreling in the Senate: Do Both Parties Do It?

Previous chapters have focused on vote buying in the House of Representatives on three bills between 1986 and 1993, all years of Democratic control. In all of those cases, policy coalition leaders were able to win House members' votes for the leaders' policy preferences by giving out distributive benefits. In this chapter, we shift the focus to the Senate, examining distributive politics first under a Democratic majority, then under Republican control. This allows us to address the two questions posed at the end of Chapter 5: First, do policy coalition leaders in the Senate, like those in the House, use pork barrel benefits to buy votes for general interest legislation? If so, are Republicans as inclined as Democrats to use pork barrel projects as a coalition-building technique?

There is some reason to doubt that either would be the case. With respect to partisan differences, the Democrats, as the party of government, have fewer doubts than Republicans about the legitimacy of using federal resources to solve problems, whether that solution comes from national policy or distributive benefits to their districts. As a consequence, Democrats are more likely to see vote buying with pork barrel projects as a fairly benign practice. On the other hand, Republicans, with their ideological commitment to economy in government and the free market as the best way to sort out problems, could be expected to take a different approach. Although fiscal conservatives of both parties often have taken aim at the pork barrel as a prime target for budget savings, Republican rhetoric in particular has been resolutely hostile to such spending. Most notably, the House Republicans' 1994 campaign manifesto, the "Contract with America," pledged that if they won control of the House, they would pass a balanced budget and tax limitation amendment to the Constitution (the "Fiscal Responsibility Act"). One clear commitment in that pledge was the elimination of pork. Although Senate candidates did not campaign on a similar common platform, voter anger at "politics as usual" that year suggests that Republican senators were subject to the same voter expectations as House members.

Yet the long term, the temptations of the pork barrel seem irresistible. It is a commonplace of popular political lore that pork helps to win elections, and, as noted previously, academic research to a significant extent backs up that belief, at least for House members. How could Republicans, particularly those at risk electorally, remain pure when they might well pay a price for withholding from their constituents benefits traditionally seen as part and parcel of the representational package? Indeed, those Republican challengers who initially campaigned against pork barreling might later feel that they had been a bit rash in condemning a practice that could help them to secure their seats into the future. But by then they could be in a bind. While some constituents might be delighted to see benefits coming home from Washington, others could react against the apparent hypocrisy of a representative who provided the benefits after so recently railing against them. In fact, there is evidence that although House Democrats obtained more distributive benefits in the 1980s, Republicans received substantial amounts as well, which suggests that they considered such benefits politically useful. However, there also is evidence that for Republicans, pork is less valuable: House Democrats profited from it at the polls, while Republicans enjoyed no significant benefit (Alvarez and Saving 1997), which should reduce Republicans' incentives to violate their party's ideological opposition to pork. Therefore, it is worth investigating whether Republicans, following their ascension to the majority in both houses of Congress, were as willing as Democrats to distribute projects, especially as a way of buying votes for important legislation.

Second, we must ask whether pork barrel benefits are as attractive to senators as they are to House members. There is some reason to think that they are not. Interviews conducted with House and Senate staffers for federal highway legislation, discussed in Chapter 3, indicated that senators initially resisted demonstration projects in highway reauthorization bills. They did so in part because for most senators, an individual project would benefit a smaller portion of their much larger constituencies. To satisfy some constituents and not others might not give a senator a net gain if some were alienated by the perception that another part of the state was more favored. Moreover, also because their constituencies normally are so much larger than those of House members, senators might be faced with unmanageable demands once they began to provide such benefits. According to one staff member, senators were less focused on getting highway demonstration projects than on gaining highway spending formulas that were most advantageous for their states, a much more efficient way to ensure that their constituents would receive broadly distributed federal benefits. As one staffer said, "formulas are the Senate's pork."

However, even with formula-based highway bills, senators brought to the conference committee a list of "priority projects." Although their projects received less generous federal funding than the House's demonstration projects, they were, nevertheless, the Senate's own version of distributive benefits. Additionally, despite the fact that most states are larger than one congressional district, there clearly is great variation in state population; as Lee and Oppenheimer argue, the closer in size a state's population is to that of a House district, the greater are the incentives for its senators to seek distributive benefits (1999, p. 126). Finally, as the section that follows shows, the Senate has become notorious in some circles over the past two decades for earmarking funds for academic institutions, another form of pork barrel benefits. Therefore, there is evidence that the Senate is not impervious to the lure of pork barrel benefits. Given that, the remaining question is whether such benefits serve as currency that facilitates the passage of general interest legislation in the Senate as it does in the House.

This chapter addresses both questions; that is, do policy coalition leaders in Republican-controlled congresses exchange pork for support, and does the Senate do so as well as the House? The focus here is on distributive benefits in Senate appropriations bills. Outsiders call them pork barrel projects, but they are officially and slightly less pejoratively known as earmarks. An earmark consists of a detailed specification of how Congress intends for appropriated funds to be spent within an individual state, typically on a discrete distributive project. Earmarks may be contained in the language of the bill itself, but they are most commonly found in the committee report that accompanies the bill. Two examples come from the Senate Appropriations Committee's FY 1996 recommendations for the Department of Agriculture and related agencies:

> The Committee makes available $1,000,000 for unanticipated costs necessary to complete the Rice Germplasm Laboratory in Stuttgart, AR;
>
> The Committee also has included $250,000, the same as the 1995 level, for continued support of agricultural development and resource conservation in the native Hawaiian communities serviced by the Molokai Agriculture Community Committee. (*Agriculture, Rural Development, Food and Drug Administration, and Related Agencies Appropriation Bill, 1996*, S. Rpt. 104–142, p. 65 and 29)

Apart from earmarks, appropriations bills can reasonably be considered general interest legislation, defined in Chapter 1 as broad-based measures that affect the whole nation or a large segment of it. The thirteen appropriations bills that Congress passes each year pay for large swaths of governmental operations, with the exceptions of the subcommittees on the District of Columbia and the legislative branch (neither of which is analyzed in this chapter). Naturally, many of the agencies and programs that they fund affect some areas of the country more than others. For example, the Interior appropriations bill most affects western states, which have more federally owned lands than the East. However, the impact of general interest legislation need not fall evenly on the whole country; it must simply be widespread and not exclusive to one state or group of people. Appropriations bills thus surely meet the test of general interest legislation, and we might expect the leaders who seek to pass these bills to use earmarks to help them, especially given the highly partisan nature of some of the issues that come to a vote during the debate of appropriations bills.

To compare the two parties' earmarking practices, this chapter examines appropriations bills passed in the last session in which the Senate was controlled by Democrats, the second session of the 103rd Congress (1994); the first session of Republican control in the 104th Congress after they won the majority in the 1994 election, when Republicans' ideological fervor was high; and the first session of the 106th Congress (1999), during which the Republicans were still in control, but perhaps more in touch with electoral realities.

The next section of this chapter examines the recent history of earmarking during both the Democratic and Republican eras; it provides a first cut, in narrative form, into the two parties' relative emphasis on pork barrel spending in appropriations bills in the Senate. It then describes the results of interviews with Senate Appropriations Committee staff and other close observers of the process. Then hypotheses are developed and tested in the final section, which reports the results of the statistical analysis of earmarks in appropriations bills in the three Senate sessions considered here.

EARMARKING IN APPROPRIATIONS BILLS

Recent History

Most of the attention to earmarking both in the press and in scholarship on the subject focuses on academic earmarks, which consist of funds directed to specific colleges and universities for research facilities and research and development projects. They arouse opposition for two reasons. First, like all such awards, they are seen by many as a drain on the federal budget, wasteful gifts given to constituents to increase legislators' chances of reelection. Second, these earmarks are opposed by many in the scientific community, as they are designed to circumvent the normal peer review process, which awards federal grant money strictly on the merits of the project and the qualifications of the researchers. From this perspective, earmarks weaken the scientific enterprise. An additional criticism is that too much of the money does not go to research at all; an official of the Department of Energy noted that in the FY 1987 legislation funding its operations, all of the earmarked projects were for construction, thus diverting to "bricks and mortar" money that otherwise would have been devoted to research (Norman 1986, 617).

Of course, there is an alternative view of academic earmarking. Its defenders charge that the peer-review process is unfairly biased toward a relatively few elite universities in a small number of states, while the rest of the nation's academic institutions are effectively shut out. In the House of Representatives, Manuel Lujan (R-N.M.) argued in 1986 that 51 percent of federal research funding went to thirty universities, and none of the top twenty recipients of such peer-reviewed funding was in the Southeast or the Southwest (Norman 1986, 617). The journal *Science*, a vociferous critic of earmarking, reported that in 1983 and 1984, fifteen universities had received earmarked funds totaling over $100 million (Holden 1985, 1183). As John Murtha (D-Penn.), past chair of the House Defense Appropriations subcommittee said, "A member knows better than anyone else what would go well in his district" (Schmitt 1994). And even George Brown (D-Calif.), a long-time crusader against such earmarking, conceded that without earmarks, referees of research grant applications would award all grants to a set of elite universities (Munson 1993, p. 195), a number of them in his own state of California.

Of course, other kinds of earmarking thrived at the same time that journalists focused on academic pork. In the Senate, Robert Byrd (D-W.Va.), chairman of the Appropriations Committee during the 103rd Congress and an ardent champion of all kinds of earmarking, made especially sure that West Virginia received far more than its proportionate share of federal funds. He campaigned for reelection on a promise to be a "billion dollar senator" for West Virginia by bringing that much federal money home within five years; he actually did so in two years (Munson 1993, p. 152). Although some of it was academic pork, much of it took other forms. Furthermore, an examination of almost any Appropriations Committee report would show that West Virginia was hardly the only state that benefited handsomely from the earmarking process.

However, the shift from Democratic to Republican control in the 104th Congress led to expectations that the amount of pork in all kinds of legislation would be reduced drastically. There were even indications in individual House races that the district benefits that had helped to secure so many seats for so long had begun to backfire, as constituents started, perhaps partly as a result of the Republican diatribe against pork, to see such benefits in a negative light. The rules did seem to change overnight. Just prior to the 1994 elections a glum staffer, contemplating the imminent defeat of her boss, a prominent House Democrat, speculated in an interview that for the first time his success at bringing home the bacon was hurting more than helping with constituents. Similarly, in a preelection analysis of the prospects of House Speaker Tom Foley's soon-to-be successful challenger, *Time* magazine observed that years of using his position to bring home the bacon might actually be damaging Foley:

> An unusual number of voters in eastern Washington State – and in the districts of other powerful Democrats across America – claim that they are looking beyond the local benefits of federal largesse and pondering what it's costing the country to have 435 Congressmen and 100 Senators each forcing the government to keep open another unnecessary hospital or sleepy agency office or subsidy program for well-to-do ranchers. (Tumulty 1994)

In at least one other case, an incumbent found himself disavowing a project that he probably requested and from which he doubtless had expected to benefit: *The Sunday Times* reported that an unnamed New Jersey representative agreed with his challenger that $1.4 billion appropriated for a flood control tunnel in his district was wasteful and unneeded (Neil 1994).

Some observers expected a change following the 1994 election. Gary Andres noted that academic earmarks declined precipitously during the Democratic 103rd Congress, but he attributed it to the first unified control of Congress and the presidency in twelve years. In the words of a congressional staffer, "'Letters from congressmen to the administration, phone calls, statements at hearings and other types of communications with the executive branch all can have the same effect as an earmark if the same party controls the White House and Congress'" (Andres 1995, p. 209). Nevertheless, Andres predicted that although directed spending would go up in the 104th Congress, pork barrel spending possibly would not, as Republicans used their power to force federal agencies to reorder their policy priorities rather than to earmark benefits for particular districts and states.

Reflecting that view, Ron Packard (R-Calif.), the new chair of the House Appropriations Committee's legislative branch subcommittee, predicted that the committee would be forced to turn over a new leaf:

> [U]ntil the GOP takeover, Packard helped "look after" funding for favored projects of other California House members. But today, Packard said, "the old boy network of appropriators is gone. . . . The role of the committee is no longer to look out for the pet projects of other members of Congress," he said. "Instead, the committee is cutting its own members' pet projects." While such fiscal restraint may run counter to the appropriators' habits, the panel has no choice. Before Packard and other subcommittee heads could be assured of their positions, they had to meet individually with [House Speaker Newt] Gingrich and sign letters promising to end pork-barrel spending. Gingrich, Packard suggested, is not to be trifled with in such matters. Any chairman violating the pledge to the speaker will lose his leadership post, Packard predicted. (Green 1995)

This speculation that the new speaker was determined to exercise strong discipline over the Appropriations Committee is confirmed by scholarly analysis (Aldrich and Rohde 2000).

In fact, the early news was that academic earmarks declined dramatically, by 50 percent, in the first Republican spending bills, those for fiscal year 1996 (Cordes and Gorman 1996). Similarly, the amount of money recommended for academic earmarks declined dramatically, from more than $529 million in 1994 to $328 million in 1995, in the Republicans' first fiscal year budget (Savage 1999, p. 3). However, an analysis by the antipork crusaders Citizens against Government Waste found much less dramatic reductions in earmarking overall when the analysis was not restricted to academic earmarking. Its "Pig Book" report on pork barrel spending for the first session of the 104th Congress reported that in seven of the eight appropriations bills that passed in 1995, pork barrel spending had declined by 11 percent; however, defense earmarks rose by 133 percent, canceling out much of the saving (Citizens against Government Waste 2000).

Within less than a year of the 1994 elections, articles began to appear in the mass media blaming the pork barrel habit for at least part of the Republicans' failure to curb government spending as much as they had promised (Wolf 1995). For example, "Such budget hawks as Georgia's Saxby Chambliss, Washington's George Nethercutt [Speaker Foley's successful challenger] and Florida's Mark Foley have fought a fierce rear-guard effort for their districts' farm subsidies" (Tumulty 1995). And as the 1996 elections approached, Republican resolve collapsed, as the same House leaders who had urged spending restraint now implored the Appropriations Committee to include earmarks for Republicans who might need them for reelection (Taylor 1996). Academic earmarks climbed steadily year after year; by 2000, the amount appropriated totaled more than $1 billion (Healy 2000). Overall, reports of growing numbers of earmarks for Republicans appeared in the media over the next four years, to the point that, perhaps predictably, conservative Republicans lost patience with their own party for squandering the newfound surplus on earmarks (Christensen 2000).

Of course, it is possible that the rise and fall of earmarks in appropriations legislation is due primarily to House action, given that appropriations bills traditionally originate there, and that the Senate, with a few legendary exceptions like Robert Byrd, adds little. The accounts described above do focus on the House; however, many of the figures are based on final appropriations bills, which reflect Senate preferences as well. There is considerable evidence that the Senate Appropriations Committee not only adds a great deal of its own pork to such bills, but does so in order to amass support for its bills on the Senate floor. But before considering the case for the argument that the Senate Appropriations Committee adds pork to buy votes for its bills, it is worthwhile briefly to describe how the appropriations process works, especially as it relates to pork barrel politics. The following section does that; the section after that describes impressionistic evidence that senators who receive earmarks are expected to support the leaders on the bills to which they are attached. In subsequent sections, I develop and systematically test hypotheses concerning the allocation of pork and its impact on roll call voting on appropriations bills in the Senate.

The Process

Within the appropriations committees in both houses of Congress, earmarks are distributed primarily by the powerful subcommittee chairs, commonly known as "cardinals" in recognition of their control over discretionary federal spending. Their power is structured by the modern budget process, particularly the 1974 Budget Act and, until FY 2003, the 1990 Budget Enforcement Act. Under the process structured by those acts, the full Appropriations Committee in each house received a total spending allotment known as the Section 302(a) allocation; that total was then divided among the thirteen subcommittees as their Section 302(b) allocations. Each subcommittee chair or, more accurately, the chair's staff, then produced a draft of the bill, known as the "chairman's mark," taking account of the allocation. Rank and file members of the subcommittee typically had little role in the process of developing the markup vehicle, and they sometimes did not even receive a copy of the bill until shortly before the markup session or even at the markup session (Savage 1991, pp. 338–339; Munson 1993, pp. 64–68; Schick and LoStracco 2000, p. 208). In fact, as one staffer said, in preparation for markup, "Subcommittee clerks turn off the phones and refuse to give out draft legislation." During the three congresses considered here, to change the chairman's mark once it came to markup session was difficult, as the subcommittees were limited by their annual spending caps and by budget-neutral rules. Those rules required that if an expenditure was added for one account, an equal amount had to be cut from another (Schick 2000, p. 208), a politically difficult feat, especially without the support of the chair.[1] Therefore, it was difficult for members to add earmarks in markup; instead, they had to contact the subcommittee chair with their funding requests, including requests for earmarks, well before that time.

A key feature of the appropriations committees in both houses traditionally has been their high degree of bipartisanship, due in part to the fact that the committees are not, under House and Senate rules, permitted to make substantive public policy. Even though their bills often do contain policy measures, the disagreements within committee are thought to be less often zero-sum and more often about how to divide dollars and cents than is true in authorizing committees. The disaggregable nature of the issues in which they deal provides a basis for bipartisan compromise (Fenno 1966, pp. 547–549). Although there is evidence that the Democratic caucus (and later, the Republican Conference) in the House pursued a partisan strategy in its assignment of members to the Appropriations Committee between 1947 and 1984 (Kiewiet and McCubbins 1991, pp. 100–133), there is a long-standing view of the Senate Appropriations Committee in particular as more bipartisan than most other committees, a perception that was substantiated by committee staff members, as seen below. Yet

[1] In addition, increases in spending on nondiscretionary entitlement programs, as well as legislation that would reduce federal revenues, were subject to a pay-as-you-go requirement, which required offsets in other spending or taxes to make up for the cost of such actions (Schick 2000, pp. 23–24, 50–52). With respect to discretionary spending, once the budget was balanced in 1998 and went into surplus, the spending caps, generally acknowledged to have been set unrealistically low in the 1997 budget-balancing agreement, were often ignored in subsequent appropriations bills by quiet, mutual agreement between the two parties.

there is also evidence that the Senate Appropriations Committee became markedly more partisan in the 1980s and 1990s.

Earmarking for Votes

Numerous accounts of the earmarking process in subcommittee support the argument developed here that earmarked projects are added to general interest bills to win votes for that legislation. Anecdotal evidence abounds in both published accounts and in my own interviews. This section describes that evidence.

Richard Munson's account of the consideration of FY 1992 spending bills in both the House and Senate Veterans Administration, Housing and Urban Development, and Independent Agencies subcommittees provides examples of the use of pork to buy votes. Bob Traxler (D-Mich.), then the subcommittee chair in the House, was quite systematic about his vote buying. He thought it was necessary to give key members a stake in the bill in order to win their votes, starting with his own subcommittee, whose members he asked to submit three project requests for his consideration. In addition, his staff assembled a list of nearly 600 other project requests; however, his own subcommittee members were especially favored with earmarks. Similarly, Barbara Mikulski (D-Md.), the corresponding Senate subcommittee chair, received more than 1,400 requests for projects; she eventually provided them for key senators in return for support for her bill. Lest the recipients not understand the purpose of their earmarks, in her letters to senators announcing their projects, Mikulski said, "'I hope I can count on your support to preserve this well-balanced bill'" (Munson 1993, pp. 65–67, 141–142). Senator Jake Garn (R-Utah), ranking minority member of the subcommittee, was more explicit during the markup: He warned members "'not to tear apart the delicate balance [of the bill]...[because] other provisions and promises could suffer'" (Munson 1993, p. 150).

As Garn's remark suggests, the possibility of retaliation for disloyalty is behind every project award; the means is the removal of a member's project in conference committee (Shepsle and Weingast 1987a, 1987b; Longley and Oleszek 1989). By one account, the cardinals punish their opponents "endlessly" with the elimination of their projects (Munson 1993, p. 6). One example of retaliation occurred in 1992 when House freshman Thomas Andrews (D-Maine) antagonized the Appropriations Committee and its defense subcommittee by opposing funding for the B-2 bomber. His punishment was the loss of one of four destroyers that would have been built in his district. Driving the point deeper, the committee transferred the funding to a shipyard in the district of Jamie Whitten (D-Miss.), chairman of the Appropriations Committee (Anderson and Binstein 1992).

One of the two major questions addressed in this chapter is whether Republican-controlled congresses also used pork barrel projects to buy votes for appropriations bills. That they did so is suggested by Senate leaders' reaction to Senator John McCain's sustained and very public criticism of pork barrel spending. Even then-majority leader Trent Lott was not immune: McCain attacked him for seeking $370 million for a helicopter carrier that, McCain charged, "the Navy does not need or want." Although Lott claimed that the Navy requested the funding, "a confidential memo surfaced in which Lott's staff instructed the Navy to request funding for the ship." As to the purpose of such earmarks, "the leaders deeply resent [McCain's] attacks on pork-barrel spending, which they regard as *a necessary tool to win the votes of lawmakers*" (Hirsh and Isikoff 2000, emphasis mine).

The Interviews

My interviews with Senate staff members and other close observers of the appropriations process corroborate the picture drawn by scholarly and journalistic accounts of distributive politics in the Senate Appropriations Committee. In both 1996 and 2000 I interviewed Democratic and Republican staff members (mainly staff directors, traditionally known as clerks) of five appropriations subcommittees, along with a former top full committee staff member, aides to Senate leaders, a chief of staff for a member of the Senate, and several lobbyists who advocate for earmarks for various clients. Because the interviewees were promised anonymity, it is not possible to identify which subcommittees were said to follow which practices. Of course, the interviews themselves do not lead to definitive conclusions about earmarking, but they do aid in the development of hypotheses tested later in this chapter about the allocation of earmarks and their intended effect.

Subcommittee staff confirmed accounts that described strong control over project allocations by subcommittee chairs. Nevertheless, they asserted that the chairs generally exercised that power in a bipartisan manner, compared with other committee chairs. One majority staff member said that her boss treated Democrats and Republicans equally well, largely as a matter of reciprocity: "He has been both ranking and chairman; when you've been treated fairly, you do the same."

However, staff members enjoyed a good deal of discretion. Although the chairs were made aware of fellow senators' project requests at some point along the way, the subcommittee staff directors made the decisions on the smaller ones. (The dividing line between small and large projects was not clear and probably varies by subcommittee in any case.) One long-time staff director said that he took to the chair and ranking member "the big stuff," but he never brought 40 percent of the requests to the chair's attention and simply made the decisions himself. Similarly, another staff member said that the majority staff made the decisions unless the senator making the request had a personal relationship with the subcommittee chair or was himself or herself an appropriations subcommittee chair; in those cases, the chair made those decisions. Nevertheless, even as they exercised their discretion, staff members normally were careful to do as their bosses would wish.

With respect to priorities in earmark allocation, several staffers indicated that subcommittee members received first preference, in part because "we need the help of senators on the subcommittee to get the bill pushed." Second, project requests from members of the full committee received priority, subordinate only to subcommittee members themselves. Additionally, some staffers said that other appropriations subcommittee chairs were favored, "because your [own subcommittee] members are asking them for things too." Thus, project requests and awards appear to operate in a system of reciprocity among appropriations subcommittees.

Finally, staff members for several subcommittees indicated that Senate leaders were favored because of their ability to facilitate consideration of their bills. The potential for blackmail of subcommittee chairs by party leaders is illustrated by one staffer's quote of a remark by former Senate Majority Leader Robert Dole, who rather threateningly said of this subcommittee's bill in the 104th Congress, "[the bill] *will* have Kansas' items by the time it comes to the floor."

Clearly, senators are treated unequally in this process. Some members get more and larger earmarks than others. For members, the art of requesting earmarks centers around establishing priorities. Wise staffers know to list their requests according to the projects' priority to their senator. They are encouraged to do so by some subcommittee clerks, who ask them to rank their requests by high, medium, and low priority. As one staffer said, "outside members [those not on the Appropriations Committee] have no expectation of a high percentage of their items being in the bill. All they ask is that their top one or two priorities be included.... If you're up for reelection in two years you get to ask for a lot more; even more if the election is in the current year." In fact, this staffer noted that the majority clerks call the chiefs of staff of those members who are up for reelection in an even-numbered year and ask for their top priorities. There are also discussions between the members. Members in jeopardy receive more help than those who are safe. The minority no doubt does the same, working through the ranking minority members.

However, it is on the last point that subcommittee clerks admitted to some advantage for the majority party. Majority staffers for one subcommittee claimed that they "work hard to treat everyone fairly." But when pressed, they admitted that, at the end of the 106th Congress, Republicans in tight races were particularly advantaged, while Democrats did not get as many projects. Another said that while his chair generally treated Democrats the same as Republicans, "the scale is tipped to Republicans" who are up for reelection.

Were these earmarks added to appropriations bills in order to buy the votes of the senators who received them? If so, did it work? As a remark quoted above indicated, leaders and their staff did grant earmarks in order to gain the recipients' support for the subcommittee bills. It was deemed especially important to have the support of subcommittee and full committee members of both parties in order to present a united front on the Senate floor, thus providing little basis for other senators to oppose the bill.

Nearly all staff members thought that the inclusion of earmarks probably helped to ensure members' loyalty. However, no one considered them critical to the passage of these appropriations bills. Rather, they were seen as a way of increasing the margin of safety for the bills by enlisting the commitment and help of project recipients. Specifically, earmarks were deemed a useful way to persuade senators to help push the bills to passage and to sway a member's vote in cases where he or she could go either way, particularly on amendments. Perhaps most important, they were seen as a way to prevent senators from offering amendments against the committee in the first place. As one staff member said, earmarks are "rarely used as a hammer but they draw people into the legislative process so they support what the process brings. It might secure their active cooperation to ensure the bill is passed into law." Another said, "We could do a clean bill [i.e., one without earmarks] and pass it, but senators couldn't be as enthusiastic" as they are when the bill contains earmarks for their states. Thus, earmarks give senators an additional vested interest in the bill's passage. From the point of view of a staff member for a majority-party senator who was not on the Appropriations Committee: "You usually hold the line if you get an earmark. All we expect is that our one or two top priorities be included. If they are, we will stick with the Appropriations Committee chairman through thick and thin."

Despite the fact that project recipients are expected to be loyal to the chair's version of the bill, staff members indicated that there are limits to the extent to which earmarks win members' support for the leaders who provide them. If the issue is a matter of conscience, constituency concern, or a campaign promise, members "get a pass" from the committee, if they have the courtesy to ask. "You don't blind-side the chairman." But "if you ask, it goes a long way" toward avoiding the chairman's ire. Another staffer made a special point of policy disagreements. In such cases, "members will thank the chairman for their projects and say they won't vote with him unless he needs them. Most of the time they're released." Yet the fact that project recipients feel that they must ask permission to deviate from the chairman's line is evidence of the expectation that votes are to be rendered in return for benefits.

To reinforce the sense that project recipients who have not received a "pass" must be loyal, there is the implicit threat of punishment for disloyalty. Those who violate the norm of returning votes for projects might be penalized in one of two ways: in conference committee with the loss of their project or with a rejection of their requests for earmarks the following year. As one staff member said, "If you vote against the bill, it's not taken in a good light. [Your project] is the first thing to go in conference." Members who vote no or offer an amendment against the committee are regarded as "trying to score political points off the committee. But it doesn't happen often when a member has a project."

Another staff member indicated that subcommittee staffers encourage the chairs to discipline such members. For example, if the subcommittee had "done a reach" for a senator by providing a project that normally would not have been given and that senator had voted no anyway, this staffer remembered it in conference and might remind the chair. The project thus "becomes more expendable" in hard bargaining. The disloyal senator is then told why he or she lost the project: "Senator X worked hard for his project and he voted with us; [you voted no] so when we had to start dropping, we dropped yours." However, even in these cases, this staff member admitted to not knowing whether such tactics made a difference in senators' inclination to support the committee. Nor did he specify how often the chairman took his advice and removed the project.

Other staff members admitted that such punishment is rarely imposed. One asserted that the staff is more inclined to punish disloyal members than the chairs: "Members have interpersonal relationships, but staff gets really pissed off if they vote 'no' when you busted your buns to get them what they need. If it were up to staff they'd be gone in a heartbeat." However, there is a technique for avoiding such discipline, staffers noted. A senator may join with the other senator from his state and with members of the state's House delegation to request earmarks. When that happens, it is much more difficult to remove a project from an offending senator's state, as doing so would penalize other members, at least some of whom probably voted with the chair. The disincentive to punish the innocent is great. Thus, it is unclear just how much power the threat of retaliation has to hold members to the position of the subcommittee chair.

I also asked interviewees whether they had seen a change in the use of earmarks between the Democratic 103rd and the ostensibly antipork Republican 104th congresses. Several respondents noted that due to funding cuts the number of earmarks was limited in the new Republican Congress. Staffers put less stress on ideological opposition to the pork barrel than did media accounts, but some did comment on it. When asked in 1996 whether the Republicans were handling earmarks the same way that the Democrats had, one staffer, a Democrat, said cynically, "They want to but they're trying not to; there are too many people watching." A Republican staffer expressed a similar sentiment: "There is a lot of talk, but there may not be a lot of change." However, as the tables in the next section show, in a short-lived spate of self discipline, there was in fact a reduction in earmarking between the last year of the 103rd and the first year of the 104th congresses. When asked about the subsequent increase in earmarks between the 104th and 106th congresses, one Republican staff member said, "Republicans have a more schizophrenic relationship to appropriations than Democrats. Since 1994, the decline and fall of [resistance to] earmarks can be explained as the transition from their original revolutionary fervor to the desire to become a permanent ruling majority."

Despite the temporary decline in the number of earmarks, there is no indication that subcommittee chairs' reasons for adding them to appropriations bills changed between the Democratic and Republican congresses. The preceding quotations about the presumed effectiveness of earmarks as a tool to win senators' votes came from staffers for both parties in Republican- and Democrat-controlled congresses.

EARMARK ALLOCATION AND IMPACT ON ROLL CALL VOTING

Overview

The major hypotheses of this chapter are two. The first is that Senate Appropriations subcommittee chairs add earmarks to spending bills to fill out a winning coalition for their preferred version of their annual appropriations bills. Second, the recipients of those benefits are indeed more likely to support the chair's version of the bill. That this sort of coalition building occurs in the House has already been demonstrated in the preceding chapters; the interviews with Senate insiders suggest that it also occurs in the Senate. However, there is a question as to whether the Republican majority was as invested in this strategy as their Democratic predecessors. This section discusses in general terms the impact of the 1995 shift from a Democratic to a Republican majority on three phenomena: the numbers of projects given by the appropriations subcommittees, the allocation strategy used by subcommittee leaders in handing out projects, and the impact of projects on the recipients' roll call votes. The three sections following this one develop specific hypotheses for each of those questions and present the analysis of the data on appropriations subcommittee earmarks.

The evidence thus far presents conflicting perspectives on the distribution of appropriations pork. While the media accounts of earmarking described earlier suggest that Republicans initially were true to their antipork rhetoric, distributing less than the Democratic majority that preceded them, there is also evidence that they began to backslide as the 1996 congressional elections approached. Moreover, the Republican majority seemed to grow even more wedded to the distribution of pork as time went on, giving out more and more from one Congress to the next.

With respect to the reasons that subcommittee chairmen distribute pork, Republican and Democratic subcommittee clerks alike said that they expected project recipients to vote with the chairs on the bills to which their benefits were attached. There is no evidence in the interviews of any real change in the attitudes of the chairs on that score. But there is a partisan consideration that could bear on Republican chairmen's inclination to use pork barrel projects to form policy coalitions: Partisan voting in Congress increased substantially during the 1990s compared with the 1980s; the mean annual percentage of votes that qualified as party unity votes (those on which a majority of one party opposed a majority of the other party) climbed from 45 percent in the 1980s to 57 percent in the

1990s; the difference between those means significantly exceeds the .001 level of confidence. Not surprisingly, party unity reached its peak in 1995, the first year of the Republican takeover of the 104th Congress. That year, majorities of the two parties in the Senate opposed each other on 69 percent of all roll call votes, an extraordinary level of partisan voting for the Senate (Parks 1999; Ornstein, Mann, and Malbin 2002, p. 172).

More to the point, there is evidence that partisanship in the Senate Appropriations Committee increased significantly between the 100th and 104th Congresses, notwithstanding committee staffers' claims of bipartisanship (Marshall et al. 1997). Additionally, appropriations bills became more subject to challenges on the floor, especially from the minority, including minority party members on the committee. The authors concluded that the committee majority's efforts were increasingly directed toward serving majority party interests and away from protecting bipartisan committee agreements. Thus, that most famously bipartisan committee began to resemble the full Senate.

The question that arises from these findings is the following: At a time when partisanship seemed to rule, did senators sell their votes for projects for their states? To put it differently, even if committee leaders would have liked to be able to buy their colleagues' votes, *could* they do so in an increasingly partisan chamber? This question has implications for both project allocation and the impact of those projects on roll call votes.

With respect to allocation strategy, heightened partisanship could produce one of two effects. First, it could increase leaders' sense that they need to buy votes. To the extent that partisanship on the committee grew, subcommittee chairs might increasingly have tried to mitigate its effects on their bills by evenhandedly bestowing their distributive largesse. We saw in Chapters 4 and 5 that policy coalition leaders did so in the House. At first glance, this scenario might appear to contradict the workings of partisanship: To the extent that chairs could rely on the members of their own party for support on grounds of party loyalty itself, one might think that they have less need to buy votes. As I argued in Chapter 2, when a party has a large majority and voting is driven by party loyalty, vote buying is unnecessary for the majority, as amendments from the minority can be defeated without calling on more individual, material incentives such as pork. However, in recent years, no party has had a sufficiently comfortable majority to enable it regularly to muster the sixty votes needed to break filibusters that are now frequent in the Senate. Thus, even if the majority always voted together, its leaders would need votes from the minority on many issues. In that case, the addition of earmarks could buy a cushion of safety for the chairs, augmenting the support that they could gain on the basis of partisan loyalty alone. Therefore, we might expect to continue to see the bipartisan distribution of earmarks.

Alternatively, heightened partisanship could produce another effect on the allocation of earmarks: In a more partisan time, pork barrel projects could become part of the majority party's strategy for maintaining its electoral position, especially if, in the extreme, the party does not need to use projects to buy members' votes for its legislation. It is important to keep in mind the reason that pork works to grease the legislative wheels: Members believe that it helps to get them reelected. Majority party leaders, including the powerful cardinals, might then distribute projects in a partisan fashion to help their members retain their seats; concurrently, they could deprive minority party incumbents of projects, making them more vulnerable to a majority party challenge in the next election. Thus, Republican leaders, so newly in control of the Senate, might have become inclined to use earmarks to retain control. If that were the case, we could expect to see a pattern of increasing partisanship over time in the distribution of appropriations pork.

To summarize, this discussion suggests conflicting expectations concerning the impact of members' partisanship on project allocation in an increasingly partisan Senate. On the one hand, pork can be used to mitigate partisan divisions, buying the votes of those who might oppose the committee and ensuring the support of those who are generally inclined to do so. In that case, the cardinals would grant it to Republicans and Democrats alike in order to increase the chances of presenting a united front to a divided Senate in hopes of winning over minority party members on the floor. On the other hand, they might take a party-enhancing approach, giving projects to their own majority party members, hoping to help keep them in office and their party in the majority. In this case, partisan divisions are taken as given and reinforced by the distribution of pork. Any temptation for majority senators to wander on individual amendments that might be offered by the minority in hopes of dividing the majority would thus be counteracted.

This discussion has similar implications for the second hypothesis, which states that senators who receive projects are more likely to comply with the wishes of the chairman who bestowed them. In the bills examined in the House, the two transportation bills and NAFTA, the hypothesis was supported by the data. However, members may be more willing to sell their votes for pork under some partisan circumstances than others. When the issues in an election are nationalized, as they arguably were in 1994, Congress tends to display much more party unity, at least for a while. That is because nationalization of issues involves a convergence of local issues with national ones, imposing on legislators a strong constituency-based incentive to vote the national party line (Brady 1988). During such a period, members may see the issues themselves as being electorally relevant and their party's position as a sufficient draw; in such a case, members may not change their votes in return for a project.

Therefore, to the extent that partisanship grew in the 104th Congress, it is possible that district projects became less relevant to members' voting on Appropriations Committee bills, whether because of perceived pressure from the district on the issues or the strength of members' own partisanship and ideology. Rather, projects may serve purely as a device to preserve the majority party's numerical advantage by helping its members get reelected. However, even if that is the case, as time passes after a nationalizing election, we can expect partisan unity to decline; thus, by the 106th Congress, pork can be expected to be more effective at winning senators' votes.

To examine all of the possibilities raised above, Senate appropriations bills for one fiscal year in each of three congresses are considered here: FY 1995, considered in 1994, the last year of the 103rd Congress and the last year of Democratic control before the 1994 elections; FY 1996 bills, considered in 1995, the first year of the Republican majority; and FY 2000, taken up in the 106th Congress in 1999, also during Republican control.

The Volume of Earmarking

The preceding discussion suggests the following expectation: The overall amount of earmarking declined between the Democratic 103rd Congress and the Republican 104th; however, as time went on and the value of earmarks began to reassert itself in the minds of the Republican majority, earmarking probably increased substantially compared with the 104th Congress.

To examine the overall distribution of earmarks in those three fiscal years, I tallied the number of projects awarded to all states by the Senate Appropriations Committee subcommittees. For my purposes, nine of the thirteen subcommittees were relevant. Three of the four that were not examined here have no jurisdiction over matters in the fifty states: They are the subcommittees on the Legislative Branch, District of Columbia, and Foreign Operations. The last of these is full of earmarks for specific countries that may indeed be added to satisfy groups of constituents in certain states; however, as it was not possible to determine that from a reading of the record, that subcommittee was excluded. Additionally, the Department of Defense subcommittee was omitted. Although that subcommittee is well known for earmarking specific weapons systems to help certain defense contractors and the constituents they employ, it was not practical to devise a reliable way to identify all of the states that would benefit from an earmark. The problem has two levels: first, identifying the primary builder of the system and all of its relevant facilities, and, second (and even more difficult), identifying the subcontractors, who may be located in a number of other states. The earmarks included in the bills of the other nine subcommittees were identifiable by state; all of these were included in the count of earmarks reported here.

The documents used to tally earmarks for each of these subcommittees were the subcommittee reports and the accompanying bills as reported to the Senate by the Appropriations Committee. Virtually all of the earmarks were contained in the reports rather than the bills themselves. Although projects in report language do not have the full force of law, they express Congress's legislative intent. Perhaps more to the point, they send a strong signal to the relevant executive department that the way to stay in the good graces of Congress and keep the money flowing with minimum restrictions is to follow Congress's instructions in its reports. Of course, the reports used here were the initial committee reports, not the final conference reports, as it is on the basis of the former that members cast their preconference votes on the floor of the Senate.

The criteria for inclusion in the tally were as follows: For each subcommittee an individual project was counted if it was recommended by the Senate subcommittee, a specific state was named, and a dollar amount was included.[2] A number of these projects were also House earmarks or were earmarked by the administration in its funding request. Nevertheless, for several reasons, all earmarks recommended by the Senate were counted regardless of who else included them. First, Savage (1991) found that House and Senate earmark lists were nearly identical, as senators and representatives on the subcommittees had decided to support the same projects.[3] Additionally, my own interviews indicated that House members

[2] If a project implicitly included several states, such as the Mexican border, all states were included in the tally. If the report instead used such identifiers as a university, river, or national park, the state or states involved were ascertained (if not named) and included.

[3] Additionally, outside requests for earmarks may go to the full congressional delegation; for example, the governor of Connecticut traditionally writes a letter to the state's delegation listing the projects for which, in his view, the state needs funding (Lightman 1995).

and senators tend to work together on earmarks. Finally, regardless of who had the initial idea for an earmark, if it is recommended by the Senate in its subcommittee report, it is because a senator has requested it. If a senator wants it, it is a potential bargaining chip for the committee.

The last point raises the question of which senator from a state should get credit for an earmark. Given enough time and cooperation from subcommittee staff in interviews, every earmark could be traced to one senator (unless both worked on it together, of course). However, once a project is granted, both senators can take credit for it; indeed, in the interviews, several senators were cited as taking credit for projects that the other senator from that state actually won.[4] Moreover, in the House, there is evidence that members receive an electoral benefit from federal spending in all other districts within the state as well as from state-wide federal spending (Levitt and Snyder 1997); it is not unreasonable to assume that senators would enjoy a similar advantage. Therefore, in this analysis, both senators get credit for an earmark for their state.

Table 6.1 displays the distribution of projects by the nine subcommittees whose project awards were tallied. Several things stand out. First, all of these subcommittees engaged in earmarking in all three congresses. Second, they varied widely in the extent to which they did so: The number of earmarks given in the second session of the 103rd Congress ranged from thirty-six by the Labor and Health and Human Services subcommittee to 1,492 by the Energy and Water Development subcommittee. Not surprisingly, the labor subcommittee deals with many of the major public policy issues that define the differences between the Democratic and Republican parties; those issues are probably more compelling to members than any pork barrel projects that the subcommittee might distribute. By contrast, the Energy and Water subcommittee stands astride the quintessential pork barrel jurisdiction. True to its tradition, it gave out an enormous number of earmarks. Additionally, four of the subcommittees, including Energy and Water, gave earmarks to virtually every state (three gave to 49 states and one gave to 48 states). All but two gave to well over half the states.

[4] A particularly vivid example was reported in *Roll Call* ("Heard on the Hill," August 5, 2002) during the run-up to the crucial 2002 Senate elections. Kit Bond (R-Mo.) was reportedly "furious" that Jean Carnahan (D-Mo.), involved in a tight and ultimately unsuccessful race for reelection, had taken credit for earmarks in the transportation subcommittee's bill. This despite the fact that it was Bond, not Carnahan, who was a member of that subcommittee and had actually gotten the money for Missouri. The subcommittee chair, Patty Murray (D-Wash.), who was also chair of the Democratic Senatorial Campaign Committee, allegedly refused even to give a copy of the bill to Bond until after Carnahan had already taken credit for the projects. In fact, Carnahan claimed credit even before the subcommittee markup.

TABLE 6.1 *Earmarks Given to States by Nine Senate Appropriations Subcommittees, by Congress*

	Agriculture			Commerce, Justice, State			Energy and Water			Interior			Labor, Health and Human Services		
	103rd	104th	106th	103rd	104th	106th	103rd	104th	106th	103rd	104th	106th	103rd	104th	106th
Total number of projects	234	166	431	132	65	395	1492	1659	1837	306	156	448	36	16	49
Number of states with projects	44	39	48	21	39	48	49	49	50	49	44	50	15	9	14
% projects to subcommittee	43.6	45.8	38.9	43.2	35.4	42.3	34.0	26.3	22.2	21.9	45.5	48.2	55.5	43.8	63.3
% projects to committee	71.4	70.5	67.5	93.9	55.4	67.5	74.4	54.6	58.2	68.3	60.1	72.5	94.4	87.5	89.8

	Military Construction			Transportation			Treasury, Postal Service			VA/HUD		
	103rd	104th	106th	103rd	104th	106th	103rd	104th	106th	103rd	104th	106th
Number of projects	491	390	172	227	390	243	102	35	18	229	97	301
Number of states with projects	49	47	40	48	50	47	31	18	12	42	50	49
% projects to subcommittee	12.4	12.1	25.0	38.8	28.7	37.9	26.5	14.3	27.8	33.6	25.8	38.2
% projects to committee	68.0	47.2	67.4	74.0	53.3	70.4	85.3	68.6	66.7	80.3	55.7	75.7

Note: % projects to subcommittee and % projects to committee refer to the percentage of all projects given by the subcommittee to members of the subcommittee and the full committee, respectively. Data are for one fiscal year in each Congress: 1995, 1996, and 2000, respectively.

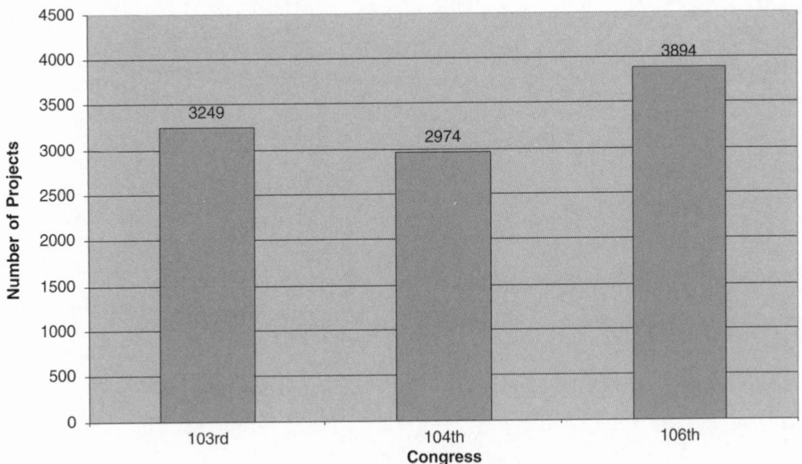

FIGURE 6.1. Projects earmarked in nine appropriations bills for one fiscal year in three congresses.

Did earmarking decline dramatically with the ascension of the Republican majority? Figure 6.1 provides a summary of the total numbers of projects distributed by these nine subcommittees in each of the three congresses (recall that one fiscal year is examined in each congress); clearly, Republicans earmarked less, at least initially, than the Democrats had done before them. Looking at the individual subcommittees in Table 6.1, we see that most of them earmarked less in the first session of the 104th Congress than the Democrats had in the second session of the 103rd. On seven of the nine subcommittees, the number of earmarks declined between the 103rd and 104th Congresses, in five cases drastically. Only two of them earmarked more in the 104th than the 103rd: Energy and Water and Transportation. Both of those subcommittees are particularly known for catering to demands for infrastructure projects for senators' states.

Was the change a lasting one, or did the Republican majority eventually surrender to the temptations of pork, especially following their historic loss of seats in the 1998 midterm elections? Temptation evidently won out, as both Figure 6.1 and Table 6.1 show. Overall on these nine subcommittees, earmarks increased by 31 percent between the first sessions of the 104th and 106th Congresses. With only three exceptions among the nine subcommittees – Military Construction, Treasury, Postal Service and General Government (Treasury Postal Service), and, surprisingly, Transportation – Republican earmarks for FY 2000 exceeded, often greatly, not only their own for FY 1996, but also Democratic earmarks for FY 1995. Moreover, the distribution of projects in the 106th was even more universalistic than in the generous 103rd Congress. Six of the subcommittees in the 106th Congress gave projects to forty-seven or more states, compared with four subcommittees that did so in the 103rd.

The extent to which members of the Appropriations Committee were favored is dramatic, particularly in the 103rd Congress. Twenty-nine senators served on the full committee, yet in that Congress, every subcommittee awarded more than two-thirds of the earmarks to states represented by committee members. The pattern of awards is less favorable for full committee members in the two Republican congresses, although they are more favored in the 106th than in the 104th, suggesting once again that over time, Republican behavior more strongly resembled that of the Democrats. In the 106th Congress, seven subcommittees concentrated project distribution even more than they had done in the 104th.

In addition, most subcommittees also strongly favored their own members. In the 106th Congress, Republicans gave a lower percentage of earmarks to full committee members than Democrats had, but within five subcommittees, they actually concentrated project distribution even more than Democrats had done.

Thus, Senate Republicans never eschewed earmarks, not even during the first year of their ascendancy, although they did exert more discipline over their distribution in 1995 than the Democrats who immediately preceded them in the majority. Although their behavior over time came to resemble that of the Democrats and even exceeded them in generosity, several additional factors probably contributed to the high level of project awards in 1999. First, Senate Republicans watched as their House counterparts lost seats the 1998 midterm elections when, with a Democrat in the White House, the normal dynamic would have been for them to gain seats; moreover, Senate Republicans failed to attain their normal midterm gain (although they did not lose seats). Such outcomes must have reminded them of the virtues of constituency service, including earmarks. Finally, there was the newfound luxury of a budget surplus, an event that occurred far earlier than congressional leaders and the president dreamed when they negotiated the 1997 budget-balancing accord that produced it. In fact, the budget was balanced only a year later, in 1998. The next year, President Clinton took advantage of the new surplus by encouraging Congress to exceed the spending caps imposed under the Budget Enforcement Act (Schick 2000, p. 26), which effectively removed any brakes that might have restrained earmarking. Therefore, the extent to which earmarking increased between the 104th and 106th Congresses cannot be laid entirely at the feet of a normalization of Republican behavior following the ideological fervor of the 104th. It was simply easier and even more tempting to do politically and procedurally, once the budget was in surplus and the spending caps were effectively dismissed. Even senators who previously had opposed earmarks as fiscally irresponsible could now excuse them on the grounds that they could more easily be afforded. Thus, the Republicans more than reverted to the practices of the last Democratic majority in awarding projects: They exceeded their predecessors.

Patterns of Earmark Distribution

The preceding section deals to some degree with how the appropriations subcommittees distributed earmarks. Table 6.1 provided a first cut into the data, showing that projects went more to members of the subcommittee and full committee than anyone else. However, as the interviews indicate, other considerations probably influenced projects distribution. This section analyzes those patterns more fully; it specifies a model of project distribution that includes a variety of factors that might influence subcommittee chairs as they decide which senators are to be favored with earmarks. The section following this one models the impact of those projects on senators' support for the subcommittee chairs' favored positions when their bills reached the Senate floor, answering the question of whether subcommittee chairs were able to use earmarks to buy the votes of the recipients.

Four of the nine subcommittees examined in the preceding section were selected for detailed analysis of allocation patterns and the impact of project awards on roll call voting. Those subcommittees were Agriculture, Rural Development and Related Agencies (which, for convenience will be referred to as Agriculture); Commerce, Justice, State and Judiciary (CJS); Treasury/Postal Service and General Government; and Veterans Administration, HUD, and Independent Agencies (VA/HUD).

Why choose these subcommittees for close analysis? A review of the reports of the nine subcommittees included in Table 6.1 indicates that some appeared primarily concerned with distribution of benefits to various interests and constituencies, while others concentrated primarily on broad national public policy. The four subcommittees listed above were chosen for the extent to which they concentrated on each type of policy. Given Fenno's finding that committees with different goal structures have different decision-making processes, it was important to account for goals in selecting subcommittees for detailed analysis (Fenno 1973). From different degrees of emphasis on broad public policy in a subcommittee, different member goals can be inferred. In this case, those goals are reelection and good public policy, two of the three goals that Fenno finds on congressional committees. For senators influence is not a separate goal; to be sure, senators have been found to be attracted to the Appropriations Committee for its influence, but that goal is combined with and usually outweighed by reelection (or constituency service) and good public policy (Fenno 1973, p. 144; Bullock 1985; Smith and Deering 1990, p. 100).

Each appropriations subcommittee typically subsumes the jurisdiction of one or more authorizing committees; thus, using Deering and Smith's (1997, p. 80) classification of senators' motives for requesting particular authorizing committees, it was possible to derive a dominant goal structure for appropriations subcommittees. Two examples of each were chosen: to represent the reelection/constituency service goal, the subcommittees on Agriculture and VA/HUD were chosen. For the good public policy goal, the subcommittees on CJS and Treasury/Postal Service were selected, although it should be noted that constituency figures as a motivation on these two subcommittees as well, just not to the same extent as on Agriculture and VA/HUD. To think of the goals in terms of a continuum might be more accurate, moving from the most constituency-oriented to the most policy-oriented, as follows: Agriculture, VA/HUD, CJS, and Treasury/Postal Service.[5]

The expectation here is that although the reelection subcommittees give out more earmarks (as we would predict) both types of subcommittees are likely to try to buy votes using the projects that they do give. The policy-oriented subcommittees, which are more likely to be divided by party and ideology, might use projects to try to buy the votes of those who otherwise would oppose the chairs on a partisan basis. Thus, we

[5] I categorized these subcommittees by examining the list of agencies funded by each subcommittee and matching them with those agencies' authorizing committees. The dominant goal structure for each authorizing committee was then taken from Deering and Smith (1997, p. 80) and applied to the corresponding appropriations subcommittee. The resulting classification is as follows (the shortened authorizing committee names with their associated goal structures follow the name of the relevant Appropriations subcommittee): *Agriculture*: Agriculture-constituency. *VA/HUD and Independent Agencies*: VA, not desired by senators, but serving a clear constituency; HUD, policy/constituency; Environment (EPA): constituency/policy. *CJS*: Judiciary, policy; Commerce, constituency; Small Business, constituency/policy; Foreign Relations, policy. *Treasury/Postal Service*: Government Affairs, policy; Banking, policy/constituency; Finance (IRS), policy/constituency. Although the subcommittees are mostly driven by mixed motivations, on each, one outweighs the other.

can determine whether such projects overcame partisan impulses in an increasingly partisan Appropriations Committee.

With respect to which senators received projects, the likely impact of partisanship, and the closely related variable of ideology, is unclear, as discussed above. The increasingly partisan pattern of the committee members' voting on the committee's own bills might lead either to bipartisan distribution of projects in an effort to mitigate the effects of partisanship or to more partisan distribution in a shift from a vote-buying strategy to an incumbent-protection strategy by the majority party. That is, sure of the majority party members' votes, the chairs might favor them in project distribution to help protect their seats and to avoid helping minority party members. Thus, the alternative expectations are that there is a bias toward members of the majority party and members of the majority's dominant ideological bent, or, if the committee is pursuing a bipartisan strategy, no relationship between either of these variables and the receipt of earmarks.

Certain additional expectations concerning the pattern of project distribution can be derived from the interviews as well as from previous chapters. Solidifying the support of the chairman's own subcommittee and the full Appropriations Committee are perhaps the paramount considerations in the distribution of earmarks in the Senate. And there could be another reason for favoring the subcommittee: Its members may have a particularly high demand for the policies within the their jurisdiction. As discussed in Chapter 2, there is disagreement among scholars about the extent to which committees are composed of high demanders. Nevertheless, there is evidence that the Senate Appropriations Committee has been populated by advocates for the programs under its jurisdiction (Fenno 1966, p. 504), although in the House, at least, which subcommittees attract high demanders is subject to change depending on which party holds the majority (Adler 2000). To the extent that any subcommittee is composed of such members, its tendency to be generous to its own will be even greater. Therefore, for both reasons, we expect a positive relationship between service on the subcommittee and full committee and receipt of projects.

Additionally, several staff members indicated that leaders, especially other Appropriations Committee leaders, also received preference due to their ability to facilitate either the subcommittee chair's own project requests from other subcommittees or the chamber leaders' ability to facilitate passage of the bill itself. However, in the case of this committee, virtually everyone is both a member and a leader of one of the thirteen subcommittees. With twenty-eight or twenty-nine members, depending on the congress, and thirteen subcommittees, there are twenty-six leadership positions, counting the subcommittee chairs and ranking minority members (the full committee chair and ranking minority member each also hold those positions on a subcommittee). So satisfying other subcommittee leaders is equivalent to satisfying other members of the full committee. Hence, in the statistical analysis, the variable for leadership consists only of the chamber leaders. Like Appropriations Committee members, Senate leaders are expected to get more projects than other members.

Seniority also is expected to affect project allocation. More senior members typically have more to bargain with in efforts to gain earmarks; for example, they may chair an authorizing committee that the subcommittee chair considers important in coalition building on this bill.

In addition to the preceding considerations, interviewees stressed the role of the Senate election cycle in the distribution of earmarks. Members up for reelection in the current two-year cycle were, according to some subcommittee clerks, given extra servings of pork. Of course, the expected closeness of the upcoming race may also be a factor; those most at risk would be considered most in need of extra benefits. To the extent that the subcommittee is partisan in its benefit distribution, this variable would operate in conjunction with the member's party. That is, the chair would most likely give benefits to members of his or her own party who were expected to experience a difficult election.

A key difference between the House and Senate is, of course, the difference in the size of members' constituencies, a difference that varies from state to state. The consequences of the variation in state size for policy making, especially the distribution of federal spending, has been explored by Lee and Oppenheimer (1999). They argue that pursuit of distributive benefits is a more efficient reelection strategy for small-state senators than for large-state senators. That is because any given benefit affects a larger proportion of small-state constituents; large-state senators, on the other hand, are more likely to engage in position taking and policy activism to impress their constituents (Lee and Oppenheimer 1999, pp. 124–125). Accordingly, small-state senators are more likely to gravitate to reelection committees, such as appropriations (p. 131). Not surprisingly, in appropriations for nondiscretionary formula programs and discretionary distributive programs, small states do proportionately better than larger states. The authors attribute the small-state advantage in part to the fact that in building coalitions, it is cheaper for Senate coalition leaders to give proportionately more benefits to small states to win their senators' votes, thus disadvantaging the larger states in relative terms (pp. 160–165, 173–183). Similar patterns occurred in the distribution of funds in the 1991 and 1998 highway reauthorization bills (Lee 2000).

There is reason to think that such considerations would affect the allocation of earmarks as well, especially if committee chairs use projects to buy members' loyalty to the chairman's mark. If this pattern obtains for earmarks, we would expect an inverse relationship between state size and earmarks. If, on the other hand, subcommittee chairs respond mainly to the demand for projects, which is likely to be driven by state size, we should expect a direct relationship between the size of the state and the number of projects. That is because the larger the state, the greater the number of potential demanders and the more House members with whom senators can coordinate project requests. Nevertheless, although the relationship between state size and the number of projects may be positive, at the same time small states might be given relatively more projects than large states. That is, even if small states are given disproportionate benefits overall, it is to be expected that the larger the state, the larger its total distributive benefit.

To place the preceding discussion in terms of a model of projects granted by a subcommittee, the following was estimated for each of the four subcommittees:

Number of projects = fn(Subcommittee, Appropriations, Leader, Seniority, No. of Congressional Districts (CDs), Small State, Republican, Conservatism, Reelection, Percent Farming (in models for Agriculture only))

Number of Projects: This consists of the number of projects that a senator's state received from the subcommittee.

Subcommittee: This takes the value of 1 if the senator served on the subcommittee that reported the bill, 0 otherwise.

Appropriations: This is a dummy variable that takes the value of 1 if the senator served on the Appropriations Committee, 0 otherwise.

Leader: This is a dummy variable that takes the value of 1 if any of the following conditions hold (and 0 otherwise): The senator is majority or minority leader of the Senate or majority or minority whip.

Seniority: This is the number of years the senator had served as of the year in which the votes were taken.

Number of Congressional Districts (CDs): This consists of the number of congressional districts in the senator's state as of the 1992 elections; it serves as a control for the size of the senator's state and the number of House members working with senators to request projects.

Small State: This is a dummy variable that takes the value of 1 if a state has four or fewer congressional districts. It is intended to measure any special advantage that small states enjoy relative to large states as a result of equal representation in the Senate.[6]

Republican: This is a dummy variable that takes the value of 1 for Republicans, 0 for Democrats.

Conservatism: For the 103rd Congress, this is the senator's 1993 Conservative Coalition support score as calculated in *Congressional Quarterly Almanac* (1993). This was used in preference to the senator's score for the entire 103rd Congress because the seven of the twenty-three votes used for the 1994 scores were also used to calculate the subcommittee support scores that serve as endogenous variables in the present analysis. A similar problem exists for the 104th Congress, and the senator's 1996 Conservative Coalition score was used, as the votes taken here occurred in 1995.[7] For the 106th Congress, the senator's 2000 American Conservative Union scores (the votes examined here were taken in 1999) were used, as *CQ Weekly* noted that the Conservative Coalition itself had been reduced to virtual irrelevance by 1998, made moribund by the shift of the South toward the Republican Party and the concurrent reduction in the number of conservative southern Democrats (Gettinger 1999).

Reelection: Several alternative measures of electoral status were included here; they are discussed in detail below.

Percent Farming: This is the percentage of the state's population living on farms as of the 1990 Census. It is included in the models for agriculture only.[8]

[6] Bruce Oppenheimer suggested the number four; while it is somewhat arbitrary, using a specific number has the advantage of not being highly correlated with the number of congressional districts (r = −.55); it performed as well or better than other measures of the small state effect.

[7] For the 103rd Congress, the correlation between the 1994 and 1995 Conservative Coalition Support Scores is .96. For the 104th Congress, the correlation between 1995 and 1996 Conservative Coalition Support scores is .95.

[8] Other measures of state interests were either not available or not obvious, given the diverse jurisdictions of the other three subcommittees.

An additional note on the measurement of party and ideology in the equations for the 106th Congress is in order here. As *CQ Weekly* noted (Gettinger 1999) in early 1999, there was less and less crossing of party lines by Southern Democrats to activate the old conservative coalition. In the data examined here, the correlation between party and ideology rises with every Congress; from an absolute value of .70 in the 103rd Congress to .80 in the 104th to a remarkable .96 in the 106th. Even accounting for the fact that a different measure of conservatism was used for the 106th, it seems clear that partisanship increased over this time period. For the 106th Congress, therefore, it was necessary to choose between party and ideology due to the high collinearity between the two. I chose ideology for both models, not because it trumps party but because, in attempts to estimate the committee support equations, in two equations no estimates could be obtained (i.e., statistical convergence was not achieved) due to the fact that some of the votes included in the subcommittee support scores were straight party votes on one or both sides.[9] However, the equations were successfully estimated when I substituted conservatism for party. But keep in mind that for the 106th Congress, party and ideology are virtually equivalent.

These equations were estimated using OLS regression. The coefficient estimates for the twelve equations are presented in Table 6.2. With only three exceptions, two of them in the 104th Congress, subcommittee membership had a significant impact on a senator's chances of getting projects. In two of the three years when this was not the case, full committee members were favored. These results refine those reported in Table 6.1, which shows a strong tendency to favor members of the full committee and the relevant subcommittee. In Table 6.2 we see that subcommittee members are really the ones who are favored. For example, on agriculture, subcommittee members received at least 3.8 more projects than other senators in the 104th Congress.

With respect to the agriculture subcommittee, state-based demand also played a role, as the percentage of the state's residents who were engaged in farming had a significant impact on the number of projects received by their senators. For every percentage-point increase in farming in a state, its senators got 2.3 more earmarks. Nevertheless, with that variable accounted for, subcommittee membership still played a role, suggesting

[9] In such cases, a type of collinearity arises in logistic regression, which is used here for the second set of models, due to the fact that the "dependent variable is invariant for one or more values of a categorical independent variable," and it is therefore impossible to obtain unique estimates of the coefficients (Menard 1995, 65–67).

TABLE 6.2 *Determinants of Earmark Allocation by Appropriations Subcommittees, by Congress*

	Agriculture			Commerce, Justice, State		
	103rd	104th	106th	103rd	104th	106th
Subcommittee	6.017[a]	3.859[a]	6.486[a]	4.201[b]	1.018[b]	5.464[b]
	(1.743)	(1.273)	(2.728)	(1.941)	(0.470)	(2.521)
Appropriations	0.307	0.316	1.071	−0.035	−0.132	0.938
	(1.204)	(0.899)	(1.921)	(1.317)	(0.323)	(1.726)
Leader	−1.530	1.911	4.653[c]	−0.613	−0.003	0.474
	(2.318)	(1.691)	(3.529)	(2.593)	(0.617)	(3.284)
Republican	−0.481	1.178	–	−0.345	0.291	–
	(1.276)	(1.111)		(1.426)	(0.401)	
Conservative	−0.015	−0.046	0.005	0.032	0.001	0.029[b]
	(0.022)	(0.018)	(0.019)	(0.024)	(0.007)	(0.016)
Seniority	0.020	−0.001	0.024	−0.011	0.025[b]	0.257[a]
	(0.054)	(0.037)	(0.074)	(.061)	(0.014)	(0.070)
CDs	−0.137	0.015	0.056	0.608[a]	0.128[a]	0.310[a]
	(0.059)	(0.043)	(0.090)	(0.065)	(0.016)	(0.083)
Small State	−0.632	−0.323	−1.410	5.270[a]	0.413	3.739[a]
	(1.092)	(0.818)	(1.714)	(1.229)	(0.296)	(1.579)
Percent Farming	2.314[a]	2.752[a]	3.808[b]	–	–	–
	(1.413)	(1.038)	(2.119)			
Constant	4.878[a]	3.376[b]	4.634[b]	−6.709[a]	−0.567	−1.873
	(1.717)	(1.334)	(2.390)	(1.856)	(0.472)	(2.006)
Adjusted R^2	.158	.172	.100	.484	.452	.265

	Treasury, Postal Service			VA/HUD		
	103rd	104th	106th	103rd	104th	106th
Subcommittee	2.591[b]	0.307	0.808[b]	0.806	0.233	3.459[b]
	(1.037)	(0.490)	(0.398)	(1.324)	(0.366)	(1.537)
Appropriations	0.737[c]	0.476[b]	−0.004	2.361[a]	0.273	1.646[c]
	(0.510)	(0.237)	(0.195)	(0.907)	(0.260)	(1.088)
Leader	−0.487	−0.244	−0.056	−0.935	−0.147	−0.385
	(1.105)	(0.498)	(0.400)	(1.753)	(0.485)	(2.035)
Republican	−0.554	−0.322	–	0.407	0.680[b]	–
	(0.608)	(0.324)		(0.965)	(0.317)	
Conservative	0.016	0.005	−0.003	−0.031[b]	−0.009	0.005
	(0.010)	(0.005)	(0.002)	(0.016)	(0.005)	(0.010)
Seniority	−0.003	−0.001	−0.002	0.045	−0.000	0.078[b]
	(0.026)	(0.011)	(0.009)	(0.041)	(0.011)	(0.042)
CDs	0.166[a]	0.089[a]	0.014[c]	0.156[a]	0.017[c]	0.052
	(0.028)	(.013)	(0.010)	(0.045)	(0.012)	(0.051)
Small State	0.249	0.473[b]	0.444[b]	0.639	−0.356	1.347[c]
	(0.523)	(0.238)	(0.196)	(0.833)	(0.232)	(0.980)
Constant	−0.513	−0.553[c]	0.246	3.330[a]	2.052[a]	2.995[a]
	(0.787)	(0.383)	(0.249)	(1.250)	(0.369)	(1.243)
Adjusted R^2	.381	.359	.051	.261	.083	.153

[a] $p < .01$.
[b] $p < .05$.
[c] $p < .10$.

Note: The first entry in each cell is the estimated coefficient; the number in parentheses is the standard error. Significance tests are one-tailed.

that preference in awarding earmarks for subcommittee members goes beyond their tendency to be high demanders based on state need.

If subcommittees favored leaders, it was done so selectively that it hardly leaves a statistical trace. The only exception is the agriculture subcommittee in the 106th Congress, and even then the coefficient significant only at the .1 level of confidence. Otherwise, there was no systematic relationship between the number of projects a senator received and his or her leadership position. Similarly, seniority had little impact on senators' success in gaining earmarks in the 103rd and 104th Congresses; it was significant in the 104th for one and in the 106th for two subcommittees.

Additionally, state size does make a difference. With the exception of the agriculture subcommittee, senators representing larger states did get more projects, as one would expect on the basis of the likely volume of constituent demand; in eight of the twelve equations the larger the state (as measured by the number of congressional districts), the more projects its senators were awarded. However, in no case did an additional congressional district result in more than a fraction of an additional project. Once that relationship is accounted for, in five of the twelve cases small states received additional projects across the three congresses, particularly from the CJS and Treasury/Postal Service subcommittees, probably reflecting the strategic advantage held by small-state senators in the project distribution process.

With respect to the impact of party on the distribution of projects, these four subcommittees appear to have adhered mostly to the norm of bipartisanship. In only two cases, the VA/HUD subcommittee in the 104th Congress and CJS in the 106th, were majority party members favored in the distribution of projects. Recall that in the 106th Congress, ideology is equivalent to party, so the positive sign on the "conservative" variable means that Republicans were also favored. Whatever the increase in Appropriations Committee partisanship, it is not reflected in the distribution of earmarks on these subcommittees.

Consistent with that finding, variables measuring the impact of electoral needs had absolutely no impact. A number of measures designed to capture such an effect were included in the allocation equations: a dummy variable indicating whether or not the senator was up for reelection in the next reelection year, the senator's previous reelection margin, and the margin he or she actually received in the subsequent election (as a measure of his or her actual vulnerability). In addition, variables that would reflect an interaction between the electoral variables and majority party membership were used. None of those variables had any effect on the number of projects (or their value; those estimates are described below) that the member received in any of the twelve equations, and they were dropped from the model. If reelection is a consideration that garners an extra serving of pork, the pattern is not clear enough to show up in systematic analysis of the allocation of earmarks.

There are other ways to quantify earmarks. The equations reported in Table 6.2 use the number of earmarks as the dependent variable. In previous chapters, I used a dichotomous variable as the measure of distributive benefits. In those cases, the dichotomous variable performed as well as or better than other measures, such as the value of the benefits or the number of benefits to each legislator. However, when I estimated the equations in this chapter using a dichotomous variable as the dependent variable, the results were much worse than the results for the number of projects model. That is likely because senators typically represent far more people than House members and need more earmarks to get any electoral benefit, yet there is far more variation in the numbers of earmarks granted by the Senate Appropriations Committee than in those benefits granted in the cases in previous chapters.

Another way to look at project allocation is to consider the total value of earmarks for a senator's state, instead of the number of earmarks. That question is especially interesting in view of evidence that small state senators are more likely to be bought by coalition builders because their support costs less, due, presumably, to lower demand (Lee 2000). Thus, the project allocation model was estimated using the total dollar value of the projects earmarked by a subcommittee for a senator's state. The results are not presented here, but can be summarized as follows: For eight of the twelve subcommittees across the three congresses, the R^2 is much lower, usually half the size of those seen in Table 6.2. In terms of the significance of the explanatory variables, the differences are small, although, typically, fewer variables are significant in the estimates of the value of the projects. One might conjecture that here, in the projects' value rather than their number, we would see an advantage for leaders and more senior members; however, that is not the case, except for one subcommittee in the 106th Congress, CJS. High-ranking members are actually more advantaged in the number of projects that they receive than the projects' value. Moreover, given prior research, we might expect small states to have a particular advantage in the value of projects, but for the most part, that is not the case; in fact, there are subcommittees in which the small state variable was significant in the number of projects model, but not in the value of projects model. Overall, the most important result is that it is far harder to explain statistically the value of the projects given to senators than the number of projects given.

To summarize the results of the estimates of the project allocation equations: Apart from favoring members of their own subcommittees, the chairs did not exhibit strong evidence of strategic behavior in awarding projects to their fellow senators across the three congresses. That is, with the exception of the 106th Congress, they did not give more projects to leaders or more senior members who might have helped to facilitate the bills or provided important voting cues to other senators. Rather, the most consistent finding across subcommittees and congresses is that these subcommittees gave projects to their own members and to senators from larger states. These results substantiate the remarks of staff members that giving projects is designed to "draw people into the legislative process" and to "secure their active cooperation to ensure the bill is passed into law" with little thought as to who is most likely to do so, beyond members of the subcommittee. Although there appears to be no finely honed distribution strategy, perhaps the subcommittee chairs' approach is sufficiently strategic: Their own subcommittee members are particularly important in the effort to send a bipartisan signal to the full Senate that their bill is something that all members, regardless of party, should support.

To look at the results another way, were there distinctive patterns of project allocation under Republican versus Democratic control? Three differences stand out. First, there appears to be a growing disadvantage for large states in Republican congresses: By the 106th Congress, the number of subcommittees declined in which the number of congressional districts was significantly and positively related to number of projects received, as the number of subcommittees that gave an advantage to small states grew. Additionally, the Republican 106th was the only congress in which leaders were particularly favored. Overall, however, although the Republicans temporarily slowed the flow of earmarks during their first year in the majority, there was otherwise not a great deal of change in how projects were distributed from one congress to the next, regardless of changes in partisan control.

The Impact of Earmarks on Roll Call Voting

The second major question is, did earmarks work? That is, did senators who received projects from a subcommittee support the chair's position to a greater degree than those who were not so favored? We have seen non-systematic, impressionistic evidence from the interviews that the purpose of earmarks is to win the recipients' loyalty to the subcommittee chair's bill. In this section, I estimate the impact of senators' earmarks on their roll call votes on the bill to which the projects were attached. The major hypothesis is that the more projects a senator receives, the greater the support he or she gives to the subcommittee chair's preferences on the bill. Additionally, it is expected that members of the full committee and the subcommittee in question will support their own subcommittee at higher rates than other senators. In part, that may be due to the efforts of the chair and ranking minority members to unite subcommittee members in order to present a solid front in full committee and on the floor. However, to the extent that the traditionally bipartisan Appropriations Committee became more partisan in the late 1980s and mid-1990s, this effect can be expected to decline over time.

As a result of the same partisan phenomenon, conservatives and Republicans are expected to be less supportive of the subcommittee in the 103rd Congress and more supportive in the two Republican congresses. For the agriculture subcommittee model, the Percent Farming variable was included to control for senators' state interest in the bill on its merits. The higher the percentage of a state's population occupied in farming, the greater the senator's support for the bill is likely to be regardless of earmarks or partisanship.

The model for voting on each subcommittee's bill is as follows:

Subcommittee Support = fn(Number of Projects, Subcommittee, Appropriations, Republican, Conservatism, Percent Farming (for agriculture only))

Subcommittee Support is the number of nonunanimous recorded votes on which the senator supported the position taken by the subcommittee chair. I used a support score for each subcommittee rather than individual votes as in Chapters 4 and 5 because of the large total number of votes. The number of recorded votes taken on the bills ranged from a low of two in the case of two subcommittees to a high of twelve votes, with the rest ranging from three to six votes each. Those votes are described in the Appendix to this chapter. When the dependent variable is so limited in range, OLS regression is not an appropriate estimation technique; therefore ordered logit analysis was used. All other variables are the same as in the project allocation model.[10]

[10] Inspection of the two models immediately leads to the question of whether the system is recursive, in which case OLS regression can be used to estimate the project allocation

Table 6.3 displays the results. It shows a substantial difference between Democratic and Republican congresses in the effectiveness of vote buying with distributive projects. In the 103rd Congress, in all cases but one (the policy-oriented CJS subcommittee), the more projects a senator received, the more votes he or she was likely to cast in support of the positions of the subcommittee chair. Thus, the strategy of giving projects to enlist support was clearly successful in the Democratic Party–controlled Senate. However, in the 104th Congress, the first year of Republican control, only for the agriculture subcommittee did receipt of projects influence members' voting. Even more strikingly, in the 106th Congress, in no case did projects influence votes.[11] This lack of positive impact is especially surprising given the fact that Democratic and Republican staffers alike,

model and ordered logit analysis can be used for the roll call voting model (Committee Support), or nonrecursive, in which case a technique such as two-stage least squares must be used. The variable that might be suspected of causing a violation of the assumptions of recursive equation systems is Number of Projects in the second model. To resolve the question, consider the requirements for a recursive model: (1) The system must be hierarchical; that is, no pair of variables can be reciprocally related. In this case, project awards are clearly temporally prior to the floor votes, so this condition is met. (2) "Each error term is uncorrelated with (a) all the exogenous variables and (b) all the other error terms in the model" (Berry 1984, 11–13). Here the potentially troublesome requirement is (a). If the relationship between project awards and committee support were reciprocal, the error term of the Committee Support model would be correlated with Number of Projects in that model. For an explanation of why that is so, see Asher (1983, p. 27).

To determine whether the error terms in the second set of models are correlated with Number of Projects, I used a diagnostic technique developed by Hausman (1978), in which for each Congress, I estimated the second model as specified, but also included the saved residuals from the first (Number of Projects) model. Significance for the residuals variable would indicate that the error term for the second model is correlated with Number of Projects. In that case, the Number of Projects variable in the second model would be shown to be correlated with the error term of the Committee Support model (see note 8) and an instrument for Number of Projects would have to be substituted. In none of the estimations for the twelve bills did the residuals variable from the Number of Projects model attain the .05 level of confidence in the Committee Support model. Thus, it was possible to estimate both models using single-equation techniques, which are appropriate for recursive models.

11 There is a factor here that might attenuate the relationships between projects and votes. Although both of a state's senators may take credit for an earmark, and they may indeed have worked together to get it, some are no doubt given on the request of one senator. Does the other show equal loyalty to the subcommittee? As noted earlier, chairs are unlikely to withdraw a project from the member who asked for it, if that member is loyal, just to punish one who did not ask for one, did not *directly* receive one, and voted against the committee. Because of this difficulty, the relationship between projects and votes may not be as strong as it would be if we could discern who asked for each project, as we were able to do in the House of Representatives. Nevertheless, the relationships are significant for the 103rd Congress.

TABLE 6.3 *Earmarks and Voting on Appropriations Bills, by Congress*

	Agriculture			Commerce, Justice, State		
	103rd	104th	106th	103rd	104th	106th
Number of projects	0.121[a]	0.234[a]	0.020	−0.026	0.213	−0.046
	(0.045)	(.062)	(0.027)	(0.034)	(0.194)	(0.026)
Republican	−2.268[a]	0.362	–	−1.605[a]	6.759[a]	–
	(0.586)	(.615)		(0.620)	(1.497)	
Conservative	−0.013[c]	0.043[a]	0.082[a]	−0.005	0.059[a]	0.096[a]
	(0.009)	(.011)	(0.011)	(0.010)	(.020)	(0.014)
Appropriations	1.707[a]	0.762[c]	−0.136	0.068	−0.815	0.529
	(0.525)	(0.481)	(0.480)	(.541)	(0.686)	(0.546)
Subcommittee	−2.015	0.877	−0.303	1.285[c]	0.098	−0.660
	(0.773)	(0.712)	(0.753)	(.804)	(1.002)	(0.802)
Percent Farming	1.171[b]	1.127[b]	0.698[c]	–	–	–
	(0.587)	(0.587)	(0.542)			
Pseudo R^2	.163	.183	.267	.091	.555	.398

	Treasury, Postal Service			VA/HUD		
	103rd	104th	106th	103rd	104th	106th
Number of projects	0.151[b]	−.146	−0.058	0.126[b]	.068	−0.038
	(0.073)	(.180)	(0.320)	(0.057)	(.229)	(0.051)
Republican	−0.840[c]	.320	–	−3.429[a]	5.454[a]	–
	(0.550)	(.781)		(0.654)	(1.133)	
Conservative	−0.043[a]	.074[a]	−0.013	0.006	.058[a]	0.004
	(.010)	(.016)	(0.007)	(.010)	(.014)	(.005)
Appropriations	0.876[b]	.331	−1.122	0.725[c]	.615	1.297[b]
	(0.494)	(.585)	(0.649)	(0.500)	(.608)	(0.566)
Subcommittee	1.329[c]	−1.204	1.809[c]	0.132	−.169	−0.447
	(0.992)	(1.152)	(1.241)	(0.713)	(.907)	(.785)
Pseudo R^2	.198	.324	.057	.191	.424	.033

[a] $p < .01$.
[b] $p < .05$.
[c] $p < .1$.
Note: The first entry in each cell is the estimated coefficient; the number in parentheses is the standard error. Significance tests are one-tailed.

in interviews throughout this period, said that project recipients were expected to vote with the chair.[12]

[12] An alternate measure of earmarks was also used for all of these equations: The dollar value of a senator's projects was substituted for the number of projects received. As with the first model (Number of Projects) the value of a senator's projects had less impact on his or her roll call voting than did the number of projects. These results imply that members regard being able to claim credit for a project as at least as helpful to them, if not more so, as being able to boast about its value.

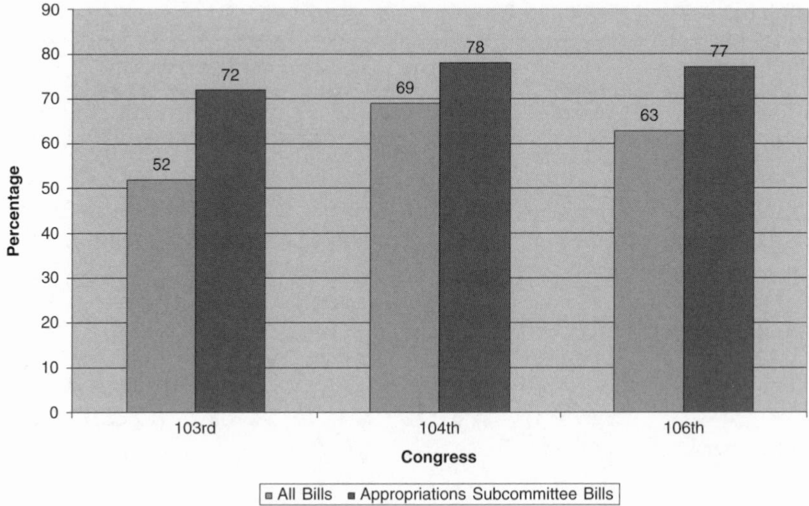

FIGURE 6.2. Party unity votes in selected congresses.

With respect to the effects of party and ideology, nine of the twelve subcommittee support scores were affected by one or the other in the predicted direction in the 103rd and 104th Congresses, reflecting the high degree of partisan/ideological voting in the 1990s. However, in the 106th Congress, senators' subcommittee support scores for the Treasury/Postal Service and VA/HUD bills were not affected by party and ideology (recall that party was omitted due to its near-perfect collinearity with ideology), at least not in the expected direction. That result is surprising in view of the level of partisanship of those votes. Figure 6.2 compares the percentage of roll call votes that qualified as party unity votes (on which a majority of one party voted against a majority of the other) on all of the bills from these four subcommittees with the overall percentage of votes that qualified as party unity votes for the same years. The most striking result is that votes on these four appropriations bills were even more partisan than overall voting in the Senate in all congresses, including the 106th.

So why was the conservatism/party variable not positively and significantly related to voting on the Treasury and VA/HUD bills in the 106th Congress? The answer lies in the individual votes that make up the subcommittee support indices. For the Treasury/Postal Service bill, there were only two roll call votes. Both were party unity votes, but on one of the two, the Republican majority opposed not just the Democrats, but also the Republican subcommittee chair. That was on a vote to table an amendment to prohibit funding for abortions for federal employees. The subcommittee chair, Ben Nighthorse Campbell (R-Colo.) is himself prochoice; he supported the motion to table the antiabortion amendment. The majority of his own party opposed him, while the Democrats supported him. A similar situation existed on the VA/HUD subcommittee, where the majority of Republicans opposed their own chair, Christopher Bond (R-Mo.), on two of the three votes. One of those was a party unity vote; the other was not. Analysis of the individual votes that make up the subcommittee support indices (discussed in more detail below) indicated that the conservatism variable was significantly related to those votes. However, because the chairs opposed their own party on several of these votes, ideology did not explain support for the *chair's* positions (the basis of the dependent variable) on the overall support scores. To put it differently, the subcommittee chairs were less partisan on these two subcommittees than the Republican Conference, therefore partisanship and ideology did not predict support for the chair.

Finally, in voting on these appropriations bills, members of the full committee and each of the subcommittees were more loyal to the cardinals in the Democratic 103rd Congress, but that loyalty declined in the Republican 104th and 106th Congresses. Once other variables are accounted for, members of the Appropriations Committee and the reporting subcommittee were not consistently more supportive of their subcommittee chair than other senators.

As noted earlier, I analyzed subcommittee support scores rather than individual votes to render the results more comprehensible. Using the support scores as the dependent variable makes it practical to analyze a great many votes – a total of seventy roll calls – in twelve equations, which provide results that are easier to digest than the results of seventy separate equations. However, important detail may be lost in the support scores. Therefore, to determine whether the overall subcommittee support scores obscure relationships between projects and support for the subcommittee chair on individual votes, I also analyzed each vote separately using the same explanatory variables. Those results substantiated the ones reported in Table 6.3, although there were one or two surprises. In the agriculture subcommittee in the 103rd Congress, although the number of projects a senator received was positively related to his or her support for the subcommittee chair, on individual votes, that effect occurred on only two of the eight roll calls cast. To explore that result more fully, I estimated the individual votes separately for Democrats and Republicans and found that projects affected Democrats on six of the votes, a result more consistent with the estimates for the overall support score.

Returning to the analysis of individual votes for Democrats and Republicans together, for Treasury/Postal Service and VA/HUD in the 103rd Congress, projects had an impact on half or more of the votes. However, the results were very different for the two Republican congresses. With the exception of agriculture in the 104th, projects did not have an impact on a single roll call vote. That finding is identical to the results for the overall subcommittee report scores. Moreover, it strongly supports the inference that in Republican congresses, earmarks did not buy votes.

If the parties were as internally unified and pitted against each other as Figure 6.2 suggests, we would expect that earmarks would be useful mainly as a way to influence minority party votes, as the votes of the majority should be assured for these highly partisan bills. That is, we would expect to see that subcommittee chairs added to their margin of support by buying some of the opposing party's votes, a phenomenon that we saw clearly for highway demonstration projects and, in a different way, on NAFTA. Did earmarks affect the votes only of minority party members, who would not otherwise have supported the majority on these now highly partisan appropriations bills?[13] To answer that question, I analyzed the impact of earmarks on subcommittee support scores separately for Democrats and Republicans. This analysis allowed an examination of the possibility that the chairs were able to peel off members of the minority party with pork barrel benefits.

The results appear in Table 6.4. For economy of presentation and ease of comparison, I have reported only the estimates of the coefficients for the Number of Projects variable for each party on each committee in the three congresses; however, with the obvious exception of the variable for party, which is omitted, the model is identical to that reported in Table 6.3.

Unlike the results of a similar analysis of the highway bills and NAFTA, vote buying on these subcommittees was not clearly partisan. Here I find that majority party votes are affected as often as minority party votes. In the 103rd Congress, minority party votes were influenced on the Treasury/Postal Service and VA/HUD bills, but only majority votes were

[13] This question cannot be answered in as intuitively appealing a manner as it was in Chapters 4 and 5, where I calculated probabilities of a no versus a yes vote for Democrats and Republicans based on whether or not they received a district benefit. Here, it was necessary to use ordered logit to estimate the coefficients; ordered logit is not amenable to such calculations, as logit is. The separate analyses for Democrats and Republicans performed in this chapter are instructive, nonetheless.

TABLE 6.4 *Impact of Earmarks on Support for Subcommittee by Democrats and Republicans, by Congress*

	103rd		104th		106th	
	Republicans	Democrats	Republican	Democrats	Republicans	Democrats
Agriculture	0.089	0.175[a]	0.163[b]	0.303[a]	0.029	0.061
	(0.077)	(.060)	(0.091)	(0.095)	(0.034)	(0.050)
Commerce	0.067	−0.137	0.404[b]	–	−0.054	−0.021
	(0.054)	(0.085)	(0.248)		(0.029)	(0.069)
Treasury	0.194[b]	0.086	−0.188	0.015	−0.089	−0.121
	(0.099)	(0.114)	(0.215)	(0.400)	(0.669)	(0.407)
VA/HUD	0.453[a]	−0.061	0.498	−0.263	−0.070	−0.042
	(0.113)	(0.068)	(0.396)	(0.317)	(0.063)	(0.099)

[a] $p < .01$.
[b] $p < .05$.
Note: The model is identical to that in Table 6.3, except that it is estimated separately for Democrats and Republicans. Only the coefficients for the Number of Projects variable are reported; the coefficients are estimates of the impact of earmarks on the member's support for the subcommittee chair. The numbers in parentheses are the standard errors. Significance tests are one-tailed. In the 104th Congress, Democrats were almost perfectly united on votes on the Commerce subcommittee bill; thus, there was no variance for the model to explain.

bought on the agriculture bill. That is, in the 103rd, Republicans who received projects were more likely to support the Democratic chairs of the Treasury/Postal Service and VA/HUD subcommittees, while the same was true for Democrats on agriculture. In the Republican-controlled 104th and 106th Congresses, projects did not buy minority Democratic support for the bills, except on agriculture in the 104th, where Republican votes were also affected by projects. Moreover, in the 104th Congress, majority party votes were affected on an additional subcommittee, CJS.[14] Given that majority and minority votes were influenced in three cases each, we must conclude that there is no pattern in the partisan effect of pork barrel projects on these votes. In the 106th Congress, as in previous analyses, we see no impact for pork barrel projects on members of either party. Thus, these results reinforce the picture of the disappearing impact of pork barrel benefits on roll call voting in the Senate. The findings drive home the point that in a highly partisan Senate, it takes more than a little pork to persuade minority party senators to break ranks with their own party.

To understand what prevented Republican subcommittee chairs from effectively exploiting the pork barrel, I conducted an additional set of interviews in late 2000 with Senate staff and other observers of the process. In those interviews, I summarized the results of the statistical analysis and asked staffers their opinions about this apparent new dynamic in Senate appropriations. Those interviews offer clues but no conclusive arguments as to why the discipline formerly bought by the pork barrel broke down in the Republican congresses. The answer seems to reside in part in Republicans' general ambivalence about pork. On one hand, they dislike it in principle, often condemning it as a misuse of government funds. On the other hand, many of their constituents expect it, and it is hard to resist a benefit that might help them to secure their seats. Staffers noted this ambivalence. As one said, "Republicans have a more schizophrenic relationship to appropriations than Democrats." Another staff member, who had worked for both Republicans and Democrats on the Appropriations Committee, was more specific: "On the Republican side there's a shadiness or a game they play, where they want to have it both ways." They are in favor of a balanced budget and believe that pork is bad, but

[14] That might seem anomalous for CJS, as overall, projects had no impact. However, analysis of the individual votes (as opposed to overall subcommittee support scores) separately for Democrats and Republicans shows that on CJS, Republicans were affected on only one of three votes. Overall, the analysis of individual votes by party produced the same results as the Committee support measure by party.

"they still have to show they're doing something for their constituents." Democrats, on the other hand, are less conflicted; this staffer argued that Democrats see pork barrel benefits as something that government should provide. Republican ambivalence may not keep them from asking for projects, but it might well make the idea of selling their votes for such benefits unacceptable.

However, the interviews suggest a more practical reason for less vote selling. Several staff members noted that the issues that come to the floor in appropriations bills had changed. As one said, "Increasingly, votes are on highly charged substantive policy matters – a senator would come to [the Appropriations Committee chairman] and say, 'Look, I have to vote X on guns – it's an important political issue in my state. I hope you keep that in mind and don't disadvantage me on projects.'" He noted that the Republican leader, Trent Lott, expected far more allegiance from his caucus than had other leaders before him. There are, he said, "more caucus votes than before, where the party leader tells you how to vote." As a result, there is less room for project-for-votes trading.

This increase in votes on policy issues as opposed to less divisive questions of simple dollars and cents mirrors a change in the House Appropriations Committee instituted by Gingrich at the beginning of the 104th Congress. Aldrich and Rohde (2000) demonstrate that the new speaker decided to use the appropriations process to enact substantive policy changes that would have been more difficult to pass through the normal authorization process. As a result, between the 103rd and 104th Congresses the number of partisan amendments proposed on appropriations bills in the House rose from fourteen to 133, nearly a tenfold increase between the two congresses (Aldrich and Rohde 2000, p. 17).

A concurrent development appears to have been an increasing sense among members that they could get away with not voting with the chair who gave them earmarks because they doubted that they would be disciplined for doing so. As one staffer said, mournfully, "There are so few people who are willing to enforce discipline – for generations it was accepted that if you got a project, you voted for the bill; if not, you lost the project. But at some point sanctions started breaking up and people got away with it." And in this person's opinion, it was too late for leaders to reassert discipline: "People have no shame. They vote no and take the dough. I don't know what you can do about it."

Another concurred: "The committee doesn't want to discipline itself or others"; therefore, "you *can* have it both ways," getting projects and then voting as the party leadership (outside the committee) or consciences dictate. This person suggested a different spin on the influence that comes with an appropriations subcommittee chairmanship: Senators use that influence to help their colleagues. As this staffer said, "the chairman and ranking member are human; they like to please their colleagues." Although they may have received something in return, it typically was not the support of those colleagues on their appropriations bills. Nevertheless, it is difficult to believe that they did not want those members' support for their policy preferences; that is traditionally one of the benefits of an Appropriations Committee chairmanship and an expectation acknowledged by staff members.

Finally, one staffer suggested a more personal reason for the decline in the Appropriations Committee's leverage over project recipients. "I sense a change in people's attitudes toward appropriators: [Appropriations Committee] Chairman Stevens threatens people. Stevens is more confrontational than his predecessors, and people may be more tired of it." This staffer said that he felt a growing animus toward the appropriators from the authorizers. The chairs of authorizing committees "are having trouble getting their bills through, and the appropriators are throwing authorizations into their bills." As a result, "there's more shouting at appropriators in Republican caucus than historically."

Thus, two major factors seem to have influenced the decline in the utility of pork barrel benefits for buying votes for Senate Appropriations Committee bills: First, the issues coming to the floor in the committee's bills were more partisan, which itself was most likely a result of the increase in partisanship in the Senate overall. The difficulty in passing authorization bills and the resulting increase in policy add-ons in appropriations bills surely exacerbated that tendency. Recall that one of the necessary conditions stated in Chapter 2 for pork to be an effective means of winning votes is for members to care more about the pork than they do about the measure for which it is intended to buy their vote. It appears that for the Senate Appropriations Committee in the 104th and 106th Congresses, due to increased partisanship, that condition was no longer met. That change in the partisan complexion of those votes meant that members had more pressing considerations than distributive benefits as they decided how to cast their votes. Second, as members grew more driven by partisan or ideological considerations and cast more votes contrary to the wishes of their benefactors, they came to see that they were unlikely to lose their projects in the current bill or to be denied them in the future, even if they did vote against the subcommittee chairs. Thus, the incentive to comply with the wishes of the chairs declined.

CONCLUSIONS

For the 103rd Congress, these results support the argument that Senate Appropriations subcommittee chairs positively influenced the loyalty of other senators by giving their states projects in the FY 1995 appropriations process. Some Appropriations Committee staff members argued that their bills would have passed without projects. Given the special status of such bills, that is most likely true. However, subcommittee chairs want more than final passage of their bills; they seek passage of their own version, the "chairman's mark." To attain that, they must win floor votes on amendments that would undermine their version of the bill, many of which are far closer than the final votes on the bills. Indeed, nearly all of these appropriations bills won final passage with great ease. With only two exceptions, all of the controversial votes were on amendments. Here, the danger to the chair's preferences is significant, because an amendment, for example, to eliminate funds for an Internal Revenue Service tax compliance initiative does not strike at any pork barrel projects that the Treasury funding bill contains. Thus, senators could have voted in favor of that amendment without stripping the bill of their projects. But by including projects with the implicit understanding that the recipients are to support the subcommittee chair, the chair hopes to prevail against such amendments.

Taken together, the interviews and the quantitative results suggest that subcommittee chairs found it necessary to give the lion's share of projects to their own committee and subcommittee members just to try to assure committee solidarity on floor votes. Despite, or perhaps because of, the increase in partisanship in the Senate overall as well as in the Appropriations Committee, the subcommittees generally gave out projects in a bipartisan manner. In three-quarters of the cases examined here, neither party nor ideology affected project distribution.

Given that chairs typically gave projects to subcommittee members regardless of party, they might expect that those members would remain loyal to them or at least would not actively fight them in full committee or on the floor. However, that hope was in vain in the Republican-controlled congresses. In the 104th and 106th Congresses, more than one-fourth of all hostile amendments were offered by members of the subcommittee, nearly all of them Democrats. In the Republican congresses, all of the subcommittee members offering hostile amendments had received earmarks in the bill; indeed, two-thirds of them received more than the mean number of awards given out by the subcommittee. The contrast with the 103rd Congress could not be more stark. In that Congress, only one of the twenty-five amendments proposed to the four subcommittee bills was offered by a subcommittee member. Of course, it is possible that even more amendments would have been offered by subcommittee members in the 104th and 106th Congresses in the absence of project awards; nevertheless, it is undeniable that earmarks won less loyalty in amending activity in the Republican-controlled Senate than in that controlled by the Democrats.

Even if project awards cannot prevent some members from offering hostile amendments on the Senate floor, the chair normally expects project recipients to vote against such amendments. Yet even that hope was futile in the 104th and 106th Congresses. Only in the 103rd Congress did projects reliably buy loyalty. Thus, although the famed bipartisan culture of the Appropriations Committee continued in the distribution of projects, it was dead in 1995 with respect to amending activity and floor votes, projects or no projects.

If projects did not buy fealty to subcommittee chairs, why did they distribute them in such massive numbers, especially in the 106th Congress? There were, of course, politically tinged budgetary reasons for doing so: the budget was in surplus, and the president himself had ignored the spending caps in his budget requests. But from the point of view of the Republican majority, the fact that members wanted projects for reelection purposes was evidently a strong prod to subcommittee chairs. To be sure, they distributed them in a bipartisan manner, true to the committee's tradition. That is, they did not favor their own party's members and deprive Democrats so as to weaken the latter electorally. Nevertheless, giving out projects promised to benefit their own incumbents as well, thus helping to protect the status quo and their majority status. To reiterate what one staff member said, "The decline and fall of [Republican resistance to] earmarks can be explained as the transition from original revolutionary fervor to the desire to become a permanent ruling majority."

In this chapter, we find qualified support for the major hypothesis of this book, which is that policy coalition leaders use pork barrel projects to buy the votes of members of Congress for general interest legislation. Democrats were clearly more successful at using the strategy than Republicans, although on the agriculture subcommittee, the effectiveness of earmarks carried over from the Democratic 103rd to the Republican 104th Congress. Overall, however, partisanship appears to have taken over on these votes.

This chapter concludes the case studies of the use of distributive benefits to buy members' votes. Chapter 7 analyzes the patterns found in these chapters, considers the implications for coalition building and governance, and identifies areas for further study.

APPENDIX

The following is a description of the votes and the partisan division of the votes for all votes included in the subcommittee support scores for each Congress. The descriptions are taken from *Congressional Quarterly Almanac* for 1994 and 1995. Page numbers are noted at the end of each entry. For 1999, the quotations are from *CQ Weekly*, with the specific issue cited in the text.

103rd Congress

Agriculture Subcommittee Votes

HR 4554. "Market Promotion Program. Appropriations Committee amendment to provide up to $90 million for the Market Promotion Program, which subsidizes overseas advertising of U.S. agricultural products. Adopted 62-38: R 34-10; D 28-28 (ND 19-23, SD 9-5), July 19, 1994" (1994 C.Q.A., 35-S).

HR 4554. "Food Stamps Demonstration Initiatives. Bumpers, D-Ark., motion to table . . . the McCain R-Ariz., amendment to [allow] food stamp 'cash out' demonstration initiatives, which would allow the Secretary of Agriculture to authorize states to experiment with providing cash benefits rather than food stamps to low-income individuals. Motion rejected 37-62: R 1-43; D 36-19 (ND 27-14, SD 9-5). July 19, 1994" (1994 C.Q.A., 36-S).

HR 4554. "Food Stamps Demonstration Initiatives. McCain amendment," described above. "Adopted 63-34; R 43-1; D 20-33 (ND 14-26, SD 6-7) July 19, 1994" (1994 C.Q.A., 36-S).

HR 4554. "Research Facilities Closure. Leahy, D-Vt., amendment . . . close 19 Agricultural Research Service facilities specified in the president's fiscal

1995 budget. Adopted 76-23; R 36-8; D 40-15 (ND 33-8, SD 7-7), July 19, 1994" (1994 C.Q.A., 36-S).

HR 4554. "Agriculture Research Buildings. Bumpers, D-Ark., motion to table the Bradley, D-N.J., amendment to cut the amount appropriated for construction and repairs of Agricultural Research Service buildings and facilities from $38.7 million to $25.7 million. Motion rejected 50-50; R 25-19; D 25-31 (ND 16-26, SD 9-5), July 19, 1994" (Bradley amendment later rejected.) (1994 C.Q.A., 36-S).

HR 4554. "Agriculture Research Buildings. Bradley, D-N.J., amendment to cut the amount appropriated for construction and repairs of Agricultural Research Service buildings and facilities from $38.7 million to $25.7 million. Rejected 46-54; R 18-26; D 28-28 (ND 24-18, SD 4-10) July 19, 1994" (1994 C.Q.A., 36-S).

HR 4554. "Tobacco Tariffs. McConnell, R-Ky., motion to table the Brown, R-Colo., amendment to require tobacco producers to pay for compensation to foreign producers, required by the General Agreement on Tariffs and Trade, that could result from a U.S. tariff on imported tobacco. Motion agreed to 63-37; R 20-24; D 43-13 (ND 29-13; SD 14-0), July 20, 1994" (1994 C.Q.A., 36-S).

HR 4554. "Departmental Homosexual Policy. Helms, R-N.C., amendment to require a public hearing prior to the removal of an Agriculture Department employee from a job position because of remarks made by the employee outside of work in opposition to departmental policies regarding homosexuals. The amendment also would reinstate any person removed for such reasons prior to the date of enactment. Adopted 59-41; R 36-8; D 23-33 (ND 14-28, SD 9-5), July 20, 1994" (1994 C.Q.A., 36-S).

CJS Subcommittee Votes

HR 4603. "Legal Services Corporation. Specter, R-Pa., motion to table . . . the Gramm, R-Tex., amendment to prohibit the Legal Services Corporation from using federal money to raise legal challenges in behalf of the poor against welfare reform. Motion agreed to 56-44; R10-34; D 46-10 (ND 41-1, SD 5-9). July 21, 1994" (1994 C.Q.A., 38-S).

HR 4603. "National Endowment for Democracy. Dorgan, D-N.D., amendment to reduce the amount for the National Endowment for

Democracy from $35 million to $25 million. Rejected 39-57; R 15-27; D 24-30 (ND 19-22, SD 5-8), July 22, 1994" (1994 C.Q.A., 38-S).

HR 4603. "Motion to Recommit. Smith, R-N.H., motion to recommit the bill to the Appropriations Committee with instructions to report it back with an amendment reducing the total appropriation to an amount not greater than the fiscal 1994 level without cutting programs intended to reduce crime. Rejected, 24-71; R 21-21; D 3-50 (ND 3-37, SD 0-13), July 22, 1994" (1994 C.Q.A., 39-S).

HR 4603. "Illegal Immigrants Incarceration Costs. Hollings, D-S.C., motion to table . . . the Dole, R-Kans., amendment to transfer $350 million from the U.S. contribution to the United Nations for international peacekeeping operations to reimburse states for the incarceration of illegal aliens. Motion rejected 44-52; R 8-34; D 36-18 (ND 29-12, SD 7-6), July 22, 1994." Dole amendment later adopted by voice vote (1994 C.Q.A., 39-S).

HR 4603. "Death Penalty Statistics. Hatch, R-Utah, amend. to the Dole, R-Kans., amend., to prohibit . . . officials [from using] evidence that race was a statistically significant factor in the decision to seek the death penalty. (The Hatch and Dole amends. were essentially similar.) Rejected 33-54; R 32-7; D 1-47 (ND 0-37, SD 1-10). July 22, 1994" (1994 C.Q.A., 39-S).

Treasury/Postal Service Subcommittee Votes

HR4539. "IRS Compliance Initiative. DeConcini, D-Ariz., motion to table the Grassley, R-IA, amendment to strike $405 million for an IRS tax compliance initiative in FY 1995." Passed 54-43; R 9-35; D 45-8 (ND 35-5, SD 10-30). June 21, 1994 (1994 C.Q.A., 27-S).

HR4539. "Fiscal 1994 Level. DeConcini, D-Ariz., motion to table the Smith, R-N.H., motion to . . . [cut] the bill by $1.1 billion to the fiscal 1994 level. Passed, 56-38: R 11-30; D 45-8; (ND 33-6, SD 12-2), June 21, 1994" (1994 C.Q.A., 27-S).

HR4539. "Border Crossing Fee. Deconcini, D-Ariz., motion to table the Reid, D-Nev., amendment to delete language in the bill that would have prohibited the Customs Service from charging border crossing fees along the US-Mexican border. Rejected 44-55; R 18-26; D 26-29 (ND 21-20, SD 5-9). June 22, 1994" (1994 C.Q.A., 27-S).

HR4539. "Recreational Diesel Fuel. [Technical amendment to protect] the Gorton amendment [that] would allow marinas to sell dyed diesel fuel intended for tax-exempt commercial use to recreational boaters, provided that the marina collects taxes on the fuel when sold. Motion agreed to 79-20; R 42-2; D 17-18 (ND 24-27, SD 13-1). June 22, 1994... (Subsequently,... the Gorton amendment was adopted by voice vote.)" (1994 C.Q.A., 27-S).

HR4539. "Employment Floors. DeConcini, D-Ariz., motion to table the McCain, R-Ariz., amendment to eliminate the full-time equivalent employment minimum staffing requirements from the bill. Motion agreed to 66-33: R 19-25; D 47-8 (ND 35-6, SD 12-2), June 22, 1994" (1994 C.Q.A., 27-S).

HR4539. "Passage. Passage of the bill to provide $23.6 billion in new budget authority for the Treasury Department, the U.S. Postal Service, the Executive Office of the President and certain independent agencies for fiscal 1995. The administration had requested $24,570,064,000. Passed 72-27: R 22-22; D 50-5 (ND 38-3, SD 12-2), June 22, 1994" (1994 C.Q.A., 28-S).

VA/HUD Subcommittee Votes

HR 4624. "Space Station. Bumpers, D-Ark., amendment to terminate the space station program, cutting $1.9 billion from the bill. Rejected 36-64: R 6-38; D 30-26 (ND 23-29, SD7-7). Aug. 3, 1994" (1994 C.Q.A., 43-S).

HR 4624. "Ethanol Mandate. Mikulski, D-Md., motion to table the Johnston, D-La., amendment to prohibit the EPA from implementing its renewable oxygenates rule for re-formulated gasoline, which would require a minimum of 15% and eventually 30% of the oxygenates used in reformulated gasoline to come from renewable sources, such as ethanol. The amend. also would have cut NASA's procurement budget by $29.3 million. Motion agreed to 512-50; R 19-25 D 31-25 (ND 26-16, SD 5-9), with Vice President Gore casting a 'yea' vote. Aug. 3, 1994" (1994 C.Q.A., 43-S).

HR 4624. "VA Inpatient Facilities. Rockefeller, D-W.Va., motion to table the Murkowski, R-Alaska, amendment to restrict the use of $87.7 million in the bill to build or modernize three inpatient facilities as veterans hospitals in Tennessee, California, and Hawaii. Motion agreed to 62-36: R 7-36, D 55-0 (NC 42-0, SD 13-0), Aug. 4, 1994" (1994 C.Q.A., 44-S).

HR 4624. "Pension Fund Housing Investment. Mikulski, D-Md., motion to table . . . the Cohen, R-Maine, amendment to eliminate the $350 million in the bill for a government subsidy program to encourage investment by pension funds in low-income housing. Motion agreed to 55-43; R 4-39, D 51-4 (ND 39-3, SD 12-1), Aug. 4, 1994" (1994 C.Q.A., 44-S).

HR 4624. "Community Development Block Grants. Smith, R-N.H., amendment to eliminate the $135 million in "special purpose grants" under the Department of Housing and Urban Development and to redistribute the money through the Community Development Block Grant Program. Rejected 27-71; R 23-20; D 4-51 (ND 3-39, SD 1-12), Aug. 4, 1994" (1994 C.Q.A., 44-S).

HR 4624. "Clean Water Revolving Fund. Smith, R-N.H., amend. to eliminate $697.2 million earmarked for specific waste water treatment construction projects and redistribute the money through the formula established in the Clean Water State Revolving Fund. Rejected 37-60; R 25-18, D 12-42 (ND 8-33, SD 4-9), Aug. 4, 1994" (1994 C.Q.A., 44-S).

104th Congress

Agriculture Subcommittee Votes

HR 1976. "Cotton Disaster Assistance. Cochran, R-Miss., motion to table . . . the Kerrey, D-Nebr., amendment to eliminate the provision that provides up to $41 million to cotton farmers who suffered crop insect damage in 1995, and instead transfer the money to [various rural development accounts]. Motion rejected 37-53: R 28-21; D 9-32 (ND 3-28; SD 6-4), Sept. 18, 1995. (Subsequently, the Kerrey amendment was adopted by voice vote.)" (1995 C.Q.A., S-71).

HR 1976. "Market Promotion Program. Cochran, R-Miss., motion to table . . . the Bryan, D-Nev., amendment to cut the $110 million Market Promotion Program, which provides subsidies to companies that advertise American agricultural products overseas. Motion agreed to 59-41: R 32-22; D 27-19 (ND 20-16; SD 7-3), Sept. 19, 1995" (1995 C.Q.A., S-71).

HR 1976. "Poultry Regulation. Boxer, D-Calif., motion to table . . . the Committee amendment to block a new federal regulation that would allow poultry to be sold as 'fresh' only if it was never chilled below 26 degrees F. Currently, poultry can be chilled to nearly zero and still be labeled as 'fresh.' Motion rejected 38-611: R 7-46; D 31-15 (ND 30-6; SD 1-9), Sept 19, 1995. (Subsequently, the Committee Amendment was adopted by voice vote.)" (1995 C.Q.A., S-71).

HR 1976. "Mink Exports. Cochran, R-Miss., motion to table . . . the Kerry, D-Mass., amendment to cut $2 million provided for market promotion assistance to the U.S. Mink Export Council. Motion rejected 18-78: R 15-36; D 3-42 (ND 3-33; SD 0-9), Sept. 19, 1995. (Subsequently, the Kerry amendment was adopted by voice vote.)" (1995 C.Q.A., S-72).

HR 1976. "Under Secretary for Natural Resources and Environment. Bumpers, D-Ark., motion to table . . . the Stevens, R-Alaska, amendment to delete funding for the assistant under-secretary for Natural Resources and Environment. Motion rejected 42-51: R 0-51; D 42-0, Sept. 19, 1995. (Subsequently, the Stevens amendment was adopted by voice vote.)" (1995 C.Q.A., S-72).

HR 1976. "Research Grant Bidding. Cochran, R-Miss., motion to table . . . the Feingold, D-Wis., amendment to require that grants made by the Dept. of Agriculture (USDA) be subject to scientific peer review by scientists outside the USDA and that all research grants be awarded on a competitive basis. Motion agreed to 64-34; R 40-13; D 24-21 (ND 18-18; SD 6-3), Sept. 20, 1995" (1995 C.Q.A., S-72).

HR 1976. "Deficiency Payments. Conrad, D-N.D., amend. to establish a $35 million forgiveness program that would provide farmers with up to $2,500, if they are required to repay advance deficiency payments for a 1995 crop but have suffered a loss in excess of 35% due to weather or related conditions. Rejected 34-64; R. 8-45; D 26-19 (ND 19-17; SD 7-2), Sept. 20, 1995" (1995 C.Q.A., S-72).

HR 1976. "Revised Market Promotion Program. Cochran, R-Miss., motion to table . . . the Bumpers, D-Ark., amendment to reduce the appropriation from $110 million to $70 million for the Market Promotion Program which provides subsidies for companies that advertise American

Agricultural products overseas. Motion rejected 36-62: R 26-27; D 10-35 (ND 8-28; SD 2-7), Sept. 20, 1995. (Subsequently, the Bumpers Amendment was adopted by voice vote.)" (1995 C.Q.A., S-72).

CJS Votes

HR 2127. "Legal Services Corporation. Gramm, R-Texas, motion to table . . . the Domenici, R-N.M., amendment to preserve the Legal Services Corp., a federal legal assistance service for the poor, by providing the corporation with $340 million. . . . Motion rejected 39-60: R 38-16; D 1-44 (ND 1-34; SD 0-10), Sept. 29, 1995. (Subsequently, the Domenici amendment was adopted by voice vote.)" (1995 C.Q.A., S-77).

HR 2127. "Social Crime Prevention. Kohl, D-Wis., amend. to add $80 million for social crime prevention programs and offset the cost by cutting FBI funding by an equal amount. Adopted 49-41: R 9-40; D 40-1 (ND 31-1; SD 9-0) Sept. 29, 1995" (1995 C.Q.A., S-77).

Treasury/Postal Service Votes

HR 2020. "Federal Health Policy Abortions. Committee amendment to strike bill provisions to prohibit federal employees or their families from receiving abortion services through federal health insurance policies except when the life of the woman would be endangered. Adopted 52-41: R 15-35; D 37-6 (ND 33-2; SD 4-4), Aug. 4, 1995. A 'yea' was a vote in support of the president's position" (1995 C.Q.A., S-61).

HR 2020. "Federal Health Policy Abortions. Nickles, R-Okla., amendment to the Appropriations Committee amendment to prohibit federal employees or their families from receiving abortion services through their federal health insurance policies except when the life of the mother would be endangered or in cases of rape or incest. Adopted 50-44: R 40-10; D 10-34 (ND 5-31; SD 5-3), Aug. 5, 1995. A 'nay' was a vote in support of the president's position" (1995 C.Q.A. S-61).

HR 2020. "Federal Health Policy Abortions. Mikulski, D-Md., amendment to the Appropriations Committee amendment, to prohibit federal employees or their families from receiving abortion services through their federal health insurance policies except when the life of the woman would be endangered or in cases of rape or incest or where abortion is determined to be medically necessary. Rejected 45-49: R 9-41; D 36-8 (ND 33-3; SD 3-5), Aug. 5, 1995" (1995 C.Q.A., S-61).

VA/HUD Votes

HR 2099. "Space Station Termination. Bumpers, D-Ark., amendment to terminate the space station program.... Rejected 35-64: R 12-41; D 23-23 (ND 19-17, SD 4-6) Sept. 26, 1995. A 'nay' was a vote in support of the president's position" (1995 C.Q.A., S-74).

HR 2099. "National Service Program. Mikulski amendment to provide $426.5 million for the ... AmeriCorps program ... [offsetting the increase] by reducing funding for assisted housing. The bill would terminate the National Service program. Rejected 47-52: R 6-47; D 41-5 (ND 32-4; SD 9-1), Sept. 26, 1995. A 'yea' was a vote in support of the president's position" (1995 C.Q.A., S-74).

HR 2099. "Mentally Disabled Veterans. Rockefeller, D-W.Va., motion to waive the Budget Act ... [in order to allow] the Rockefeller amendment [to] strike from the bill limits on compensation for certain mentally disabled veterans and offset the cost by limiting proposed tax cut benefits to those families making less than $100,000 per year. Motion rejected 47-53: R 2-52; D 45-1 (ND 35-1; SD 10-0); Sept. 27, 1995. A three-fifths' majority vote (60) of the total Senate is required to waive the budget act" (1995 C.Q.A., S-74).

HR 2099. "Veterans Medical Care. Rockefeller, D-W.Va., motion to waive the Budget Act ... [in order to allow] the Rockefeller amendment [to] increase [funding] for veterans medical care ... to the level requested by the president.... [offsetting] the cost by limiting proposed tax cut benefits to those families making less than $100,000 per year. Motion rejected 51-49: R 6-48; D 45-1 (ND 35-1; SD 10-0); Sept. 27, 1995. A three-fifths' majority vote of the total Senate is required to waive the budget act. (Subsequently, the chair upheld the ... point of order and the Rockefeller amendment fell.)" (1995 C.Q.A., S-75).

HR 2099. "Health and Environmental Regulations. Baucus, D-Mont., amendment to enable the EPA administrator to disregard provisions in the bill that would weaken environmental protection or public health. Rejected 39-61: R 5-49; D 34-12 (ND 30-6; SD 4-6), Sept. 27, 1995" (1995 C.Q.A., S-75).

HR 2099. "Homeless Assistance. Bond, R-Mo., motion to table ... the Sarbanes, D-Md., amendment to restore homeless assistance funding to the 1995 level, and offset the costs by reducing funds for the renewal of expiring subsidized private housing contracts. Motion agreed to 52-48: R 52-2; D 0-46 (ND 0-36; SD 0-10), Sept. 27, 1995" (1995 C.Q.A., S-75).

HR 2099. "Superfund. Lautenberg, D-N.J., motion to waive the Budget Act ... [in order to allow] the Lautenberg amendment [to] increase [funding for the] Superfund program, restoring the program to the 1995 level ...; [offsetting the cost] by limiting a proposed tax cut to those families making less than $150,000 per year. Motion rejected 45-54: R 1-52: D 44-2 (ND 34-2; SD 10-0); Sept. 27, 1995. A three-fifths' majority vote of the total Senate is required to waive the budget act. (Subsequently, the chair upheld the ... point of order and the Lautenberg amendment fell.)" (1995 C.Q.A., S-75).

HR 2099. "Passage of the bill to provide about $81 billion in fiscal 1996 budget authority for VA, HUD, and independent agencies, ... about $8.9 billion less than the administration requested and [the] fiscal 1995 [appropriation]. Passed 55-45: R 54-0; D 1-45 (ND 1-35; SD 0-10), Sept. 27, 1995. A 'nay' was a vote in support of the president's position" (1995 C.Q.A., S-75).

106th Congress

Agriculture Subcommittee Votes

S 1233. "Patients' Bill of Rights. Lott, R-Miss., motion to table (kill) the Lott second-degree amendment to the Dorgan, D-N.D., amendment that would insert the text of S. 6 into the underlying appropriations bill. The Lott amendment would replace the text of the Dorgan amendment (S 6), which would ... protect consumers in managed care plans and other health coverage, with the text of S 326, which would improve the access and choice of patients to quality, affordable health care. June 22, 1999. Motion rejected by a vote of 45-55: Republicans 0-55; Democrats 45-0 (Northern Democrats 37-0, Southern Democrats 8-0)" (*CQ Weekly*, June 26, 1999, 1570).

S 1233. "Patients Bill of Rights. Lott, R-Miss., motion to table (kill) the Dorgan, D-N.D., amendment that would ... protect consumers in managed care plans and other health coverage. Motion agreed to by a vote of 53-47: Republicans: 53-2; Democrats 0-45 (Northern Democrats 0-37, Southern Democrats 0-8)" (*CQ Weekly*, June 26, 1999, 1570).

S 1233. "Unilateral Food and Medicine Sanctions. Helms, R-N.C., motion to table (kill) the Ashcroft, R-Mo., amendment to the Daschle, D-S.D., amendment. The Ashcroft amendment would terminate U.S. unilateral sanctions on agricultural and medicinal goods and bar the president from imposing such sanctions against a country without congressional approval, with certain exceptions. Motion rejected by a vote of 28-70: Republicans 17-36; Democrats 10-34 (Northern Democrats 8-28, Southern Democrats 2-6); Independents 1-0. Aug. 3, 1999. (Subsequently, the Ashcroft amendment was adopted by voice vote.)" (*CQ Weekly*, December 4, 1999, 2943).

S 1233. "Motion to invoke cloture (thus limiting debate) on the bill to provide $60.7 billion in new budget authority for the Agriculture Department, the Food and Drug Administration and rural development and nutrition programs in fiscal 2000. The bill would provide $417 million less than provided in fiscal 1999 and $6.2 billion less than requested by President Clinton. Motion rejected by a vote of 50-37: Republicans 50-0; Democrats 0-37 (Northern Democrats 0-30, Southern Democrats 0-7). June 28, 1999. Three-fifths of the total Senate (60) is required to invoke cloture" (*CQ Weekly*, July 3, 1999, 1642).

S 1233. "Republican Emergency Farm Aid Plan. Daschle, D-S.D., motion to table (kill) the Cochran, R-Miss., amendment to the Daschle amendment. The Cochran amendment would strike the Daschle language and instead provide $7 billion in emergency aid to farmers, mostly in supplemental market transition payments. Motion rejected by a vote of 47-51: Republicans 2-50; Democrats 45-0 (Northern Democrats 37-0, Southern Democrats 8-0); Independents 0-1. Subsequently, the Cochran amendment was withdrawn. Aug. 3, 1999" (*CQ Weekly*, Aug. 7, 1999, 1967).

S 1233. "Democratic Emergency Farm Aid Plan. Lott, R-Miss., motion to table (kill) the Harkin, D-Iowa, amendment [that] would provide $10.8 billion in emergency aid to farmers and ranchers.... Motion agreed to by a vote of 54-44: Republicans 51-1; Democrats 2-43 (Northern Democrats 1-36, Southern Democrats 1-7); Independents 1-0. Aug. 3, 1999" (*CQ Weekly*, Aug. 7, 1999, 1967).

S 1233. "Milk Prices. Motion to invoke cloture (thus limiting debate) on the Lott, R-Miss., motion to recommit the bill to the Senate Appropriations Committee with Jeffords, R-Vt., instructions to add language to prohibit funding for the Agriculture Department to implement proposed changes in milk marketing orders in fiscal 2000. Motion rejected by a vote of 53-47: Republicans 27-27; Democrats 25-20 (Northern Democrats 17-20, Southern Democrats 8-0); Independents 1-0. Aug. 4, 1999" (*CQ Weekly*, Aug. 7, 1999, 1967).

S 1233. "Emergency Farm Aid Plan. Cochran, R-Miss., motion to table (kill) the Roberts, R-Kans., amendment [which] would strike the Daschle language and instead provide $7.6 billion in emergency aid to farmers, mostly in supplemental market transition payments, but including $400 million for disaster assistance, [and] to require congressional approval before imposing U.S. unilateral sanctions that restrict agricultural and medicinal goods to a foreign country. Motion agreed to by a vote of 66-33: Republicans 21-32; Democrats 45-0 (Northern Democrats 37-0, Southern Democrats 8-0); Independents 0-1. Aug. 4, 1999. Subsequently, a modified Cochran amendment . . . was adopted by voice vote" (*CQ Weekly*, Aug. 7, 1999, 1968).

S 1233. "Sugar Program. Cochran, R-Miss., motion to table (kill) the McCain, R-Ariz., amendment, [which] would prohibit the Agriculture Department from using funds in the bill for the sugar program, which provides loans, import restrictions and price-supports for the industry. Motion agreed to by a vote of 66-33: Republicans 34-19, Democrats 32-13 (Northern Democrats 24-13, Southern Democrats 8-0), Independents 0-1. Aug. 4, 1999" (*CQ Weekly*, Aug. 7, 1999, 1968).

S 1233. "Democratic Emergency Farm Aid Plan. Cochran, R-Miss., motion to table (kill) the Dorgan, D-N.D., amendment [which] would strike the Daschle language (as replaced by the Cochran amendment) and instead provide $9.8 billion in emergency aid to farmers and ranchers, including funds for disaster assistance, income loss payments and emergency trade provisions. Motion agreed to by a vote of 55-44: Republicans 52-1; Democrats 2-43 (Northern Democrats 1-36, Southern Democrats 1-7); Independents 1-0. Aug. 4, 1999" (*CQ Weekly*, Aug. 7, 1999, 1968).

S 1233. "Compromise Emergency Farm Aid Plan. Cochran, R-Miss., motion to table (kill) the Conrad, D-N.D., amendment, [which] would provide $8.8 billion in emergency aid to farmers, mostly in supplemental market transition payments. Aug. 4, 1999. Motion agreed to by a vote of 51-48: Republicans 47-6; Democrats 3-42 (Northern Democrats 2-35,

Southern Democrats 1-7); Independents 1-0" (*CQ Weekly*, Aug. 7, 1999, 1968).

S 1233. "Fuel Additive Effects on Health. Boxer, D-Calif., motion to table (kill) the Chafee, R-R.I., substitute amendment to the Boxer amendment. The Chafee amendment would express the sense of the Senate that the Environment and Public Works Committee should review EPA findings on the fuel additive methyl tertiary butylether (MTBE) and report to the Senate. The Boxer amendment would express the sense of the Senate that MTBE should be phased out in order to address the threats it poses to public health and the environment, and renewable ethanol should be promoted to replace MTBE. Aug. 4, 1999. Motion agreed to by a vote of 52-43: Republicans 14-38; Democrats 38-4 (Northern Democrats 33-2, Southern Democrats 5-2); Independents 0-1. Subsequently, the Boxer amendment was adopted and the underlying $70 billion bill was passed by voice vote" (*CQ Weekly*, Aug. 7, 1999, 1969).

CJS Votes

S 1217. "Cloture. Motion to invoke cloture (thus limiting debate) on the motion to proceed to the bill that would provide $35.3 billion in new budget authority for the departments of Commerce, Justice and State and the federal judiciary in fiscal 2000. The bill would provide $918 million less than in fiscal 1999 and $11.6 billion less than requested by President Clinton. Motion rejected by a vote of 49-39: Republicans 48-1; Democrats 1-38 (Northern Democrats 1-31, Southern Democrats 0-7). June 28, 1999" (*CQ Weekly*, July 3, 1999, 1642).

S 1217. "Underage Drinking Media Campaign. Lautenberg, D-N.J., amendment that would provide $25 million for a media campaign to prevent alcohol use by individuals under 21 years old. Rejected by a vote of 43-54: Republicans 5-47; Democrats 38-6 (Northern Democrats 31-5, Southern Democrats 7-1); Independents 0-1. July 22, 1999" (*CQ Weekly*, July 24, 1999, 1819).

S 1217. "FCC Accounting Requirements. Hollings, D-S.C., motion to table (kill) the Enzi, R-Wyo., amendment that would prohibit the FCC from requiring the utilization of any accounting method that does not conform to 'generally accepted accounting principles.'... Motion rejected 45-52. R 6-46; D 39-5 (ND 31-5, SD 8-0); I 0-1. July 22, 1999. (Subsequently, the Enzi amendment was adopted by voice vote.)" (*CQ Weekly*, July 24, 1999, 1819).

S 1217. "Prisoner Injunctive Relief. Gregg, R-N.H., motion to table (kill) the Wellstone, D-Minn., amendment that would exempt juveniles and the mentally ill from current laws that limit the power of federal courts to grant injunctive relief on the basis of prison conditions. Motion agreed to 56-40. R 50-1; D 5-39 (ND 5-31) SD 0-8); I 1-0. July 11, 1999" (*CQ Weekly*, July 24, 1999, 1819).

S 1217. "Tuna Importation. Gregg, R-N.H., motion to table (kill) the Boxer, D-Calif., amendment that would prohibit importation of tuna from any nation in the Inter-American Tropical Tuna Commission in any year in which the nation has not paid a proportionate share of the commission's expenses. Motion rejected by a vote of 35-61: Republicans 33-19; Democrats 2-41 (Northern Democrats 0-35, Southern Democrats 2-6); Independents 0-1. Note: Subsequently, the Boxer amendment was adopted and the $35.3 billion underlying bill was passed by voice vote. July 22, 1999" (*CQ Weekly*, July 24, 1999, 1819).

Treasury/Postal Service Votes

S 1282. "Alcohol Use by Minors. Campbell, R-Colo., motion to table (kill) the Lautenberg, D-N.J., amendment that would add alcohol use by minors to the topics addressed by the national anti-drug media campaign intended to reduce youth drug use. Motion agreed to by a vote of 58-40: Republicans 48-6; Democrats 10-34 (Northern Democrats 6-30, Southern Democrats 4-4). July 1, 1999" (*CQ Weekly*, July 3, 1999, 1643).

S 1282. "Abortion Coverage. Boxer, D-Calif., motion to table (kill) the DeWine, R-Ohio, amendment that would prohibit funding for abortions or for administrative expenses of federal health plans that provide coverage for abortions, except where the life of the mother is endangered or the pregnancy is the result of rape or incest. Motion rejected 47-51; R 7-46; D 40-5 (ND 33-4; SD 7-1). July 1, 1999. (Subsequently the DeWine amendment was adopted and the $22.7 billion underlying bill was passed by voice vote.)" (*CQ Weekly*, July 3, 1999, 1643).

VA/ HUD Votes

HR 2684. "Veterans' Medical Care. Wellstone, D-Minn., motion to waive the Budget Act [and allow an] amendment [that] would increase funding for veterans' medical care by $1.3 billion. Motion rejected by a vote of 36-63: Republicans 9-44; Democrats 26-19 (Northern Democrats 24-13, Southern Democrats 2-6); Independents 1-0. Sept. 22, 1999. A three-fifths majority vote (60) of the total Senate is required to waive the Budget Act. (Subsequently, the chair upheld the point of order, and the amendment fell.)" (*CQ Weekly*, September 25,1999 2250).

HR 2684. "Veterans' Benefits, AmeriCorps. Bond, R-Mo., motion to table (kill) the Smith, I-N.H., amendment that would reduce funding for the AmeriCorps national service program by $225 million and reallocate $210 million for veterans' medical benefits, $5 million for homeless veterans and $10 million for construction of veterans' extended care facilities. Motion agreed to by a vote of 61-38: Republicans 16-37; Democrats 45-0 (Northern Democrats 37-0, Southern Democrats 8-0); Independents 0-1. Sept. 22, 1999" (*CQ Weekly*, September 25, 1999, 2250).

HR 2684. "Atomic Veterans Benefits. Wellstone, D-Minn., amendment that would express the sense of the Senate that lung cancer, colon cancer and brain and central nervous system cancer, afflictions developed by some 'atomic' veterans who were exposed to radiation . . . should be added to the list of radiogenic diseases that are presumed . . . to be service-connected disabilities. Adopted 76-18: R 32-18; D 43-0 (ND 35-0; SD 8-0). (Subsequently, the underlying bill was passed by voice vote.) Sept. 24, 1999" (*CQ Weekly*, October 2, 1999, 2329).

7

Conclusions

The argument of this book is that vote buying with pork barrel projects is useful, even essential, under some conditions for passing general interest legislation in a legislative body whose majority party leaders lack powerful sanctions for enforcing party discipline on each and every issue. The U.S. Congress is certainly such a body, despite its increasing partisanship. In his influential analysis of the role of parties in the House of Representatives in assembling majority voting coalitions, David Rohde (1991) describes a system of "conditional party government," in which the party caucuses expect their leaders to use the tools in their possession to enforce discipline, but only on those issues on which broad intraparty agreement exists. Rohde explicitly recognizes that there are issues on which no such agreement exists (pp. 31–32); in such cases or where policy coalition leaders wish to buck the party leadership, they must use other resources to assemble a majority. Pork is one such resource. The preceding chapters show that it is one that is often effective at winning votes.

There are many potential opportunities for leaders to use this method of forming coalitions, despite the fact that the proportion of votes that is counted as party unity votes has risen over the past twenty-five years (Ornstein, Mann, and Malbin 2002, p. 172). The standard scoring system for a party unity vote requires only that a simple majority of one party vote in opposition to a simple majority of the other. This means that a vote on which 50 percent minus one member dissents from a bare party majority is classified as one on which the party was unified. Thus, there was still a need on at least some of those votes to augment coalitions founded on policy agreement, and plenty of opportunity to do so, especially for leaders with access to distributive benefits. That access is more readily available to majority party coalition leaders than to those in the minority, as majority party leaders (including committee chairs) control the agenda. This means that they have control over what is considered and when; in particular, they control, at least initially, the legislative vehicle for dealing with a particular policy problem. Certainly, majority party coalition leaders' preferred version of a bill might ultimately lose in committee or on the floor to a minority substitute proposal. But by controlling the agenda early on, they have an opportunity to structure their own preferred proposal so as to gain votes in any way possible short of altering the bill so much that it is no longer worth the effort of moving it.

Chapter 2 briefly reviewed the debate among theorists of distributive politics as to whether projects in purely distributive legislation go to all members who want one (universalistic distribution) or only to as many as are needed to form a bare majority (minimal winning) coalition. When coalition leaders seek to pass general interest legislation, as opposed to a massive pork barrel bill, they do not necessarily need to give projects to more than a minority of members, as the legislation in question can attract a base of support on its own merits.

Nevertheless, it may be dangerous to give projects to enough members only to round up support to a bare majority. First, if the threat of a presidential veto hovers over the bill, they need to give enough projects, especially to members of the president's party, to override a veto, as House Public Works and Transportation Committee leaders did in the 1987 highway reauthorization. Second, in the Senate, the need to obtain sixty votes to break a filibuster provides adequate reason to assemble an extraordinary majority. Finally, and more broadly, the danger of amendments that would undermine the coalition leaders' policy goals (amendments that might seem harmless to members who generally support the bill) increases the attractiveness of a relatively policy-neutral form of currency with which to buy votes. Thus, coalition leaders have a choice of two possible approaches to coalition size. First, they can give projects as if they were following an efficient strategy of giving only to members whose votes are both attainable and absolutely needed to protect the leaders' preferred version of the bill: those who are on the fence or are only slightly opposed to the bill. However, this strategy has disadvantages. To the extent that leaders try to distribute projects efficiently, they encourage members who otherwise favor the bill on its merits to behave strategically, concealing their true preferences in order to persuade leaders that their votes must be bought. Such an obvious incentive, clearly evident in the interviews on the highway bills and NAFTA, along with leaders' uncertainty as to how many votes they will need to prevail on as-yet unknown amendments, might well recommend a less discriminating approach to awarding projects. Thus, leaders can more profitably eschew the strategic distribution of projects as a futile quest and, instead, follow a second distribution strategy: Give benefits indiscriminately to all who ask. The first approach would approximate most closely a minimal winning coalition strategy; the second is essentially a strategy of universalism.

The evidence in this book supports the less discriminating approach to project distribution, particularly on the second and later rounds of vote buying. We have one example with which to examine both the first and second times that policy coalition leaders gave out distributive benefits to buy votes, and that is the transportation case. There we see that the first time leaders used the pork barrel strategy, they made their decisions as to who should get projects in a moderately strategic way. That is, the more supportive members were likely to be, the more likely they were to get a project. While that might seem to be a less efficient approach than giving projects to fence-sitters, it is a way to ensure support on weakening amendments that otherwise supportive members might find appealing. However, on the second bill, the relationship between members' expected support for the leaders' preferences and the receipt of a project disappeared. Whether because members had learned to conceal their true voting intentions or leaders just felt they had to respond to massively increased demand in order to maintain good will, the leaders did not distribute projects on that bill on the basis of members' likely support. In fact, one of the most important findings overall is that leaders were willing to give benefits in order to attract members of both parties, support that is especially important if some majority party votes are not forthcoming. Additionally, policy coalition leaders give benefits to members of the subcommittee or full committee of jurisdiction, whose unified support sends cues to members of both parties that they can, as a matter of politics, and should, as a matter of policy, support the bill. There is also some tendency to give disproportionately to leaders (especially in the House on the highway bills) who themselves have a disproportionate influence on the fate of the bill. In addition, in most cases in which measurement was possible, constituency demand had an impact on project distribution.

Beyond those considerations, little else matters to the distribution of pork barrel projects. Notable for its omission is the party of the recipient. In nearly every case (the few exceptions appearing in two out of twelve

Senate appropriations bills), projects were distributed in a bipartisan manner. This is further evidence of a universalistic or at least a supermajority distributive strategy. Leaders give to members of their own party to hold their loyalty through various challenges on the floor. They also give to members of the other party, who might be won by pork barrel benefits away from support for their own party's position if it is in opposition to the bill.

Finally, a look at the amount of variance explained by the project allocation equations reinforces the conclusion that pork is not distributed according to any finely honed strategy. Across all of the allocation equations estimated here, the mean R^2 is .242. Although the maximum R^2 among the equations is .488, in only four of the seventeen equations does it exceed .30. Thus, much variance in the distribution of projects is left unexplained by hypotheses that encompass only leaders' strategy of coalition building, along with member and constituency need, measured imprecisely in some equations with demographic variables. We are left with the likelihood that the variance that is unexplained statistically can actually be accounted for by member demand above and beyond their own value as coalition partners and measurable constituency need. Leaders meet this excess demand as best they can. By using a generous distribution strategy, coalition leaders obviate the need to try to determine members' true voting intentions and thereby court the broadest possible support for their version of the legislation. In effect, leaders use projects to buy themselves insurance against veto threats, Senate filibusters, and the possibility of a variety of amendments intended to undermine their preferred version of the bill. Nevertheless, the project allocation equations do show that leaders also distribute benefits as if they were trying to influence key members' votes.

Now we turn to a summary of the actual impact of projects on members' roll call votes. First, vote buying with pork barrel projects was remarkably effective in the House of Representatives. On all three bills considered in the House, two highway program reauthorizations and NAFTA, distributive benefits influenced recipients to support the positions of their leaders on all votes on which those leaders took a clear stance. On the two highway bills, the Big Four committee leaders took positions on thirteen of the recorded votes. Demonstration projects affected members' votes in the expected direction on all of those votes. The same was true for the vote on NAFTA.

Just as interesting as the fact that projects won votes is the question of whose votes were affected when the projects' impact on Democrats and Republicans is considered separately. In both the House and Senate, members of both parties were affected. On the 1986–1987 highway bill, while demonstration projects affected the votes of Democrats on two issues, they pulled Republicans away from their own party's majority on three of seven issues on which there was a leadership position. That finding gains additional significance when we consider members' initial propensity to support the leaders. Table 4.3 showed that there were four votes on which the typical Republican was initially inclined to vote against the Big Four. On three of those four votes, receipt of a project converted such a member to support for the leaders' position. For Democrats, the results are similar: On two of the three votes on which the typical Democrat would have opposed the leaders without a project, that member supported the leaders if he or she received one.

The impact of demonstration projects on members' voting on the 1991 highway bill was even more striking. Three of six recorded votes concerned the contentious rule under which the bill was to be considered. On all of those, Democrats were virtually unanimous, following the majority party's custom of supporting its leadership-crafted rules. Republican project recipients, on the other hand, opposed the large majority of their partisan colleagues and voted to support the Big Four on the rule. Indeed, on this bill, Republicans were pulled away from the majority of their party on four of the five votes on which the Big Four were unified and sought to enforce discipline.

On NAFTA, the tables were turned on the majority party. Although district benefits had a statistical effect on the votes of both Democrats and Republicans, the Democrats were most opposed to NAFTA. As Table 5.3 showed, the mean Democrat who received a special benefit from the president changed his or her vote from opposition to support for NAFTA. This time, a Democratic president joined forces with the more unified House Republicans to pick off votes from the already badly divided Democrats, one of whose leaders headed the opposition to his own party's president.

Thus, in the House, perhaps the most interesting effect of pork proved to be its ability to pull members away from their own party's majority when awarded by leaders of the other party. It matters not whether that party is in the majority or the minority, but, given the majority's superior access to such resources, it is usually the case that leaders of the majority party peel away members of the minority. And within the majority party, pork reins in those who are tempted to stray on other grounds, such as ideology.

The pattern on Senate appropriations bills in the Democratic 103rd Congress is similar to that in the House. When the roll call votes of Democrats and Republicans were analyzed together, earmarks influenced members to vote with the subcommittee chair on nine of twenty-five individual votes that make up the subcommittee support indices. When the individual vote models for Democrats and Republicans were estimated separately, earmarks affected the voting of members of one party or the other on fourteen of the twenty-five votes. As was true in the House, there was no clear pattern of minority party members being influenced differentially. Minority party votes were affected on two subcommittees, Treasury/Postal Service and VA/HUD, but majority party votes were affected on Agriculture.

However, an important feature of these Appropriations committee votes is that they concerned public policy issues of major importance. For example, in the 104th Congress, there were votes on insurance coverage for abortion services for federal employees, on restricting the ability of the Legal Services Corporation to bring lawsuits challenging welfare reform on behalf of the poor, on killing the Legal Services Corporation (long a target of conservatives) outright, on funding an antismoking advertising campaign aimed at young people, and so on through a large variety of partisan, ideological issues. (Those votes are described in the Appendix to Chapter 6.) Recall that pork barrel benefits influence recipients' votes only when they care more about the projects than about the issue on which their votes are sought. Therefore, when the issues activate partisan or ideological conflict, especially when the parties are internally unified over them, such material benefits are relatively weak inducements for members to defect.

Still, the lack of evidence for vote buying with pork in the Republican Senate, with the exception of the agriculture subcommittee in the 104th Congress, is striking. It is not that Republicans did not give out earmarks; they gave them out in large and increasing numbers as time went by. Nor is it the case, as the interviews with Appropriations Committee staff directors show, that leaders did not intend to influence members' votes: They expected the loyalty of the senators to whom they gave earmarks. However, Democratic project recipients not only failed to comply, a number of them committed the ultimate sin: They offered hostile amendments to the chairman's mark, something that Republican committee members did not do in the 103rd Congress, when they were in the minority. At the same time, although partisanship was already high on the four appropriations subcommittees examined here in the 103rd Congress, it increased following the Republican takeover, as it did on all Senate votes, as Figure 6.2 showed. Why did projects stop buying votes? What changed between the 103rd and 104th Congresses? Was it the growth of partisanship?

Follow-up interviews offered several explanations; partisanship plays a role in two of them. First, staffers argued that the Senate leaders, especially Majority Leader Trent Lott, used appropriations bills to pass policy measures that they could not get through the authorizing process. Second, Lott expected a high degree of loyalty from Republicans. On the other side of the aisle, such partisanship apparently motivated Democrats to stick together regardless of the wishes of the Appropriations subcommittee chairs who had given them earmarks. Third, staffers noted that members had discovered that they would not be punished for voting against the leaders who gave them their projects. If they can renege with impunity, there is little incentive for them to toe the subcommittee chair's line.

What about Republicans in the House? Were they similarly unsuccessful at using pork to buy votes once they attained majority status? This study does not include a case from the Republican-controlled House, but there is evidence that during this same time period, Republican policy coalition leaders were more successful at using pork in this way than their counterparts in the Senate. In an analysis of the 1998 highway reauthorization bill in the Republican-controlled 105th Congress, Frances Lee (2002) found that the 1,506 demonstration projects in that bill did indeed affect the roll call votes of the members who received them. Thus, the Republican takeover of Congress did not, in fact, signal the end of the effectiveness of this coalition-building technique.

In fact, as this book goes to press at the end of the first session of the 108th Congress, it appears that House Republicans are beginning to use earmarks in an explicitly partisan way for the purpose of passing appropriations bills in exactly the form that they prefer. In an extraordinary move, the chairman of the Appropriations subcommittee on Labor, Health and Human Services, Ralph Regula (R-Ohio), retaliated against members who voted against the subcommittee's bill in 2003 by removing all of their earmarks from the bill. Because Democrats voted against the bill as a block due in part to funding for education that was, in their view, inadequate, Regula struck all of their earmarks from the bill (Morgan and Eilperin 2003; Ornstein 2003). While the move was decried by Democrats and outside observers alike as putting the traditionally bipartisan Appropriations Committee on a downward slide into the virulent partisanship that has infected much of the rest of the House of Representatives, the move is surely a logical consequence of a strategy of using pork barrel benefits to build majority coalitions.

The next few years will demonstrate whether the House intends regularly to enforce the implicit terms of the trade of policy for pork. If so, we shall see whether removing the projects of noncompliant members will produce more compliance with policy coalition leaders' wishes or greater bitterness and resulting difficulties in passing essential appropriations bills. That is, it is possible that while policy coalition leaders are able to use pork as both a carrot and a stick, the ultimate outcome might be an eradication of all of the residual goodwill that years of earmarking have created for the cardinals, resulting in the need for the majority party to corral nearly all of their members on every vote. In this situation, earmarks would still be useful, but mainly to enforce party discipline and not to create bipartisan coalitions. Nevertheless, this dust-up resembles the situation observed in the Senate in the sense that in both cases, Appropriations Committee majorities are insisting on passing increasingly partisan measures for which members of the minority party cannot afford to vote, earmark or no earmark. For them to do so would be to violate one of the conditions of trading one's vote for pork: The pork barrel benefit must be more important to them than the policy to which it is attached. When that policy is among the central issues that divide the parties (and their constituent bases), most members of the minority party in an increasingly polarized Congress cannot afford to make that trade. Thus, a tougher approach to enforcing the terms of the trade of pork for votes could be both a cause and an effect of greater partisanship. That does not mean, however, that this coalition-building technique is dead, nor does it mean that it will be used in a purely partisan way on every issue.

THE LITERATURE ON THE USE OF PORK: AN ASSESSMENT

In Chapter 1, I discussed several prominent theories of policy making in Congress with respect to the role that they assign to distributive benefits in the resolution of Congress's collective action dilemma. It is worthwhile now to return to that discussion and see how those theories' approaches to distributive politics fared in view of my own analysis.

The findings here have the most to say about partisan theories. Cox and McCubbins in particular argue that pork can be used to round up a coalition in support of a piece of legislation (1993, pp. 123–125). But in their analysis, vote buying operates in the context of partisan policy making, as each party seeks to build a record of public policy that will win favor with the voters back home. That is, majority party leaders use distributive benefits to close divisions in their own ranks and help them to pass collective benefits that will provide the party with electoral rewards. The case studies in this book show that such a strategy is effective. Especially in the House, leaders of the majority party can win the votes of their own members for broad-based legislation. But my findings show that while leaders use pork as Cox and McCubbins describe, they can and do go farther. They also give benefits to members of the other party and thereby often win some of their votes as well. In so doing, they can increase the size of the coalition for their legislation without compromising its central provisions. Moreover, by adding support from the other party, coalition leaders can afford to lose some of their own members' votes, if those members have ideological or constituency-based reasons for opposing the legislation. Thus, with the exception of most of the Republican appropriations bills in the Senate, distributive benefits are used both to shore up the majority party's coalition and to drive a wedge into the minority.

With respect to informational theory, Krehbiel is surely right when he says, "Pork may be a lubricant for the legislative machine, but it is not the machine's main product" (Krehbiel 1992, p. 95). That is, in part, the argument of this book. However, it is clear that pork is used for much more than just rewarding committee members, as Krehbiel argues, in return for transmitting their expertise to the chamber as a whole. The cases in this book show that pork is distributed widely in order to lubricate parts of the machine beyond the committee system. It is given out to many members across the House and Senate to influence their votes for general interest legislation.

Douglas Arnold (1990) incorporates distributive benefits more broadly into his theory of legislative coalition-formation. Chapter 1 describes in some detail the process by which he envisions that coalition leaders add broad categories of benefits to win key votes for their general interest bills, one of several ways in which leaders form majority coalitions. According to Arnold, when leaders use a distributive strategy to gain additional supporters, they typically do so by broadening the categories of eligible benefit recipients so that the districts of key members qualify. However, he underestimates the ability of policy coalition leaders to insert benefits for specific members. Indeed, he argues that coalition leaders do not target individual members with exclusive benefits; rather, "all [leaders] can do is try to affect legislators' general expectations by modifying a program's character," by writing the bill to increase the probability that any one member's district will receive distributive benefits in the bureaucratic allocation process, rather than by directly providing such benefits in the legislation or the accompanying committee report (Arnold 1990, p. 114). We have seen here that policy coalition leaders also provide targeted benefits, thus allowing them more efficiently (and probably less expensively) to influence individual members.

Finally, Mayhew (1974) does not envision pork barrel politics as a way of resolving Congress's collective action dilemma. Rather, he sees it as central to the dilemma, a part of the problem. The solution, as he sees it, has been to give special status and power to the control committees that are charged with resolving the collective action dilemma. Distributive benefits continue, but those committees are charged with mitigating their effects on the budget. However, we have seen that the control committees themselves engage in the distribution of pork and that they do so, albeit with varying success, to gain votes for their bills. In addition to the evidence (however mixed) from the Senate Appropriations Committee, I have also discussed accounts of vote buying in the House Ways and Means Committee and the Senate Finance Committee for the 1986 reform of the tax code, described in Chapter 1. Thus, we see that congressional policy coalition leaders harness such benefits as another means of resolving the collective action dilemma that the drive for such benefits creates.

These theories were discussed in Chapter 1 because they, like this book, address the difficulty faced by Congress in marshaling its resources to pass general benefit legislation, given members' strong electoral incentives to concentrate on gaining pork barrel benefits for their constituents. If we accept the reasonable assumption that members of Congress care very much about general interest policy, then we can accept the proposition that they are receptive to means of overcoming their own incentives to concentrate on particularized benefits, as long as those means do not damage their reelection prospects. It is then not difficult to argue that they are receptive to leaders' use of such benefits to help to forge majority coalitions for general benefit legislation.

While it is undeniably true that pork barrel benefits are used to pass more particularized measures as well, such as the benefit to the billboard industry in the 1986 highway bill, the case studies show that they have also helped to pass or protect broad-based measures, such as NAFTA and the 55 mph speed limit. Thus, distributive benefits are useful tools for resolving Congress's well-known collective action problem as it relates to collective benefits.

PORK FOR POLICY: WHEN AND HOW OFTEN?

For reasons elaborated below, it is virtually impossible to devise a research design that could tell us comprehensively who uses this technique for forming majority coalitions and how often they do so. The case studies in this book involved data that were relatively (if not always readily) accessible, in part because they involved geographic benefits. But because many instances of the use of pork are not so available, it is necessary to infer, rather than demonstrate, the circumstances under which policy coalition leaders use pork barrel benefits to buy votes for broader policy measures. In Chapter 2, I specified four conditions that must exist for coalition leaders to execute such trades: First, leaders must have access to distributive benefits to trade for members' support for their favored legislation. Second, they must be willing to distribute them, and to do so for this purpose. Third, members themselves must be attracted to the benefits for their presumed electoral benefits and, to trade their votes for a project, they must like the pork more than they dislike the policy to which it is attached (assuming that they have not concealed actual support for the policy in order to get the pork). Finally, the leaders must be motivated by some combination of the goals of making good public policy and achieving influence in the chamber. The justification for these conditions is laid out in Chapter 2.

Except for the president, who has access to a vast bureaucratic treasure trove of benefits, leaders probably rely on congressional committees as the main source of benefits to trade for policy. Which committees are they? The best perspective from which to approach that question is Fenno's (1973) tripartite goal structure. He found that members sought committee assignments in the House to serve their goals of reelection, good public policy, and influence; in the Senate, reelection and good public policy were the dominant goals, given the high degree of influence that all senators enjoy by virtue of the office itself. Several scholars have divided committees in the House and Senate according to the dominant goals of those who seek assignment to them (Fenno 1973; Bullock 1976; Deering and Smith 1997). The obvious candidates for vote buying are the reelection-oriented committees, of which there are seven in the House and nine in the Senate (although four of those nine are also policy committees; Deering and Smith 1997, pp. 64 and 80). Those committees, of which Transportation is one, are most likely to deal in the particularized benefits that can be used as currency for general interest policy. The seven constituency-oriented House committees, Deering and Smith say, "are the classic pork-barrel committees of the House" (1997, p. 75). They include Agriculture, which deals with particular commodity programs; Science, which increasingly deals in benefits to particular universities (although, like most of these committees, it cannot actually commit the money); Armed Forces; and Veterans' Affairs, among others. In some cases, their bills might be omnibus bills of benefits for members. However, these committees also deal with broad policy matters. For instance, a major policy issue in the debate over the 2002 agriculture bill, the Farm Security and Rural Investment Act, concerned the conservation of farmlands. Whenever committees mix broad policy issues with constituency benefits, their leaders have the opportunity to trade pork for policy. Moreover, in both the House and Senate, the appropriations and tax-writing committees offer similar opportunities. Both deal with general interest legislation, but they can and do also offer individual benefits for members' constituents in the form of earmarks and special tax benefits. The pure policy committees, such as Judiciary and Labor in the Senate and Foreign Affairs in the House, may have less opportunity to use this coalition-building technique. That does not mean that those committees are completely lacking in such possibilities; but they probably enjoy fewer of them.

Thus, the range of committees to which this strategy is available is rather wide. The extent to which they actually use it is another question, one that is particularly difficult to answer, for two reasons. First, the data-gathering challenge is daunting. To see why, let us consider ways in which a scholar might try to approach it. The special geographic benefits found in the case studies in this book were, except for NAFTA, listed in either the bills themselves or the reports accompanying the bills. If these were the only kind of distributive benefits given, we could imagine a painstaking survey of all legislation reported from congressional committees over the course of one or more Congresses. One would, of course, have to assess whether the bill to which they were attached was simply an omnibus bill of pork barrel benefits or was, on the whole, a general benefit bill. Then it would be necessary to determine whether those benefits were added to buy votes for the bill. The way to do so would be to do as I have done: interview participants in the process of passing the bills. Then, of course, to determine whether it worked, a roll call analysis of each of the votes would be necessary. Such a comprehensive task is possible in principle, of course, but due to its magnitude, it is not especially practical.

A second obstacle to determining the frequency of this type of vote buying is the variety of forms that it takes. I have concentrated on benefits to specific districts and states, benefits that can be precisely located. However, particularized benefits are not always targeted to congressional districts; they also go to economic interests that can support members' reelection efforts. It is much harder to connect such nongeographical benefits with particular members of Congress. The 1986–1987 highway bill contains many examples, one of which follows:

> This section . . . [adds] to the projects and activities eligible for 100 percent Federal financing of the cost of construction to include the installation of traffic signs, highway lights, guardrails, and impact attenuators. ("Surface Transportation," H. Rpt. 99–665, p. 14)

Was this a general benefit to the states? Or was it a benefit to manufacturers of those devices, several of whom testified before the Transportation Committee asking for such funding? If we conclude, based on interviews or other evidence, that it was the latter, which members' constituents or contributors stood to benefit? It clearly is not feasible to gather such data in a reliable way.

It is due to the difficulties associated with collecting data on pork barrel benefits to business or other interests that I have concentrated here on explicitly geographic benefits. The only exception is the case study of NAFTA, where many of the benefits were to economic interests. That was practical only because such benefits were reported in the local news media and collected by an interest group that opposed them. And in fact, the likely reason that such deals were reported in the local media is because on such a high-visibility, controversial issue, members needed political cover for casting a vote that might otherwise damage the economic interests of their constituents. On many other issues, credit claiming is not done in the mass media. As a result, it is often impossible to connect the benefits with particular members or even to know which economic benefits were added for such a purpose or were instead added because bill-writers considered them good national policy.

Finally, pork-for-policy trades can occur across bills as well, adding another layer of complexity to the task of quantifying the frequency with which the technique is used. For example, during the Senate's consideration of Yucca Mountain in Nevada as a nuclear waste depository, Harry Reid (D-Nev.) exerted Herculean (and ultimately unsuccessful) efforts to defeat the choice. As majority whip, he had considerable clout, but that was not the route he chose to influence his colleagues' votes. As the *New York Times* reported, "Senator Reid . . . has been using all his influence in search of votes – including his power as chairman of a key appropriations subcommittee to support projects" (Mitchell and Wald 2002, p. A18).

The subcommittee in question was Energy and Water Development, one especially well suited for such an effort. Nevertheless, without such inside knowledge, one could not know that projects were given out in Reid's bill for a vote unconnected to the Appropriations Committee. Indeed, some of the statistical relationships in this book were probably attenuated due to exactly such cross-bill trades.

Thus, as a practical matter it is impossible to say how often policy coalition leaders use distributive benefits to form majority coalitions. But as this discussion indicates, it is probably more common than is recognized by outsiders. Nevertheless, I do not make the argument that such vote buying is ubiquitous; rather, I argue that it is one technique by which leaders build policy coalitions, a technique that, however dear it is to legislators, has previously not been fully recognized by scholars.

A final consideration, one that also is likely to affect the use and effectiveness of this technique for forming majority coalitions, is the importance of a particular general interest issue to the parties or, more precisely, its centrality among the issues that unite the parties internally and divide them from each other. Such issues are likely to be of high visibility and salience. Hence, members and their constituents alike have reason to care about them and may indeed care about them more than any district benefits that legislators could bring home. In David Rohde's (1991) terms, when the conditions are right for party government, members will stick with their party and allow their leaders to use their powers to the fullest to achieve their policy goals. On such issues, the majority leadership has little need for distributive benefits, and the minority has little access to them.

Indeed, members usually cannot cast a vote contrary to party and ideology on a major policy matter and expect to be protected by a little bit of pork. Recall that one of the necessary conditions for this technique to be effective is that members must care more about the benefit than the policy to which it is attached. That condition is less likely to be met on issues that are central to the identity of the party. In these cases, majority party leaders can probably use distributive benefits only at the margins, if at all, to add the last few members to their coalition, as Cox and McCubbins note. If there is no veto risk or filibuster threat in the Senate, they need only their own majority and may give distributive benefits only to those few members who need them for political cover back home. In fact, many of the benefits offered by President Clinton to Democrats probably served that purpose, as evidenced by members' very public announcements of support for NAFTA in return for protection for their tomato farmers, broomcorn growers, flat glass manufacturers, cut flower growers, and so on. However, to the extent that party leaders can use such benefits to shore up a partisan coalition for general interest legislation, pork barrel projects can expand the number of issues on which conditional party government is possible.

EVALUATING THE USE OF PORK TO BUILD MAJORITY COALITIONS

I have endeavored to present this analysis of trading projects for votes in an objective manner. It is part of the legislative process, and as such, it is worthwhile to clarify its workings. As I noted at the beginning of Chapter 1, however, many observers of this process are not so detached. Consider the introduction to the 2002 "Pig Book" published on the Web site of Citizens Against Government Waste, which tracks appropriations earmarks:

> The opening scene of *The Godfather* depicts the head of a New York "family," Don Vito Corleone, agreeing to perform certain "favors." Corleone does this with the caveat that the favor may have to be returned some day. This scene is reminiscent of what happens when the President's budget gets into the hands of the appropriators. Members of Congress approach the appropriators asking for favors, promising votes in return. They get the goods through a form of legal money laundering, but taxpayers receive only inflated taxes and a bloated bureaucracy. (http://publications.cagw.org/ PigBook2002/introduction.htm)

Such characterizations of this practice in the media are common. Indeed, the term that I have used throughout, "vote buying," could be taken as an implication of corruption. I have not intended that implication, nor do I consider it fair, as I noted in Chapter 1. It is not corrupt for members of Congress to determine whether a district benefit is more important to them and their constituents than a general interest program. Legislators must always try to achieve a balance between local and national interests. Nor is it corrupt for them to bargain strategically for such a benefit even when they favor the larger program, although that behavior, however inevitable, is perhaps more troubling, as it produces more pork barrel spending than necessary to build majority coalitions. The legislative process, even with strong, disciplined parties, is at heart a process of cutting deals of various kinds in order to form majority coalitions. Most of the time, this process is conducted out of public view; when the public does get a glimpse of it, they react with horror at the divergence between the real process of coalition-formation and the naive civics-book vision of nationally focused debate on the pure merits of general interest legislation. Certainly, debate and decision making on the merits occur, but so does deal making, especially when a majority cannot be formed purely on the merits. Some of the deals modify the policy itself, but policy coalition leaders must determine how much they can change general interest legislation and still accomplish their policy goals.

Is such deal making a force for good or ill? Journalistic accounts of pork barrel politics typically heap scorn on legislators who give and receive pork, condemning the practice as a waste of taxpayer money. Implicit in such criticism is the idea that it comes at the expense of the greater good: It must be either pork or broader national policy; either pork or a balanced budget. This book shows that in reality, it can be both: pork and national policy, or more accurately, pork for national policy; pork and balanced budgets, as Republican pork barreling increased when the budget was balanced (or, more precisely, in surplus). Although some journalistic accounts recognize that pork may be traded for policy, they fail adequately to appreciate that such benefits may be crucial to passing legislation that accomplishes national purposes, especially when individual members need to be able to take something home to their constituents in order to justify a vote, as they did on NAFTA: No one doubts that NAFTA would have failed if the president and his allies in the House had refused to deal with individual members.[1]

Of course, the worthiness of such national purposes is in the eye of the beholder. Overall, I do not believe that a blanket evaluation of using district benefits to form majority coalitions is possible. However, it is possible to think about some of the implications of doing so. Let us consider some of the potential negative consequences of leaders holding the line on the content of the general interest policy and adding local benefits in exchange for votes. Four possibilities come to mind.

From the point of view of majoritarian democracy, the first two consequences of vote buying are worst-case scenarios of the practice. First, the general interest policy that is crafted with the aid of pork may well be contrary to the preferences of the majority in Congress and the public at large. The purpose of adding such benefits is, after all, to protect coalition leaders' policy preferences, which are by no means necessarily the preferences of the majority; if their positions were reflective of majority

[1] As is the case throughout this book, the phrase "accomplish national purposes" is intended not to imply approval of the policy, but rather to indicate a policy with national implications.

views on all matters pertaining to the bill, such benefits would not (in the absence of strategic bargaining for benefits by members) be necessary.

The second implication of using pork to build majority coalitions is actually an extreme version of the first: When bills are written in private by leaders and their staff, members may not even know, when they accept their pork, exactly what they are trading their votes for. Yet they may still agree to the deal if coalition leaders can offer them distributive benefits that are so valuable that members are willing to gamble that such benefits will outweigh anything that could be in the general interest bill to which they are attached. As Chapter 6 indicates, that was once the case with appropriations bills. Another apparent example of this scenario is an omnibus energy bill (H.R. 6) that, as of the end of the first session of the 108th Congress, had passed the House but was blocked by a Senate filibuster. Media accounts noted that the House-Senate conference committee version of the bill was written in secret in a process closed to all but top Republicans (Anselmo and Stevens 2003). A *Washington Post* editorial reflected the common understanding of the strategy that the leaders followed: "Much of the conference negotiating has involved attempts to buy off wavering members with pork" ("Uncivil Society" 2003). Although the *Post* notes that Republican negotiators gave Democrats drafts of parts of the bill during those negotiations, Democrats did not have a chance to evaluate the complex bill fully until just a few days before the floor votes. Thus, it is unlikely that they knew exactly what they were trading off. The strategy worked in the House. However, the fact that Republican negotiators were unable to overcome the objections of the sixty senators needed to break the filibuster reminds us that the strategy is not foolproof. But when members trade their votes for a distributive benefit under these conditions, they are necessarily unaware of how much the bill might diverge from their own or their constituents' preferences.

A third consequence of the strategy of building majority coalitions with pork is that pork barrel benefits might eventually overwhelm the general interest provisions in a bill, adding to its cost and possibly even dragging it down with their weight. We have seen that there is a strong likelihood that pork barrel benefits will proliferate once leaders have revealed their willingness to engage in this kind of horse trading. Chapters 2 and 3 examine this tendency, but it is worth reiterating here as a negative effect of vote buying. If rank-and-file members find that they can extract constituency benefits for their votes, such benefits and their attendant expense will multiply greatly, as the highway bills examined in Chapter 3 show. In fact, ironically, the pork barrel strategy can backfire and defeat a bill by overloading it, as some observers thought was the case for the energy bill (Hulse 2003).

This brings us to the fourth consequence, which is closely related to the third: the cost of the deals. In many cases, as with NAFTA, for example, costs are difficult to estimate. But in other cases, costs can be calculated. In the case of the highway bills, as Table 3.4 indicates, the cost of highway demonstration projects multiplied more than six-fold between 1987 and 1998 as the number of projects proliferated across three highway reauthorization bills.

Although these four implications of vote buying with pork are significant, there are mitigating factors for all of them. First, it is clear that there are limits on members' ability to vote contrary to district opinion on broad national policy matters and survive for long. As I have argued, if the national policy is highly salient to the district, members usually cannot go against their districts, except as they did for NAFTA, where they received promises of specific protections for their constituents. Otherwise, if members do sell their votes on salient national policy, their constituents will probably feel that the trade is not worthwhile and may judge their representatives to be beholden to someone other than themselves and therefore not deserving of reelection. The possibility of voter retaliation surely controls much of what members of Congress do. Given the risk of negative electoral consequences, it is likely that members normally trade votes for pork on issues that are not important to their constituents or bargain for benefits for policies that they already favor. The latter circumstance (i.e., the member already favors the policy) is benign in a policy sense, if unnecessarily costly.

Thus, although the electoral process creates the conditions under which vote buying works, it can also reduce the number of situations in which pork barrel politics creates perverse, or nonmajoritarian, general interest policy. It is worth noting that similar concerns about nonmajoritarian public policy apply to strong party systems, where a structure of party discipline compels members to vote for policies that are favored by a majority of their caucus, which normally is a minority of the legislature as a whole. There as well, the incentives are particularized: the promise of a committee chairmanship or the threat of removal from one; promises to facilitate, or threats to block, one's pet bills.

Thus, it is common for democratic legislatures to use techniques to forge majorities by means other than policy compromises that attract a majority on the basis of the merits of the policy alone. To deal with the problems that citizens expect the government to ameliorate, policy coalition leaders must make deals that will create the legislative majorities necessary to improve the status quo and protect coalition members' seats at the same time. The key to evaluating such deals is the extent to which they deviate from majority preferences on the national issue. In fact, the use of distributive benefits to form majority coalitions is probably least objectionable when constituents favor the national policy but seek compensation for its negative local effects. By contrast, the situation that should create the most concern is the one in which members sell their votes on public policy that is not currently salient to their constituents but about which they might care, and oppose, if they knew the full implications.

Thus far I have given rather short shrift to the expense of these deals, yet that issue inspires much of the anti-pork outrage among observers of the legislative process. Surprisingly, however, the actual costs can be seen as a mitigating factor, in some respects. Overall, the costs are difficult to quantify definitively for the same reasons that some of the deals are difficult to detect. Yet it is possible to quantify the cost of earmarks in appropriations bills. Given that they are probably the largest source of distributive benefits, it is worthwhile to consider how much of the budget they take up. Once again, we turn to the "Pig Book" for our information. In the FY 2002 appropriations bills, the total dollar amount of earmarks was $20.1 billion. This amount was allocated for 8,341 projects in the thirteen appropriations bills. The authors do not put that dollar amount in the context of total FY 2002 spending, but doing so provides some perspective. The budget for total discretionary spending, the spending controlled by the appropriations committees, was $660.6 billion. Earmarks thus accounted for 3 percent of that portion of the budget. In addition, the amount budgeted for mandatory spending, such as Social Security, was $1,255.4 billion. Thus, of a total federal budget of $1,916 billion, earmarks accounted for 1.6 percent. There is other pork, of course. The highway bills are notable and readily quantifiable examples. Demonstration projects in the 1986–1987 bill accounted for approximately 2 percent of the total spending in the bill (Evans 1994). In the 1998 highway bill, which allowed a large increase in the number of projects as Table 3.4 shows, demonstration projects accounted for 5 percent of the cost of the bill (Lee 2002).

Despite the fact that we cannot detect all of these deals, the numbers that we do see suggest that the federal budget is hardly a big pot of pork roast. As Allen Schick says, it is not pork, but rather "programs [that] are relatively expensive because they typically provide nationwide (rather than local) benefits. . . . [that account for] the enormous size of the federal budget" (Schick 2000, p. 215). These numbers, small relative to total spending, are not intended to suggest to the reader that there is no cause for concern about the expense of pork barrel projects. The $20.1 billion in earmarked funds for FY 2002 could have paid for a few far-reaching programs instead of being tailored to thousands of smaller beneficiaries.

However, a larger concern in this regard may be those deals tailored for organized economic interests, especially those not based in members' districts, that also aid members' chances of reelection. Examples include tax breaks whose consequences are virtually undetectable to the untrained eye, protective tariffs and import restrictions, and any number of other particularized benefits that increase the taxes of ordinary citizens and the cost of goods and services in the private market. Such benefits are given out by legislative coalition builders for the same reasons that they distribute district benefits, but as noted above, those benefits often cannot be connected with the legislator who requested them, nor can their true cost readily be quantified. Pork barrel benefits for members' districts are more defensible by comparison because members can directly be held accountable for them. If their constituents decide that pork barreling is bad public policy, as some accounts suggest that they did (temporarily) in 1994, they can retire their representatives. Benefits to large, dispersed economic interests cannot be so easily tracked.

A great many books about the legislative process conclude with proposals for reform. Given the compelling appeal of pork to members of Congress and their constituents, I will not joust at windmills here. Horse trading in the process of creating majority coalitions is natural in a democratic system based on geographically based representation. I doubt that many citizens would favor a representational scheme in which their own representatives were not beholden to them; thus, as long as granting district benefits is useful for both policy making and reelection, it will be impossible to put a stop to it. Moreover, journalists and politicians who seek to stimulate public outrage will succeed only in directing it to other people's legislators; representatives and their constituents often dispute the pork barrel label for their own benefits, a label that more objective observers would readily apply. It is probably not an exaggeration to say that politically, much of the time, pork is in the eye of the beholder. And even if constituents admitted that a benefit was pork, their likely attitude would be, "fine, if that's the only way to solve the problem."

However intractable the phenomenon of pork barreling is, there is reason to be concerned with the *collective* impact of 535 members of Congress gaining particular benefits for their constituents, even when those benefits are a small proportion of the federal budget. One reason for that concern, as noted above, is the tendency of such benefits to grow year after year in particular bills.

To the extent that Congress has tried to control such proliferation, it has treated it as a collective action problem. Disciplinary devices such as the 1974 budget process, spending caps, and the "pay-as-you-go" provisions discussed in Chapter 6 may have had some dampening effect, although as Schick notes, Congress is adept at "gaming" these devices as well (Schick 2000, pp. 66–67, 147–148). Nevertheless, such disciplinary measures are Congress's way of solving, or at least controlling, its inherent free-rider problem with respect to federal spending. No rank-and-file member of Congress has an incentive to withhold requests for district benefits, as doing so will not deter anyone else or significantly improve the budget picture. But it is in members' interest to agree to restraints on the extent to which leaders can grant their requests, as the reputation of Congress and the prestige of every one of its members depends in part on Congress's degree of fiscal responsibility.

The ultimate restraint, of course, is the voters. It is to them that members of Congress respond. And voters want contradictory things. They want pork barrel benefits, large public programs that meet widespread needs, and fiscal responsibility. Members of Congress go to great lengths to give them pork barrel benefits for which members can claim individual credit. To attain the other two goals, national policy and fiscal responsibility, legislators empower their leaders to take action to create majority coalitions. As far as national policy making is concerned, members and leaders sometimes agree to meet two of their constituents' apparently contradictory goals at once. The ironic result is that large national policy edifices are constructed, in part, with bricks of pork.

References

Adler, E. Scott. 2000. "Constituency Characteristics and the 'Guardian' Model of Appropriations Subcommittees, 1959–1998." *American Journal of Political Science* 44: 104–114.

Adler, E. Scott, and John S. Lapinski. 1997. "Demand-Side Theory and Congressional Committee Composition: A Constituency Characteristics Approach." *American Journal of Political Science* 41: 895–918.

Aldrich, John H., and Charles F. Cnudde. 1975. "Probing the Bounds of Conventional Wisdom: A Comparison of Regression, Probit, and Discriminant Analysis." *American Journal of Political Science* 19: 571–608.

Aldrich, John H., and Forrest D. Nelson. 1984. *Linear Probability, Logit, and Probit Models*. Beverly Hills: Sage.

Aldrich, John H., and David W. Rohde. 2000. "The Republican Revolution and the House Appropriations Committee." *Journal of Politics* 62: 1–33.

______. 2001. "The Logic of Conditional Party Government: Revisiting the Electoral Connection." In *Congress Reconsidered*, 7th ed., ed. Lawrence C. Dodd and Bruce I. Oppenheimer. Washington: CQ Press.

Alvarez, R. Michael, and Jason L. Saving. 1997. "Deficits, Democrats, and Distributive Benefits: Congressional Elections and the Pork Barrel in the 1980s." *Political Research Quarterly* 50: 809–831.

Alvarez, R. Michael, and Schousen, Matthew M. 1993. "Policy Moderation or Conflicting Expectations?" *American Politics Quarterly* 21: 410–438.

Anagnoson, J. Theodore. 1982. "Federal Grant Agencies and Congressional Election Campaigns." *American Journal of Political Science* 26: 547–561.

Anderson, Jack, and Michael Binstein. 1992. "Pork-Barrel Politics Teaches Hard Lesson." *Washington Post*, Aug. 10.

Anderson, Sarah, and Ken Silverstein. 1993. "Oink Oink." *The Nation* 257 (Dec. 20): 752–753.

Andres, Gary J. 1995. "Pork Barrel Spending on the Wane?" *P.S.: Political Science and Politics* 28: 207–211.

Anselmo, Joseph C., and Allison Stevens. 2003. "Regional Issues Leave Energy Bill a Hair Too Unwieldy for Senate." *CQ Weekly*, Nov. 22.

Arnold, Douglas. 1979. *Congress and the Bureaucracy: A Theory of Influence*. New Haven, Conn.: Yale University Press.

______. 1990. *The Logic of Congressional Action*. New Haven: Yale University Press.

Asher, Herbert B. 1983. *Causal Modeling*, 2nd ed. Beverly Hills: Sage Publications.

Ashworth, William. 1981. *Under the Influence: Congress, Lobbies, and the American Pork-Barrel System*. New York: Hawthorn/Dutton.

Audley, John J. 1997. *Green Politics and Global Trade*. Washington: Georgetown University Press.

Axelrod, Robert. 1981. "The Emergence of Cooperation among Egoists." *American Political Science Review* 75: 306–318.

Baker, Ross K. 1989. *The New Fat Cats: Members of Congress as Political Benefactors*. New York: Priority Press.

Balla, Steven J., Eric Lawrence, Forrest Maltzman, and Lee Sigelman. 2002. "Partisanship, Blame Avoidance, and the Distribution of Legislative Pork." *American Journal of Political Science* 46: 515–525.

Baron, David P. 1991. "Majoritarian Incentives, Pork Barrel Programs and Procedural Control." *American Journal of Political Science* 35: 57–90.

Baron, David P., and John A. Ferejohn. 1989. "Bargaining in Legislatures." *American Political Science Review* 89: 1181–1206.

Barone, Michael, and Grant Ujifusa. 1992. *The Almanac of American Politics*. Washington, D.C.: National Journal.

Barry, Brian. 1965. *Political Argument*. New York: Humanities Press.

Berry, William D. 1984. *Nonrecursive Causal Models*. Newbury Park, Calif: Sage.

Beyond Distrust: Building Bridges between Congress and the Executive. 1992. Washington, D.C.: National Academy of Public Administration.

Bickers, Kenneth N., and Robert M. Stein. 1996. "The Electoral Dynamics of the Federal Pork Barrel." *American Journal of Political Science* 40: 1300–1326.

______. 2000. "The Changing Structure of Federal Aid and the Politics of the Electoral Connection." Paper presented at the annual meeting of the American Political Science Association, Washington, D.C.

Birnbaum, Jeffrey H., and Alan S. Murray. 1987. *Showdown at Gucci Gulch*. New York: Vintage.

Bond, Jon R., and Richard Fleisher. 1990. *The President in the Legislative Arena*. Chicago: University of Chicago Press.

Box-Steffensmeier, Janet M., Laura W. Arnold, and Christopher J. W. Zorn. 1997. "The Strategic Timing of Position Taking in Congress: A Study of the North American Free Trade Agreement." *American Political Science Review* 91, no.2 (June 1997): 324–338.

Bradsher, Keith. 1993. "Administration Cuts Flurry of Deals." *New York Times*, Nov. 11.

Brady, David W. 1988. *Critical Elections and Congressional Policy Making*. Stanford, Calif.: Stanford University Press.

Brady, David W., Joseph Cooper, and Patricia A. Hurley. 1979. "The Decline of Party in the U.S. House of Representatives, 1887–1968." *Legislative Studies Quarterly* 4: 381–407.

Brown, Kirk F. 1983. "Campaign Contributions and Congressional Voting." Paper presented at the 1983 annual meeting of the American Political Science Association, Chicago.

Browne, William P. 1995. *Cultivating Congress: Constituents, Issues and Interests in Agricultural Policymaking.* Lawrence: University of Kansas.

Bryce, James. 1959. *The American Commonwealth.* New York: G. P. Putnam's Sons.

Buchanan, James M., and Gordon Tullock. 1962. *The Calculus of Consent.* Ann Arbor: University of Michigan.

Bullock, Charles S., III. 1976. "Motivations for U.S. Congressional Committee Preferences: Freshmen of the 92nd Congress." *Legislative Studies Quarterly* 1: 201–212.

———. 1985. "U.S. Senate Committee Assignments: Preferences, Motivations, and Success." *American Journal of Political Science* 29: 789–808.

Cain, Bruce, John Ferejohn, and Morris Fiorina. 1987. *The Personal Vote.* Cambridge: Harvard University Press.

Carsey, Thomas M., and Barry Rundquist. 1999. "Party and Committee in Distributive Politics: Evidence from Defense Spending." *Journal of Politics* 61: 1156–1169.

Carter, Jimmy. 1982. *Keeping Faith: Memoirs of a President.* New York: Bantam.

Chappell, Henry W., Jr. 1982. "Campaign Contributions and Congressional Voting: A Simultaneous Probit-Tobit Model." *Review of Economics and Statistics* 64: 77–83.

Christensen, Mike. 2000. "Congress's Cornucopia: A Sampler of Spending Add-Ons." *CQ Weekly* 58 (Oct. 7): 2322–2323.

Citizens against Government Waste. 2000. *Pig Book.* Http://www/cagw.org, accessed June 29, 2000.

Cloud, David S. 1991. "Momentum Grows for Gas Tax to Pay for Highway Bill." *CQ Weekly* 49 (July 13): 1881.

Cohen, Richard E. 1993a. "Clinton's NAFTA Team Battling Uphill." *National Journal* 25 (November 6): 2674.

———. 1993b. "Democratic Salvage Operation on NAFTA." *National Journal*, Sept. 25, no. 38, p. 2259.

Cohn, Jonathan S. 1998. "Roll Out the Barrel." *The New Republic* 218 (April 20): 19–23.

Collie, Melissa P. 1988. "The Legislature and Distributive Policy Making in Formal Perspective." *Legislative Studies Quarterly* 12: 427–458.

Collie, Melissa P., and David W. Brady. 1985. "The Decline of Partisan Voting Coalitions in the House of Representatives." In *Congress Reconsidered*, 3rd ed., ed. Lawrence C. Dodd and Bruce I. Oppenheimer, 272–287. Washington, D.C.: CQ Press.

"Congress OKs North American Trade Pact." *Congressional Quarterly Almanac 1993*. Washington, D.C.: CQ Press.

Conway, Margaret. 1991. "PACs in the Political Process." In *Interest Group Politics*, 3rd ed., ed. Allan J. Cigler and Burdett A. Loomis. Washington: CQ Press.

Cordes, Colleen, and Siobhan Gorman. 1996. "Congress Slashes Earmarks for Academe by 50%." *Chronicle of Higher Education* 43 (Sept. 13): 33–34.

Cox, Gary W., and Mathew McCubbins. 1993. *Legislative Leviathan: Party Government in the House.* Berkeley: University of California Press.

Dahl, David. 1993. "The NAFTA Debate; Support of Fla. House Delegation Courted." *St. Petersburg Times*, Nov. 6.

Dahl, Robert A., and Charles E. Lindblom. 1953. *Politics, Economics and Welfare.* New York: Harper & Row.

Davis, Joseph A. 1987. "Making It Work: Robert Roe: Ardent Defender of Helping Folks at Home." *Congressional Quarterly Weekly Report* 45 (October 24): 2593–2594.

Deering, Christopher J., and Steven S. Smith. 1997. *Committees in Congress*, 3rd ed. Washington, D.C.: CQ Press.

Denzau, Arthur T., and Robert J. Mackay. 1983. "Gatekeeping and Monopoly Power of Committees: An Analysis of Sincere and Sophisticated Behavior." *American Journal of Political Science* 27: 740–761.

Denzau, Arthur T., and Michael C. Munger. 1986. "Legislators and Interest Groups: How Unorganized Interests Get Represented." *American Political Science Review* 80: 89–106.

Devroy, Ann, and Kenneth J. Cooper. 1993. "Hopeful White House Edges Toward NAFTA Win; Lobby Effort Gains More Than a Dozen New Votes in House." *Washington Post*, Nov. 17.

Dillin, John. 1993. "NAFTA Opponents Dig in Despite Lobbying Effort." *Christian Science Monitor*, Oct. 12.

Dodd, Lawrence C. 1977. "Congress and the Quest for Power." In *Congress Reconsidered,* ed. Lawrence C. Dodd and Bruce I. Oppenheimer, 269–307. New York: Praeger.

Duncan, Phil. 1989. *Politics in America, 1990: The 101st Congress.* Washington, D.C.: CQ Press.

Duncan, Philip D., and Christine C. Lawrence. 1997. *Politics in America, 1998: The 105th Congress.* Washington, D.C.: CQ Press.

Dutt, Jill. 1993. "White House: It's Down to a Dozen." *Newsday*, Nov. 15.

Edwards, George C., III. 1980. *Presidential Influence in Congress.* San Francisco, Calif.: W. H. Freeman.

______. 1989. *At the Margins: Presidential Leadership of Congress.* New Haven, Conn.: Yale University Press.

Ehrenhalt, Alan. 1987. *Politics in America: The 100th Congress.* Washington, D.C.: CQ Press.

Ellwood, John W., and Eric M. Patashnik. 1993. "In Praise of Pork." *Public Interest* 110: 19–33.

Elving, Ronald D. 1994. "A Chance to Transcend Parochial Concerns." *Congressional Quarterly Weekly Report* 52 (March 26): 774.

Engel, Steven T., and David J. Jackson. 1998. "Wielding the Stick Instead of the Carrot: Labor PAC Punishment of Pro-NAFTA Democrats." *Political Research Quarterly* 51: 813–828.

Evans, C. Lawrence. 1991. *Leadership in Committee: A Comparative Analysis of Leadership Behavior in the U.S. Senate.* Ann Arbor: University of Michigan Press.

Evans Yiannakis, Diana. 1981. "The Grateful Electorate: Casework and Congressional Elections." *American Journal of Political Science* 25: 568–580.

Evans, Diana. 1986. "PAC Contributions and Roll Call Voting: Conditional Power." In *Interest Group Politics*, 2nd ed., ed. Allan J. Cigler and Burdett A. Loomis, 114–132. Washington, D.C.: CQ Press.

______. 1988. "Oil PACs and Aggressive Contribution Strategies." *Journal of Politics* 50: 1047–1056.

______. 1994. "Reconciling Pork-Barrel Politics and National Transportation Policy: Highway Demonstration Projects." In *Who Makes Public Policy? The Struggle for Control between Congress and the Executive*, ed. Robert S. Gilmour and Alexis A. Halley, 42–61. Chatham, N.J.: Chatham House.

______. 1996. "Before the Roll Call: Interest Group Lobbying and Public Policy Outcomes in House Committees." *Political Research Quarterly* 49: 287–304.

Feldman, Paul, and James Jondrow. 1984. "Congressional Elections and Local Federal Spending." *American Journal of Political Science* 28: 147–164.

Fenno, Richard F., Jr. 1966. *The Power of the Purse: Appropriations Politics in Congress*. Boston: Little, Brown.

______. 1973. *Congressmen in Committees*. Boston: Little, Brown

______. 1978. *Home Style: House Members in Their Districts*. Boston: Little, Brown.

Ferejohn, John A. 1974. *Pork Barrel Politics*. Stanford, Calif.: Stanford University Press.

______. 1986. "Logrolling in an Institutional Context: A Case Study of Food Stamp Legislation." In *Congress and Policy Change*, eds. Gerald C. Wright, Jr., Leroy N. Rieselbach, and Lawrence C. Dodd, 223–253. New York: Agathon.

Ferejohn, John, Morris Fiorina, and Richard D. McKelvey. 1987. "Sophisticated Voting and Agenda Independence in the Distributive Politics Setting." *American Journal of Political Science* 31: 169–193.

Fiorina, Morris P. 1974. *Representatives, Roll Calls, and Constituencies*. Boston: Lexington.

______.. 1981a. "Some Problems in Studying the Effects of Resource Allocation in Congressional Elections." *American Journal of Political Science* 25: 543–567.

______. 1981b. "Universalism, Reciprocity, and Distributive Policymaking in Majority Rule Institutions." In *Research in Public Policy Analysis and Management*, vol. 1, ed. John P. Crecine, 197–222. Greenwich, Conn.: JAI Press.

______. 1989. *Congress: Keystone of the Washington Establishment*, 2nd ed. New Haven, Conn.: Yale University Press.

Fleisher, Richard. 1993. "PAC Contributions and Congressional Voting on National Defense." *Legislative Studies Quarterly* 18: 391–409.

Frendreis, John P., and Richard W. Waterman. 1985. "PAC Contributions and Legislative Voting Behavior: Senate Voting on Trucking Deregulation." *Social Science Quarterly* 66: 401–412.

Frisch, Scott A. 1998. *The Politics of Pork: A Study of Congressional Appropriation Earmarks*. New York: Garland.

Gettinger, Stephen. 1999. "R.I.P. to a Conservative Force." *CQ Weekly*, Jan. 9. http://cq.com, accessed May 18, 2000.

Gilligan, Thomas W., and Keith Krehbiel. 1990. "Organization of Informative Committees by a Rational Legislature." *American Journal of Political Science* 34: 531–64.

Goddard, Stephen B. 1994. *Getting There: The Epic Struggle between Road and Rail in the American Century.* New York: Basic.

Goldstein, Steve. 1995. "Pork Barrel Politics Continue Under GOP Control." *Sun News* (Myrtle Beach, S.C.), Dec. 28.

Gopoian, David. 1984. "What Makes PACs Tick? An Analysis of the Allocation Patterns of Economic Interest Groups." *American Journal of Political Science* 23: 259–281.

Goss, Carol. 1972. "Military Committee Membership and Defense Related Benefits in the House of Representatives." *Western Political Quarterly* 25: 215–233.

Green, Stephen. 1995. "Packard Helps to Man the Barricades in House GOP's Revolution." *San Diego Union-Tribune*, March 11.

Grenzke, Janet. 1989. "Shopping in the Congressional Supermarket: The Currency Is Complex." *American Journal of Political Science* 33: 1–24.

Groseclose, Tim. 1996. "An Examination of the Market for Favors and Votes in Congress." *Economic Inquiry* 34: 320–340.

Groseclose, Tim, and James M. Snyder, Jr. 1996. "Buying Supermajorities." *American Political Science Review* 90: 303–315.

Hagle, Timothy M., and Glenn E. Mitchell II. 1992. "Goodness of Fit Measures for Probit and Logit." *American Journal of Political Science* 36: 762–784.

Hall, Richard L., and Bernard Grofman. 1990. "The Committee Assignment Process and the Conditional Nature of Committee Bias." *American Political Science Review* 84: 1149–1166.

Hall, Richard, and Frank W. Wayman. 1990. "Buying Time: Rational PACs and the Mobilization of Bias in Congressional Committees." *American Political Science Review* 84: 797–820.

Handler, Edward, and John R. Mulkern. 1982. *Business in Politics.* Lexington, Mass.: D.C. Heath.

Hausman, J. A. 1978. "Specification Tests in Econometrics." *Econometrica* 46: 1251–71.

Healey, Jon. 1993. "The States' Pipeline." *Congressional Quarterly Weekly Report* 51 (Dec. 11): 12–14.

Healy, Patrick. 2000. "Congressional Manna Falls on Campuses." *Boston Globe*, July 23.

Herndon, James F. 1982. "Access, Record, and Competition as Influences on Interest Group Contributions to Congressional Campaigns." *Journal of Politics* 44: 996–1019.

Hibbing, John R., and Elizabeth Theiss-Morse. 1995. *Congress as Public Enemy: Public Attitudes toward American Political Institutions.* Cambridge: Cambridge University Press.

"Highway Bill Passes over Reagan's Veto." *1987 CQ Almanac*, 331–336. Washington, D.C.: CQ Press.

"Highway Reauthorization Dies Amid Disputes." *Congressional Quarterly Almanac, 1986*, 284–286. Washington, D.C.: CQ Press.

"Highways, Mass Transit Funded." *1991 CQ Almanac*, 137–151. Washington, D.C.: CQ Press.

Hinds, Michael deCourcy. 1992. "Indictment of Congressman Means Little at Home." *New York Times*, May 17.

Hird, John A. 1991. "The Political Economy of Pork: Project Selection at the U.S. Army Corps of Engineers." *American Political Science Review* 85: 429–456.

Hirsh, William, and Michael Isikoff. 2000. "Senator Hothead," *Newsweek*, Feb. 21, p. 26.

Holden, Constance. 1985. "Science Board Takes on Pork-Barreling." *Science* 227, (March 8): 1183.

Hook, Janet. 2000. "Campaign 2000: In Campaign with Few National Themes to Propel It, GOP Goes Local," *Los Angeles Times*, Oct. 8, p. 1A.

Hornbeck, J. F. 1994. *Highway Demonstration Projects: Background and Economic Policy Issues.* Congressional Research Service. Washington: Government Printing Office.

Hosmer, David W., and Stanley Lemeshow. 1989. *Applied Logistic Regression.* New York: John Wiley & Sons.

Hulse, Carl. 2003. "Even with Bush's Support, Wide-ranging Legislation May have Been Sunk by Excess." *New York Times*, Nov. 26.

Hurwitz, Mark S., Roger J. Moiles, and David W. Rohde. 2001. "Distributive and Partisan Issues in Agriculture Policy in the 104th House," *American Political Science Review* 95: 911–922.

Ivins, Molly. 1995. "No More Business as Usual? Oh, Those Funny GOP Freshmen." *Hartford Courant*, Oct. 29.

Jacobson, Gary C. 1990. *The Electoral Origins of Divided Government.* Boulder, Colo.: Westview.

______. 1997. *The Politics of Congressional Elections*, 4th ed. New York: Longman.

Johannes, John R., and John C. McAdams. 1981. "The Congressional Incumbency Effect: Is It Casework, Policy Compatibility, or Something Else?" *American Journal of Political Science* 25: 512–542.

Jones, Charles O. 1995. *Separate but Equal Branches: Congress and the Presidency.* Chatham, N.J.: Chatham House.

Jones, Rochelle, and Peter Woll. 1976. *The Private World of Congress.* New York: Free Press.

Jones, Woodrow, and K. Robert Keiser. 1987. "Issue Visibility and the Effects of PAC Money." *Social Science Quarterly* 68: 170–176.

Kahane, Leo H. 1996. "Congressional Voting Patterns on NAFTA: An Empirical Analysis." *American Journal of Economics and Sociology* 55: 95–409.

Kau, J. B., and P. H. Rubin. 1979. "Self-Interest, Ideology and Logrolling in Congressional Voting." *Journal of Law and Economics* 22: 365–84.

Kearns, Doris. 1976. *Lyndon Johnson and the American Dream.* New York: Harper and Row.

Kelly, Brian. 1992. *Adventures in Porkland.* New York: Villard.

Kernell, Samuel. 1986. *Going Public: New Strategies of Presidential Leadership.* Washington, D.C.: CQ Press.

Kiewiet, D. Roderick, and Mathew D. McCubbins. 1991. *The Logic of Delegation: Congressional Parties and the Appropriations Process.* Chicago: University of Chicago Press.

Kingdon, John W. 1984. *Agendas, Alternatives, and Public Policies.* Boston: Little, Brown.

———. 1989. *Congressmen's Voting Decisions*, 3rd ed. Ann Arbor: University of Michigan Press.

Knezo, Genevieve J., and Richard E. Rowberg. 1993. *Appropriations Directed by Congress to Specific Colleges and Universities, for Research and Development and Research-Related Facilities, FY 1992*. Washington: Congressional Research Service, 93–684.

Koford, Kenneth J. 1982. "Centralized Vote-Trading." *Public Choice* 39: 245–268.

Komarow, Steve. 1993. "NAFTA and Politics on the Line in Debate." *USA Today*, Nov. 8.

Kosova, Weston. 1994. "Where's the Pork?" *The New Republic* 211 (Sep. 5): 10.

Krehbiel, Keith. 1987. "Why Are Congressional Committees Powerful?" *American Political Science Review* 81: 929–35.

———. 1990. "Are Congressional Committees Composed of Preference Outliers?" *American Political Science Review* 84: 149–63.

———. 1992. *Information and Legislative Organization*. Ann Arbor: University of Michigan Press.

———. 1998. *Pivotal Politics: A Theory of U.S. Lawmaking*. Chicago: University of Chicago Press.

Langbein, Laura I. 1986. "Money and Access: Some Empirical Evidence." *Journal of Politics* 48: 1052–62.

Latus, Margaret Ann. 1984. "Assessing Ideological PACs: From Outrage to Understanding." In *Money and Politics in the United States*, ed. Michael J. Malbin, 142–171. Chatham, N.J.: Chatham House.

Lee, Frances. 2000. "Senate Representation and Coalition Building in Distributive Politics." *American Political Science Review* 94: 50–72.

———. 2002. "Coalition Building in Transportation Policy: The Politics of Geography in the U.S. House of Representatives." Presented at the annual meeting of the Midwest Political Science Association, Chicago.

Lee, Frances E., and Bruce I. Oppenheimer. 1999. *Sizing Up the Senate: The Unequal Consequences of Equal Representation*. Chicago: University of Chicago Press.

Lee, Jessica. 1993. "Fence-sitters Targets of NAFTA Push." *USA Today*, Nov. 11.

Lee, Jessica, and Bill Nichols. 1993. "NAFTA Undecided Hold Power." *USA Today*, Nov. 16.

Levitt, Steven D., and James M. Snyder, Jr.. 1995. "Political Parties and the Distribution of Federal Outlays." *American Journal of Political Science* 39: 958–980.

———. 1997. "The Impact of Federal Spending on House Election Outcomes." *Journal of Political Economy* 105, no. 1 (Feb.): 30–53.

Lewis, Charles. 1993. "The NAFTA-Math; Clinton Got His Trade Deal, but How Many Millions Did It Cost the Nation?" *Washington Post*, Dec. 26.

Lightman, David. 1995. "Pork Still a Staple in Diet of Congress." *Hartford Courant*, Oct. 23.

Longley, Lawrence D., and Walter J. Oleszek. 1989. *Bicameral Politics: Conference Committees in Congress*. New Haven, Conn.: Yale University Press.

Loomis, Burdett. 1988. *The New American Politician: Ambition, Entrepreneurship, and the Changing Face of Political Life*. New York: Basic.

Lowi, Theodore J. 1964. "American Business, Public Policy, Case-Studies, and Political Theory. " *World Politics* 16: 677–715.

Maass, Arthur A. 1951. *Muddy Waters: The Army Engineers and the Nation's Rivers.* Cambridge: Harvard University Press.

MacDonald, John. 1996. "Pork and Scandal in a Republican Stronghold." *Hartford Courant*, Feb. 24.

Manley, John. 1970. *The Politics of Finance.* Boston: Little, Brown.

Marshall, Bryan W., Brandon C. Prins, and David W. Rohde. 1997. "The Senate Purse: A Longitudinal Study of the Senate Appropriations Committee." Michigan State University, typescript.

Matthews, Donald R., and James A. Stimson. 1975. *Yeas and Nays: Normal Decision Making in the U.S. House of Representatives.* New York: Wiley.

Mayer, Kenneth R., and David T. Canon. 1999. *The Dysfunctional Congress? The Individual Roots of an Institutional Dilemma.* Boulder, Colo.: Westview Press.

Mayhew, David R. 1974. *Congress: The Electoral Connection.* New Haven, Conn.: Yale University Press.

———. 1991. *Divided We Govern: Party Control, Lawmaking, and Investigations, 1946–1990.* New Haven, Conn.: Yale University Press.

McCain, John. 2000. "Statement of Senator John McCain on Objectionable Provisions in S. 1233, Agriculture Appropriations for FY 2000." Http://www.senate.gov/~mccain/, accessed June 29, 2000.

Menard, Scott. 1995. *Applied Logistic Regression Analysis.* Sage University Paper series on Quantitative Applications in the Social Sciences, series no. 07–106. Thousand Oaks, Calif: Sage.

Merida, Kevin, and Tom Kenworthy. 1993. "For Some, a Bitter NAFTA Taste; House Awaits Fallout from Bipartisan Vote Deal-Making." *Washington Post*, Nov. 18.

Mills, Joshua. 1993. "Business Lobbying for Trade Pact Appears to Sway Few in Congress." *New York Times*, Nov. 12.

Mills, Mike. 1990. "Skinner Steers Federal U-Turn as Interstate Dead Ends." *CQ Weekly Report* 48 (Dec. 15): 4134–4140.

———. 1991a. "Highway Bill Debate Becomes War between the States." *CQ Weekly Report* 49 (June 8): 1487–1489.

———. 1991b. "Senate Panel Passes Overhaul of Federal Highway Policy." *CQ Weekly Report* 49 (May 25): 1366–1368.

"Minnesota Ranks Near the Bottom of the Pork Barrel." 200 *Star Tribune* (Minneapolis, Minn.), April 6. 2000.

Mintz, Bill. 1993. "You Scratch My NAFTA, I'll Scratch . . . , Deals Being Bade as Vote Draws Near." *Houston Chronicle*, Nov. 13.

Munson, Richard. 1993. *The Cardinals of Capitol Hill.* New York: Grove.

Mitchell, Alison, and Matthew Wald. 2002. "Senators Declare Support for Waste Site." *New York Times*, July 9.

Morgan, Dan, and Juliet Eilperin. 2003. "Rejection of Earmarks Angers Democrats; GOP Subcommitte Chairman Says He Won't Honor Party's Projects in Bill." *Washington Post*, Nov. 7.

Murphy, James T. 1974. "Political Parties and the Pork Barrel: Party Conflict and Cooperation in House Public Works Committee Decision Making." *American Political Science Review* 68: 169–185.

"NAFTA's Bizarre Bazaar." December 1992. Washington, D.C.: Public Citizen.

Neil, Andrew. 1994. "America's New World Spells the End of Big Government." *Sunday Times* (London), Nov. 6.

Neustadt, Richard E. 1990. *Presidential Power and the Modern Presidents*. New York: Free Press.

______. 1993. "Clinton NAFTA Deals? It's Business." *Newsday*, Dec. 17.

Neustadtl, Alan. 1990. "Interest Group PACsmanship: An Analysis of Campaign Contributions, Issue Visibility, and Legislative Impact." *Social Forces* 69: 549–564.

Nichols, Bill. 1993. "Just 12 Votes May Settle NAFTA's Fate." *USA Today*, Nov. 15.

Nicholson, Richard S. 1991. "Pork Barrel 'Science.'" *Science* 254 (Dec. 6): 1433.

Niou, Emerson M. S., and Peter C. Ordeshook. 1985. "Universalism in Congress." *American Journal of Political Science* 29: 246–258.

Norman, Colin. 1986. "House Endorses Pork Barrel Funding." *Science* 233: 616–617.

Norman, Colin, and Eliot Marshall. 1986. "Over a (Pork) Barrel: The Senate Rejects Peer Review." *Science* 233: 145–146.

Olson, Mancur. 1965. *The Logic of Collective Action*. Cambridge: Harvard University Press.

Ornstein, Norman. 2003. "Don't Take Civility Out of House Appropriations Panel." *Roll Call*, Nov. 5. Http://www.rollcall.com, accessed Nov. 5, 2003.

Ornstein, Norman J., Thomas E. Mann, and Michael J. Malbin. 2002. *Vital Statistics on Congress*. Washington, D.C.: AEI.

Owens, John R., and Larry L. Wade. 1984. "Federal Spending in Congressional Districts." *Western Political Quarterly* 37: 404–423.

Palazzolo, Daniel J., and Bill Swinford. 1994. "'Remember in November'? Ross Perot, Presidential Power, and the NAFTA." Paper delivered at the annual meeting of the American Political Science Association, New York, NY.

Parks, Daniel J. 1999. "Partisan Voting Holds Steady." *CQ Weekly* 57 (Dec. 11): 2975.

Penny, Timothy, and Harris Fawell. 1993. "Silence of the Hams." *Wall Street Journal*, Aug. 9.

Pike, Otis. 1993. "On Capitol Hill, the Undecided Can Hold Out for Highest Bid." *Chicago Sun-Times*, Nov. 17.

Pincus, Walter, and Dan Morgan. 1995. "Pork Barrel Hitches Ride on Pentagon Train." *Washington Post*, March 23.

Plott, Charles. 1968. "Some Organizational Influences on Urban Renewal Decisions." *American Economic Review* 58: 306–311.

Poole, Keith T., and Howard Rosenthal. 1997. *Congress: A Political-Economic History of Roll Call Voting*. New York: Oxford.

Pound, Edward T. 1994. "How to Pull the Levers." *U.S. News and World Report* 116 (Feb. 21): 46.

"President Reagan's Radio Address." 1987. Federal News Service, March 28.

"Public Citizen Launches 'NAFTA Pork Patrol.'" Nov. 16, 1993. Washington, D.C.: Public Citizen.

Ray, Bruce A. 1980a. "Congressional Losers in the U.S. Federal Spending Process." *Legislative Studies Quarterly* 3: 359–72.

———. 1980b. "Congressional Promotion of District Interests: Does Power on the Hill Really Make a Difference?" In *Political Benefits*, ed. Barry S. Rundquist. Lexington, Mass.: Lexington Books.

Rich, Michael J. 1989. "Distributive Politics and the Allocation of Federal Grants." *American Political Science Review* 83: 193–213.

Riker, William H. 1962. *The Theory of Political Coalitions*. New Haven, Conn.: Yale University Press.

Riker, William H., and Peter C. Ordeshook. 1973. *An Introduction to Positive Political Theory*. Englewood Cliffs, N.J.: Prentice-Hall.

Ripley, Randall B., and Grace A. Franklin. 1991. *Congress, the Bureaucracy, and Public Policy*, 5th ed. Pacific Grove, Calif.: Brooks/Cole.

Rivers, Douglas, and Quang H. Vuong. 1988. "Limited Information Estimators and Exogeneity Tests for Simultaneous Probit Models." *Journal of Econometrics* 39: 347–366.

Roberts, Brian E. 1990. "A Dead Senator Doesn't Lie: Seniority and the Distribution of Federal Benefits." *American Journal of Political Science* 34: 31–58.

Rohde, David W. 1991. *Parties and Leaders in the Postreform House*. Chicago: University of Chicago Press.

———. 1994. "Parties and Committees in the House: Member Motivations, Issues, and Institutional Arrangements." *Legislative Studies Quarterly* 21: 341–359.

Roman, Sixto. 1993. "Brown Sees Gains in His Battle against Academic Earmarks." *Congressional Quarterly Weekly Report* 51 (Dec. 4): 3307–3310.

Rosenbaum, David E. 1993. "Perot Debate Seen as Way to Try to Save Trade Pact." *New York Times*, Nov. 5.

———. 1994. "A Giant Void in Congress." *New York Times*, June 1.

Rosenthal, A. M. 1993. "On My Mind; Defining Bill Clinton." *New York Times*, Nov. 19.

Rundquist, Barry S., and John A. Ferejohn. 1975. "Observations on a Distributive Theory of Policy Making." In *Comparative Public Policy*, ed. Craig Liske, William Loehr, and John McCammant. New York: John Wiley.

Rundquist, Barry S. and David Griffith. 1976. "An Interrupted Time-Series Test of the Distributive Theory of Military Policy-Making." *Western Political Quarterly* 24: 620–626.

Safire, William. 1988. *Safire's New Political Dictionary: The Definitive Guide to the New Language of Politics*. New York: Random House.

Saltzman, Gregory M. 1987. "Congressional Voting on Labor Issues: The Role of PACs." *Industrial and Labor Relations Review* 40: 163–179.

Sandler, Todd. 1992. *Collective Action: Theory and Applications*. Ann Arbor: University of Michigan Press.

Savage, James D. 1991. "Saints and Cardinals in Appropriations Committee and the Fight against Distributive Politics." *Legislative Studies Quarterly* 16: 329–348.

———. 1999. *Funding Science in America*. New York: Cambridge University Press.

Sawyer, Jon. 1993. "Trade Accord Vote Won't Be Political, Gephardt Pledges." *St. Louis Post-Dispatch*, July 29.

Schick, Allen, with the assistance of Felix LoStracco. 2000. *The Federal Budget: Politics, Policy, Process*. Washington, D.C.: Brookings.

Schmitt, Eric. 1994. "House Battle Threatens Big Research Universities with Loss of Millions." *New York Times*, Aug. 17.

Schroedel, Jean Reith. 1987. "Campaign Contributions and Legislative Outcomes." *Western Political Quarterly* 40: 371–389.

Sellers, Patrick J. 1997. "Fiscal Consistency and Federal District Spending." *American Journal of Political Science* 41: 1024–1041.

Shanahan, Eileen. 1993. "White House Acting to Ease Floridians' Fears on NAFTA." *St. Petersburg Times*, Oct. 1.

Shepsle, Kenneth A. 1974. "On the Size of Winning Coalitions." *American Political Science Review* 68: 505–518.

______. 1978. *The Giant Jigsaw Puzzle.* Chicago: University of Chicago Press.

______. 1986. "Institutional Equilibrium and Equilibrium Institutions." In *Political Science: The Science of Politics*, ed. Herbert Weisberg. New York: Agathon.

Shepsle, Kenneth A., and Barry R. Weingast. 1981. "Political Preferences for the Pork Barrel." *American Journal of Political Science* 25: 96–111.

______. 1984. "Political Solutions to Market Problems." *American Political Science Review* 78: 417–34.

______. 1987a. "The Institutional Foundations of Committee Power." *American Political Science Review* 81: 85–104.

______. 1987b. "Why Are Congressional Committees Powerful?" *American Political Science Review* 81: 936–45.

______. 1994. "Positive Theories of Congressional Institutions." *Legislative Studies Quarterly* 21: 149–179.

Sinclair, Barbara. 1978. "From Party Voting to Regional Fragmentation, 1933–1956." *American Politics Quarterly* 6: 125–46.

______. 1997. *Unorthodox Lawmaking: New Legislative Processes in the U.S. Congress*. Washington: CQ Press.

Smith, Steven S., and Christopher J. Deering. 1990. *Committees in Congress*, 2nd ed. Washington: CQ Press.

Snyder, James M. 1991. "On Buying Legislatures." *Economics and Politics* 3: 93–109.

Solomon, Burt. 1987. "Staff at Work." *National Journal* 19: 1174–1176.

Starobin, Paul. 1987. "Pork: A Time-Honored Tradition Lives On." *Congressional Quarterly Weekly Report* 45 (Oct. 24): 2581–2594.

Stein, Robert M., and Kenneth N. Bickers. 1994a. "Congressional Elections and the Pork Barrel." *Journal of Politics* 56: 377–399.

______. 1994b. "Response to Barry Weingast's Reflections." *Political Research Quarterly* 47: 329–333.

______. 1994c. "Universalism and the Electoral Connection: A Test and Some Doubts." *Political Research Quarterly* 47: 295–318.

______. 1995. *Perpetuating the Pork Barrel: Policy Subsystems and American Democracy.* New York: Cambridge University Press.

Stockman, David.1975. "The Social Pork Barrel." *Public Interest* 39 (Spring): 3–30.

______. 1986. *The Triumph of Politics: Why the Reagan Revolution Failed.* New York: Harper & Row.

Stokes, Bruce. 1993. "A Hard Sell." *National Journal* 25 (Oct. 16): 2472–2476.

Strahan, Randall. 1989. "Members' Goals and Coalition-Building Strategies in the U.S. House: The Case of Tax Reform." *Journal of Politics* 51: 373–84.

Stratmann, Thomas. 1992. "The Effects of Logrolling on Congressional Voting." *American Economic Review* 82: 1162–1176.

Taylor, Andrew. 1996. "GOP Pet Projects Give Boost to Shaky Incumbents." *Congressional Quarterly Weekly Report* 54 (Aug. 3): 2169–2172.

Taylor, Andrew, Alan Greenblatt, Lori Nitschke, Chuck McCutcheon, and Charles Pope. 1998. "GOP's War on Pet Projects Bogs Down in Temptation." *Congressional Quarterly Weekly Report* 56 (Aug. 22): 2264–2269.

Toner, Robin. 1994. "Image of Capitol Maligned by Outsiders, and Insiders." *New York Times*, Oct. 16.

Tumulty, Karen. 1994. "The Price of Pork." *Time* 144 (Nov. 7): 37–39.

———. 1995. "The Freshmen Go Native." *Time* 146 (Nov. 20): 70–71.

"Uncivil Society." 2003. *Washington Post*, Oct. 22.

U.S. Congress. House. Committee on Public Works and Transportation. 1986. *Surface Transportation and Uniform Relocation Assistance Act of 1986 (to accompany H.R. 3129)* (H. Rpt. 99–665). Washington: Government Printing Office (Y1.1/8 99–665).

U.S. Congress. Senate. Committee on Appropriations. Subcommittee on Agriculture, Rural Development, Food and Drug Administration, and Related Agencies. 1995. *Agriculture, Rural Development, Food and Drug Administration, and Related Agencies Appropriation Bill, 1996.* (S. Rpt. 104–142). Washington: Government Printing Office (Y1.1/5:104–142).

Weiner, Tim. 1994. "Sending Money to Home District: Earmarking and the Pork Barrel." *New York Times*, July 13.

Weingast, Barry R. 1979. "A Rational Choice Perspective on Congressional Norms." *American Journal of Political Science* 23: 245–263.

———. 1994. "Reflections on Distributive Politics and Universalism." *Political Research Quarterly* 47: 319–327.

Weingast, Barry R., and William J. Marshall. 1988. "The Industrial Organization of Congress; or, Why Legislatures, like Firms, Are Not Organized as Markets." *Journal of Political Economy* 96: 132–63.

Weingast, Barry R., and Mark J. Moran. 1983. "Bureaucratic Discretion or Congressional Control? Regulatory Policymaking by the Federal Trade Commission." *Journal of Political Economy* 91: 765–800.

Weingast, Barry R., Kenneth A. Shepsle, and Christopher Johnsen. 1981. "The Political Economy of Benefits and Costs: A Neoclassical Approach to Distributive Politics." *Journal of Political Economy* 889: 642–664.

"Who Ya Gonna Call? Porkbusters!" 1997. *CNN All Politics.* June 9. Http://europe.cnn.com/ALLPOLITICS/1997/gen/resources/pork/porkbusters, accessed Nov. 1, 2000.

Wilcox, Clyde. 1988. "Share the Wealth: Contributions by Congressional Incumbents to the Campaigns of Other Candidates." Paper presented at the annual meeting of the American Political Science Association, Washington, D.C.

Wilhite, Allen, and John Theilmann. 1987. "Labor PAC Contributions and Labor Legislation: A Simultaneous Logit Approach." *Public Choice* 53: 267–276.

Wilson, Rick K. 1986. "An Empirical Test of Preferences for the Pork Barrel: District-Level Appropriations for Rivers and Harbors Legislation, 1889–1913." *American Journal of Political Science* 30: 729–754.

Wines, Michael. 1993. "A 'Bazaar' Method of Dealing for Votes." *New York Times*, Nov. 11.

———. 1994. "Bringing Home Bacon Isn't Protecting Veterans." *New York Times*, Nov. 6.

———. 1995. "Congress Returning to Face Long List of G.O.P. Promises." *New York Times*, Sept. 5.

Wink, Kenneth A., C. Don Livingston, and James C. Garand. 1996. "Dispositions Constituencies, and Cross-Pressures: Modeling Roll-Call Voting on the North American Free Trade Agreement in the U.S. House." *Political Research Quarterly* 49: 749–70.

Wolf, Richard. 1995. "Ways of the Past Take the Edge Off GOP Revolution." *USA Today*, Oct. 2.

Woodward, Bob. 1994. *The Agenda: Inside the Clinton White House.* New York: Simon & Schuster.

Wright, John R. 1985. "Contributions and Roll Calls: An Organizational Perspective." *American Political Science Review* 79: 400–414.

———. 1990. "Contributions, Lobbying, and Committee Voting in the U.S. House of Representatives." *American Political Science Review* 84: 417–438.

Index